TO: JEN
I will never
forget you!

Introduction to
PSYCHOLOGY

Arno F. Wittig, Ph.D.
Ball State University

Gary S. Belkin, Ph.D.
Long Island University

An American BookWorks Corporation Project

McGraw-Hill Publishing Company

New York St. Louis San Francisco Auckland Bogotá Caracas Hamburg
Lisbon London Madrid Mexico Milan Montreal New Delhi Oklahoma City
Paris San Juan São Paulo Singapore Sydney Tokyo Toronto

About the authors

Arno F. Wittig is Dean of The Honors College at Ball State University in Muncie, Indiana, and has also taught at Hobart & William Smith Colleges. He is the author of numerous books on psychology, including college textbooks, and a Fellow of the American Psychological Association.

Gary S. Belkin teaches at Long Island University's Westchester campus in New York. A prolific author, he has written several college textbooks. Professor Belkin also maintains a private practice in cognitive psychotherapy.

Introduction to Psychology

Adapted from *Schaum's Outline of Theory and Problems of Introduction to Psychology*. Copyright © 1977 by McGraw-Hill, Inc. All Rights Reserved.

2 3 4 5 6 7 8 9 10 11 12 13 14 15 16 17 18 19 20 FGR FGR 8 9 3 2 1 0 9

ISBN 0-07-071212-3

Library of Congress Cataloging-in-Publication Data
Wittig, Arno F.
    Introduction to psychology.

    (McGraw-Hill college review books series)
    "An American BookWorks Corporation project."
    1. Psychology.   I. Belkin, Gary S.   II. Title.
III. Series.
BF121.W55   1990   150   90-13070
ISBN 0-07-071212-3

Preface

Perhaps no major area of study has grown more rapidly and with more vigor in recent years than psychology. With roots in both philosophy and physiology, psychology—the systematic study of behavior—stands today as a separate scientific discipline. In its efforts to understand how and why organisms behave as they do, psychology provides insights into every aspect of our lives: our perception of the world; our ability to use language and to learn, remember, create, and problem-solve; our emotional expression; our personality development; our sense of self; our motivation, choice-making, and ability to cope; our interpersonal relations; and our behavior in groups.

This book introduces the basic principles of psychology. It may be used in conjunction with a standard textbook, as a supplement to classroom or laboratory instruction, or as a concise text. Tightly organized by a series of subheads that represent the core topics of psychology, the book presents facts, principles, and theoretical explanations for each. Like other disciplines, psychology has a specialized vocabulary; the glossary provides definitions for easy reference and review. Familiarity with key terms is essential for anyone who wishes to have a firm grasp of the subject matter.

Throughout the text the reader will find examples based on

real-life situations or the research literature of psychology. These examples are meant to enhance understanding of the subject and, possibly, suggest areas of practical application. While each chapter can be studied independently, we have frequently tried to indicate where interrelationships exist.

Arno F. Wittig
Gary S. Belkin

Contents

CHAPTER 1

Psychology: Definition, History and the Profession Today

We are all interested in how people act. Not only do we want to know what is happening, but quite frequently we want to know why. Although these questions often are answered in a rather loose or undisciplined fashion, a more rigorous body of knowledge concerning behavior has developed. This body of knowledge is called psychology.

This chapter reviews the history of psychology and looks at some of the major figures who influenced its development. It presents a number of major theories and approaches, including introspection, structuralism, functionalism, Gestalt psychology, psychoanalysis, and behaviorism. It also delineates some of the different areas in which today's psychologists practice—clinical, counseling, social, educational, industrial, experimental, community, and so on.

Definition and Purposes

Psychology is the scientific study of behavior. As such, psychology describes behavior (the what) and tries to explain the causes of behavior (the why). The scope of this study is wide, ranging from how we learn to how we think to how we act. Psychology is truly the study of *all* behavior, across all cultures and all socioeconomic levels, over the entire life span. Psychologists study both human and animal behavior from conception to death, including conscious and unconscious influences on behavior.

Areas of Behavioral Study

The description of behavior that results from psychological study is not casual or without aim. The psychological study of behavior has as its purpose the prediction or the control of behavior. Basically, prediction of behavior occurs when the psychologist correctly anticipates events that occur naturally, whereas control means the psychologist has somehow manipulated the situation and subsequently observed an expected result. For example, teaching a child to name colors controls or changes behavior. Anticipating that the child can recognize the difference between blue and red (even if the child cannot name these colors) is prediction of behavior.

Humans and Animals

Behavior is defined as any observable or measurable response by a person or animal. Psychology is defined as the study of all behavior, including both human and animal behavior. When using human subjects for study, a psychologist must be concerned with more legal and ethical problems than animals pose, the availability of subjects, the duration of the treatment, and special expenses.

It is generally quite easy to accept psychology as the study of human behavior, but questions often arise as to why psychologists study animals. There are three basic reasons, all of which are important: (1) Sometimes animals are used in studies simply because a psychologist is interested in learning about animal behavior, since animals are important as part of the environment, and understanding their behavior may be worthwhile for that reason alone. (2) Animals are often studied because it would be improper or impossible to use humans in certain types of research. While there is considerable public pressure about the mistreatment of animals in psychological research and increasing regulation regarding their use, they still allow much more flexibility than human subjects. (3) In many cases, the behavior of animal subjects is comparable to the behavior of humans. Thus, psychologists are able to explore many problem areas with animals and can predict, on the basis of the results obtained, what humans might do in comparable situations.

Heredity and Environment

One of the questions psychology seeks to answer is whether behavior occurs as a result of inherited characteristics (hereditary influences) or because of learning (environmental influences). A controversy regarding the relative importance of these two influences has continued in psychology for a long time and remains a subject of lively speculation and intense debate.

Heredity certainly influences behavior, in both direct and subtle ways. For example, heredity may influence directly such traits as brain damage, mental retardation, color blindness, and other characteristics that are likely to have significant effects upon the types of behavior a person will be able to engage in. It also appears likely that heredity influences alcoholism, schizophrenia, and other psychopathological conditions. It also influences such positive traits as musical, artistic, and mathematical ability, and may have subtle effects on aspects of personality and social development.

The influences of heredity and environment, it is generally agreed, interact. This means the behavior observed is the result of the combined effect of hereditary background and past or current environmental experience. The relative importance of each influence cannot be separated or measured with any accuracy. Each influence may affect the other to produce a result that differs from a simple summation of the two influences.

Conscious and Unconscious Behavior

Behavior is often the product of a conscious choice. Some behaviors, however, may result from motives that are below a level of awareness. Many theorists refer to these latter motives as unconscious. Both conscious and unconscious motives may lead to responses, and psychology therefore studies both.

Normal and Abnormal Behavior

Psychology studies both normal and abnormal behavior. There is often great difficulty in deciding whether a behavior should be classified as normal or abnormal. The usual criterion is to judge behavior as abnormal if it creates a problem for the individual or for society. Obviously, the decision depends upon both the individual and the particular characteristics of the society in which the individual lives.

Age Range

Psychology studies behavior over the entire life span. Indeed, because some behaviors are dependent on hereditary characteristics as well as on learning, psychologists are concerned with the individual from the moment of conception until death. However, very few psychologists study the entire age range;

most prefer to concentrate on a distinct span, such as early childhood, adolescence or old age.

Theory or Applied

The breadth of psychological study is such that it includes both theoretical studies and the application of psychological principles to specific problems. Probably the majority of psychological specialties could be categorized as applied.

The Background and Beginning of Psychology

In the history of scientific endeavor, psychology is considered a relatively new discipline. While many other disciplines—such as biology, physics, and chemistry—have traditions of study dating back to ancient history, the usual date selected for the beginning of psychology is 1879. This date is chosen because in that year, *Wilhelm Wundt* (1832–1920), a German physiologist, established the first psychology laboratory. Wundt set up the laboratory at the University of Leipzig, in Germany.

Three major factors made Wundt's work important. First, he started psychology on its way as an independent discipline. Second, his emphasis on experimental methodology gave psychology a strong scientific footing. Third, the system of structuralism, which he espoused, tested the method of introspection, which he developed in his laboratory, and thus provided a "target" for several other systems that followed.

Other researchers, particularly physiologists, had preceded Wundt in conducting psychological investigations. *E.H.Weber,* who did research on the sense of touch, devised new methods for measuring sensitivity and gave us a formula for the relationship between stimulus and sensation (Weber's law). *Johannes Muller* formulated a theory of sensation that helped explain how the nerve cells transmit information to the brain. This theory stated that the specific sensation one experiences is primarily the result not of an external stimulus acting on the sense organs but of the specific energy residing in a given nerve. In other words, not only light but any stimulus capable of activating the optic nerve—even a touch of the eyeball—can produce a visual sensation. Muller also produced the encyclopedic *Handbook of Physiology*, in which he gave prominence to psychological matters.

Hermann von Helmholtz made many important contributions in the areas of sight and hearing, and was also the first person to measure the speed of a nerve impulse. *Gustav Fechner* developed mathematical principles to explain the relationship between a physical and a mental event.

But Wundt still is considered the founder of psychology as a distinct discipline because he was the first to declare himself a psychologist and describe his facility as a psychological laboratory. Wundt also started the first journal for psychology and wrote an early textbook in the area of physiological psychology.

Psychology did not spring suddenly onto the scientific scene. Concern with "psychological" issues and problems extends into antiquity. Indeed, human and animal behavior have always been a concern of merchants, scientists, philosophers, and all thinking people. Some of the areas of study that contributed to the development of psychology as a separate discipline include philosophy, the natural sciences, medicine, and even some non-scientific and pseudoscientific areas.

Philosophy

For thousands of years, philosophers have tried to understand behavior. Indeed, many of the basic problems of psychology—such as learning, motivation, personality, perception or physiological influences on behavior—were first discussed by philosophers. For example, psychologists have always been concerned with questions of how the human mind develops from birth to adulthood.

Philosophers have traditionally grappled with the same questions. Plato, the Greek philosopher of the fourth century B.C., believed that a human was born with certain innate, or given, mental abilities and knowledge. Aristotle, a student of Plato's, wrote impressive essays on sensation, perception, learning, memory, sleep, dreams, youth, and old age. John Locke, a seventeenth-century English philosopher, believed that the human mind was at birth a *tabula rasa*, or "blank slate," upon which impressions were made. Neither philosophers nor psychologists have definitively concluded which, if either, of these views best explains behavior, and the present tendency is to recognize a mix of environmental and innate (hereditary) factors.

What made psychology separate from philosophy was a difference in approach. As the philosophies of the eighteenth and nineteenth centuries began to develop a greater emphasis on empirical values, the eventual rise of an independent psychology became possible. An attitude of scientific inquiry became the mainstay of psychology. Many departments of psychology within colleges and universities originated in departments of philosophy and only later gained independent status.

The Sciences

Much of the methodology that accompanied the introduction of scientific inquiry into behavioral areas was borrowed or adapted from other sciences. Physics, chemistry, biology, and physiology were all important as contributors to the start of psychology. The methodologies that developed are discussed in detail in Chapter 2, but it is worthwhile to briefly mention here some of the contributions that came from these sciences.

The Experimental Method

Perhaps the most important contribution of the natural sciences to psychology was the experimental method, which is discussed in Chapter 2. This method enabled psychologists to investigate problems of human behavior, learning, and perception with the same rigor used by natural scientists. It also allowed the replication of experiments by other psychologists, thus establishing a basis for the objective verification of findings.

Subjects for Investigation

In addition, various problems and theories of the natural sciences provided psychologists with subjects for investigation. Both physics and chemistry provided not only methodology but concerns regarding sensations and perceptions. These quickly were to become part of the prevailing concerns of physiological study during this time. From biology came a concern with heredity and its effects on individual development.

Support to Developing Studies

The biological theory of evolution and findings from zoology gave strong support to the development of comparative psychology, in which the behavior of one species is compared to that of another. Biology also provided much of the information on genetics and heredity that was eventually used by psychologists considering the effects of these influences on behavior. Thus, methodology, areas for investigation, and justification for study were all taken from older scientific disciplines.

Medicine

In a somewhat indirect manner, medicine made a major contribution to the beginning of psychology. Until the early 1800s, most people exhibiting abnormal personality patterns were thought to be possessed by the devil. During the early

1800s, medical practitioners developed treatments for physical illnesses that were thought to contribute to abnormal patterns of behavior.

By the late 1870s, the attitude had changed. These abnormal patterns were classified as mental illnesses, and treatment changed accordingly. This led to the development of what is now called psychiatry and had an important effect upon the beginnings of clinical psychology.

Although the concerns of psychiatry and clinical psychology both came from a medical tradition, there are differences in the training of psychologists and psychiatrists. A person who wishes to become a *psychiatrist* must, after finishing undergraduate work, receive both a degree in medicine and subsequently specialize in psychological and psychotherapy training. As a result, a strong orientation for psychiatrists is what has come to be called the medical model. That is, the psychiatrist may treat a client as a "sick" person. But many other psychiatrists and psychologists do not accept this concept of "disease." They prefer terms such as "abnormal patterns of behavior" to describe the responses of the people they observe and treat.

Psychologists, on the other hand, are not medically trained. After completing their undergraduate work, they earn a doctoral degree in psychology, with an emphasis on a particular specialty. A clinical psychologist must also undergo a rigorous internship in a mental health facility, where he or she works directly with patients under the supervision of experienced practitioners.

Nonscientific and Pseudoscientific Influences

Some areas of psychological study arose because investigators wanted to show that commonly accepted statements about behavior were wrong. Often, these incorrect statements appeared to have some "scientific flavor"—they were labeled with sophisticated-sounding names such as physiognomy, phrenology or typology.

Physiognomists believed that the appearance of the face and head reveal personality characteristics. Phrenologists "mapped" the areas of the human skull in an attempt to label brain functions and their consequent effects on human behavior. Typologists tried to correlate body type with behavioral characteristics. Although all of these areas eventually were shown to be inaccurate (for example, fat people are not always jolly), the questions they raised did generate research that explained more about behavior. Psychological studies were often conducted as responses to nonscientific prompting.

Early Development of Psychology

Early psychology was characterized by attempts to develop unified psychological systems. These systems were attempts to explain all of behavior by using a single set of principles. These included investigations in perception, thinking, consciousness, intelligence, and other areas. Although none continues to have major importance, all contributed significantly to present-day psychology.

Structuralism

The position developed by *Wundt* in Germany and later expanded by *Edward Titchener* (1867–1927) in the United States was called structuralism. Psychology, for the structuralists, was the study of the introspective reports of normal adult humans. Trained subjects made descriptive reports of how stimuli appeared to them. These reports were supposed to allow the psychologist to interpret the structure of the mind and how it worked.

In a structuralist experiment, you might be asked to report

on how you sensed the weight, texture, and color of this book. You might also be asked to describe your feelings, if any, toward the book. Merely saying, "This is a psychology book," would not be sufficient as an introspective report.

As a system, structuralism was very limited. However, the structuralists did make important contributions to the early development of psychology: (1) by testing the method of introspection, which ultimately failed because of disagreements regarding the properties of stimuli; (2) by establishing psychology as a scientific endeavor and stressing appropriate scientific methodology; and (3) by providing a starting point that was investigated by many of the later psychological systems.

Functionalism

One of the systems that developed as a reaction to structuralism was called functionalism. The functionalists were concerned with the purposes of behavior rather than with the structure of the mind. Functionalists investigated the adaptation or adjustment the subject achieved in different environments. They started out by using the method of introspection advocated by Wundt, but gradually turned to more objective methods. Their main areas of research included learning, attention, perception, and intelligence.

Preeminent among the early functionalists was the American, *William James*. In 1890, James published *The Principles of Psychology*, a textbook that systematized much of the knowledge that had been published in fragmented form up to that time. He also established the first American psychological laboratory, at Harvard College, about the same time Wundt was establishing his laboratory in Germany.

The functionalists were not limited to the use of normal human adults as subjects for their experiments. They did not rely on introspective reports, as did the structuralists. The functionalists might, for example, investigate the ways in which very young children responded to novel problem-solving situations.

Functionalists generally adopted a broader view of psychology than did the structuralists. This allowed them to study all age groups and a variety of subjects. Many new areas of investigation resulted, including the study of motivation and emotions, child psychology, and various areas of applied psychology.

Associationism

The associationists, who were heirs to the British empiricism of John Locke, were concerned particularly with the development of associations, or bonds, between stimuli and responses. Their interests included the effects of reinforcement and punishment upon such bonds, the length of practice necessary for bonds to be established, and the relationship between these bonds and a person's physiological responses to the environment. It was felt that such bonds provided the basis for understanding behavior.

As an example, associationists might be concerned with the ways in which a child might learn to make distinctions between the parts of the human body. Through parental encouragement and reinforcement, a child might first learn the word "arm" and what it stood for. Later, the child might learn to distinguish other, more specific parts of the arm, such as the elbow and wrist.

Behaviorism

John B. Watson (1878–1958) established a system for the study of behavior in which only the observable responses made by the subject were relevant. Watson called this system behaviorism. Initially it was characterized by an interest only in the muscular movements and glandular responses of the subject.

Behaviorists denied the concepts of "mind" and "consciousness" because a mind or consciousness could not be observed.

Behaviorists were interested only in observable phenomena. A strict behaviorist would not describe a person as "happy" because happiness is a state of mind, and a mind is not observable. Instead, the behaviorist might describe the person's smile or laugh, or some other observable response to a stimulus.

Although the system soon found much criticism, it did point out the possible futility of trying to describe nonobservable activities of the subject, and it helped psychology confront the ideas of stimulus control and determinism of behavior. Direct concern with the stimuli and consequent responses has become an important part of several psychological perspectives.

Intelligence Testing

In the last half of the nineteenth century, two important researchers—Sir Francis Galton and Alfred Binet—undertook systematic investigations of human intelligence. *Galton,* a cousin of Charles Darwin, the man who developed the theory of evolution, reasoned that some people must be more fit for survival than others, more capable of adapting to situations—in short, more intelligent—and he wanted to devise a test to measure a person's intelligence. Galton investigated the influence of heredity and environment on intelligence, and published a book called *Hereditary Genius* (1869), in which he argued that intelligence is an inherited trait. But he failed to develop a testing instrument that could measure human intelligence.

That important achievement is credited to *Alfred Binet,* a Frenchman. His test of the thinking and reasoning abilities of children, developed in 1905, was revised by Lewis M. Terman at Stanford University and became known as the Stanford-Binet test. It has been widely used by educators and psychologists.

Psychoanalysis

Sigmund Freud (1856–1939), a Viennese medical doctor, was the first person to practice psychoanalysis. Freud did not at first intend for psychoanalysis to become a system, but the theories he developed to support his therapeutic techniques came to be taken as such. His extensive investigation of the development and maintenance of personality, with emphasis on such things as early-childhood experiences and unconscious sources of motivation, eventually were treated as a systematic position. This, in turn, generated much inquiry intended to evaluate the principles of psychoanalysis and affected areas such as clinical psychology, counseling psychology, educational psychology, and developmental psychology.

Freud's great contribution to psychology was his suggestion that much of human behavior arises out of motives that are unconscious—that is, motives of which a person is unaware. For example, in treating some of his patients he was able to discover phobias (fears) that were deeply hidden from the patients' conscious minds and yet seriously influenced their behaviors.

Gestalt Psychology

Gestalt psychology was developed in Germany with particular interest in perceptual problems and how these could be interpreted. In general, the Gestalt psychologists pointed out that previous attempts at explaining perception (and other kinds of behavior) were simplistic because they fragmented behavior and failed to take into account the whole environment. The phrase frequently used to describe the Gestalt position is that "the whole of behavior is greater than the sum of its parts." (Please note that the Gestalt psychology of perception discussed here is not the same as Gestalt therapy discussed in Chapter 16).

The Gestalt psychologists believed that other psychological systems were mistaken in their attempts to divide human behavior (including mental behavior) into discrete, or separate, functions. They believed that human behavior, and especially human mental behavior, is a creative process of synthesis that is more than the sum of its constituent parts. For example, to show how a person reconstructs reality from the fragments of perception, Gestalt psychologists would point to the act of watching a movie, which is experienced as a continuous visual event rather than as a series of still pictures (the separate frames of the film).

Cognitive Psychology

The work of the Gestalt psychologists in perception, thinking, and problem solving foreshadowed the development of another viewpoint, known as cognitive psychology. Cognitive psychologists disagree with the main assumptions of behaviorism. They feel that stimulus-response theory cannot explain all behavior, because the mind plays an active role in processing information from the environment, thus influencing an individual's response.

The cognitive position emphasizes the mental processes that influence behavior. These include perception and interpretation of environmental stimuli, belief systems, thinking, planning, problem solving, and other processes crucial to understanding the individual's responses to environmental events. One of the leading cognitive theoreticians was Jean Piaget, a Swiss developmental psychologist, who developed a highly original theory of the stages of intellectual, perceptual, and moral development, based on the development of a person's thinking processes.

Humanistic Psychology

By the mid-twentieth century, when behaviorism and psychoanalysis were the two major forces dominating American psychology, a new movement came into existence, which was referred to as the "third force." This term applies to humanistic psychology, which emphasizes the study of the individual as a whole person rather than just sensations, reflexes, thinking processes or habits. The individual under study is looked at as a total integrated person, unique and motivated to fulfill his or her potential for creativity, dignity, and self-worth and become what humanists call "self-actualized." In contrast to the study of behavior, this approach emphasizes a person's feelings and self-awareness.

The Fields of Psychology

The attempts to explain all of behavior by reference to only one of the systematic positions did not work out. By itself, no single system could account for all types of behavior. Eventually, systematic theorizing fell into disfavor. A common trend in psychology is toward limiting areas of study to particular aspects of behavior. Theories of learning, theories of personality, and theories of development are often much more specialized than were the broad theories and claims of the early psychological systems.

Today there are several dozen psychological specialties to choose from. One can, however, organize psychology as a discipline into several broad approaches to the study of behavior. Each of these, it should be noted, includes many subspecialties, with the number growing yearly.

Clinical Psychology

Clinical psychology is the largest field of psychology. Approximately 40 percent of all psychologists are in the clinical area. They are concerned with the use of psychological techniques to recognize and treat behavioral and emotional disorders or to conduct research into the causes of such disorders. (These disorders are considered abnormal; that is, they create a problem for the individual or for society.)

Counseling Psychology

About 15 percent of all psychologists are involved in counseling psychology. They use psychological techniques to assist individuals in coping with normal personal problems. The individuals seeking such help are not classified as abnormal or mentally ill, but are seeking help with problems, such as vocational choices or interpersonal relationships. The counseling psychologist may use psychotherapeutic techniques, but treatment of severely abnormal problems is usually referred to a clinical psychologist or psychiatrist.

Experimental Psychology

Experimental psychologists are interested in knowing about behavior even if the information obtained from their studies has no direct application. In other words, experimental psychology is oriented toward exploring the fundamental questions of behavior.

Experimental studies most frequently are conducted using the special approaches of the experimental method. (See Chapter 2.) Both human and animal subjects are used in the wide variety of behaviors that are investigated.

Physiological and Comparative Psychology

Physiological psychologists and comparative psychologists often employ experimental techniques to study problems within their areas of specialization. When they do, they can be viewed as belonging within the general field of experimental psychology. However, both are set apart by special emphasis on particular aspects of behavior and are therefore grouped separately.

Physiological psychology is the study of the physiological, or bodily, foundations of behavior. Much information in these studies is gathered purely to further the understanding of behavior, but some applications of physiological findings are important in areas such as industrial, clinical or educational psychology.

Comparative psychology often studies bodily processes, but the primary interest is in comparing the behavior of one species with that of others. A comparative psychologist may employ the experimental method or some other technique to compare the behaviors of species. For example, a test of the effect of deprivation on different species of birds may be done by raising birds of both species in complete darkness and testing what effect this has on their ability to fly or to gather food. Ultimately, the goal of the comparative psychologist, like that of other psychologists, is to understand human behavior better.

Psychometric Psychology

Psychometric psychology specializes in testing and measuring human abilities. These psychologists use a wide range of instruments (tests) including personality, intelligence, aptitude, vocational, and achievement tests, and they must be familiar with various types of statistical methods for handling the results. Today, psychometricians (as they are called) must have some familiarity with computers as well as with mathematics and statistics. They usually work for the government, a university or in industry.

Educational and School Psychology

Educational psychology is concerned with the use of psychological principles to increase the effectiveness of the learning experience. This frequently includes the study of learning facilities, curricula, teaching techniques or particular student problems. A psychologist who specifically attempts to test, counsel or guide students is referred to as a school psychologist, while the more general range of educational psychology encompasses school psychology and many other matters.

School psychologists most often work directly with students who are experiencing learning or behavioral difficulties. Educational psychologists, on the other hand, may often work with teachers in an attempt to make them more effective in the classroom. For example, educational psychologists may suggest new teaching techniques or help to develop educational materials, such as books or audiovisual materials.

Social Psychology

Psychology pertains to the behavior of individuals and groups; sociology studies the behavior of individuals in social interactions and in groups. Social psychology investigates group influence upon the behavior of individuals. Many individual behaviors (for example, applauding) may be looked at as a function of membership in a group. The behaviors of people in crowds, work groups, recreational groups, subcultural or cultural groups, and many other types of groups are studied by social psychologists.

Developmental Psychology

The study of an individual's behavior over an extended time span is called developmental psychology. Developmental psychology may concentrate on all the behaviors in only one part of the age span, such as childhood, adolescence or old age. Alternatively, emphasis may be only on the development of learning, on social development, on gender differences, or on the development of physical influences on behavior.

Other Applied Psychologies

Some psychologies are theoretical–their findings do not have immediate practical applications. Other psychologies we have discussed are applied—that is, they do have direct practical applications. Modern psychology is a broad and diverse enough discipline to include many other specialties, especially in applied psychology. A sample of these applied specialties is given here:

Industrial Psychology

Industrial psychologists apply psychological principles to the solution of work-related problems. Labor-management relations, productivity, and hiring and firing problems often are a part of industrial psychology.

Consumer Psychology

Understanding the motivation of consumers and applying this knowledge to help influence their buying habits or to make them better and more effective consumers is the prime concern of consumer psychologists. Many consumer psychologists work for manufacturers or retailers in the area of consumer market research.

Engineering Psychology

The engineering psychologist studies the relationships of people to machines with the intent of improving such relationships. This may involve redesigning equipment, upgrading the working environment, addressing the way in which people use machines, or changing the location in which the work takes place.

Community Psychology

A somewhat recent trend in psychology is the study of the effect of a community's social structure upon an individual's behavior. Community psychology is a particular type of applied social psychology. While social psychologists study all the influences of groups upon an individual's behavior, community psychologists try to improve the "quality of life" for the people within the community. In this respect, community psychology is a more practical and result-oriented (as opposed to research-oriented) discipline.

CHAPTER 2

The Methods of Psychology

Casual, undisciplined reports of behavior, such as gossip or rumors, occur quite frequently. Although these are descriptions of behavior, they are not acceptable to psychologists who are studying behavior. Psychologists require more reliable measures and accurate reports. This chapter describes the methods and statistical tools most often used by psychologists to measure, report on, and interpret behavior.

The Experimental Method

The most disciplined of the methodologies used by psychologists is the experimental method. Using this method, an experimenter manipulates a variable to be studied, chooses the response to be measured, and controls extraneous or irrelevant influences that might inappropriately affect the results of the experiment.

Information gathered in this manner is called research information. Properly conducted research satisfies several criteria.

If the following criteria are not met, the results obtained may be incomplete and subject to question.

Objective

Research should be conducted so that the collection, analysis, and interpretation of behavioral information is done with maximum objectivity. This means that any conditions that might introduce bias or prejudice must be avoided if at all possible.

Systematic

Research should be systematic, or orderly. Haphazard investigation may yield results that are inappropriate for the problem being studied. Orderliness also helps an experimenter avoid needless duplication or the omission of important data. Furthermore, orderliness helps an experimenter maintain objectivity.

Repeatable

Generally, a single research result that cannot be substantiated by some similar finding may be considered suspect and not accepted widely. To overcome this, any study should be written so that a skeptical or interested investigator has sufficient information to be able to repeat the research and either confirm or refute the reported results.

Empirical

One characteristic that helps promote repeatability is for the study to be empirical in nature. An empirical study employs variables that are measurable, avoiding concepts that may be subject to many different interpretations and that cannot be observed and recorded in an objective way.

Public

It might be fascinating to design a study that investigates ghosts' behavior, but unless the procedures and results are available publicly for questioning or repetition, the study is not a research study. Supposed observations that cannot be produced for public observation cannot be accepted and obviously would violate some of the criteria mentioned previously.

Meaningful Problem

This criterion summarizes the previous criteria. A meaningful problem is one that is public, empirical, and repeatable and that is studied in an orderly and objective manner. Research in psychology must investigate meaningful problems if the study of behavior hopes to progress in an understandable fashion.

The Hypothesis

A hypothesis is a tentative premise or proposal suggested as an explanation for a phenomenon. This proposal must be stated so that it can be tested and either confirmed or refuted. Two forms of hypotheses, the null hypothesis and the directional hypothesis, are frequently used in psychological studies.

Null Hypothesis

The null hypothesis proposes that a particular condition manipulated by an experimenter will not alter the outcome of the experiment. In other words, the results of an experiment will not be altered as the experimenter manipulates a condition of the experiment. For example, an educational psychologist wants to test the effects of room temperature on student performance on an examination. The null hypothesis would propose that changes in room temperature have no effect upon the scores obtained by the students. Disconfirming the null hypothesis becomes the way to establish a relevant finding.

Directional Hypothesis

A directional hypothesis proposes that a particular change in the conditions of an experiment will alter the outcome of the experiment. That is, as a condition of the experiment varies, the results will vary. A directional hypothesis for the "temperature-exam" study, for example, might state that students tested in a room at normal temperature (68°F) will perform better than students tested in unusual temperatures (50°F or 86°F). Another directional hypothesis might propose that the students tested in the unusual temperatures would perform better.

Experimental and Control Groups

Consider again the "temperature-exam" study. Assume that the experimenter sets out to confirm or disconfirm the null hypothesis: "Changes in temperature have no effect on the students' exam scores." To perform the experiment it would be necessary to administer the exam at least three times: once to a group who takes the exam at normal room temperature; once to a group at the high temperature; and once to the group at the low temperature. The students who take the exam at the normal room temperature would be called the control group.

The purpose of a control group is to establish a basis for comparison. The students who take the exam at either the high or low temperatures would be members of experimental groups. The performance of the students in the experimental groups could then be compared with the performance of students in the control group. Without the control group, the comparison of the results would be inconclusive, and the experimenter would not be able to either confirm or refute the null hypothesis.

By using a control group and confirming or refuting the null hypothesis, a researcher is able to draw meaningful conclusions. Suppose that the experimenter tests only two groups: the high-temperature and the low-temperature groups. Suppose also that both groups score equally well (or equally poorly) on the examination. This would not confirm the null hypothesis (that changes in room temperature have no effect on student performance). Only by examining the control group's performance could the experimenter justify a tentative conclusion, either confirming or disconfirming the hypothesis.

Independent and Dependent Variables

A condition manipulated by the experimenter is called the independent variable. The response that is measured by the experimenter is called the dependent variable. Experiments in psychology attempt to either confirm or disconfirm a hypothesis that proposes a relationship between an independent variable and a dependent variable. In the "temperature-exam" study, for example, the independent variable is the temperature of the room, which is manipulated by the experimenter. The dependent variable is the performance of the students on the exam.

It is important to remember that the experimental and control groups differ only in the amount or level of the independent variable that they experience. Furthermore, the responses of both groups are measured in terms of the same dependent variable.

By arbitrary agreement, psychologists plot the independent variable on the abscissa (x-axis) of a graph and the dependent variable on the ordinate (y-axis) of the graph. The "temperature-exam" study might be presented on a graph as in Figure 2.1.

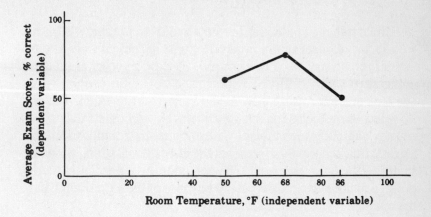

Fig. 2.1

Extraneous Variables

When preparing an experiment, the psychologist must give consideration to any possible extraneous variables, or irrelevant variables, that might influence the results of the experiment. As much as possible, such variables should be eliminated, or at least be kept constant each time the experiment is performed. Whenever possible, the experimenter should make sure that a subject's response is the result of the effect of the independent variable, and not of some extraneous variable.

While the subjects are taking the exam in the "temperature-exam" study, the psychologist would want to make certain that unusual interruptions (such as a custodian coming into the room) do not occur. In addition, other extraneous variables—such as the noise level, illumination, or humidity in the room—should be constant for each group that takes the examination.

Sampling

The number of potential subjects available for study is often very large. Consequently, a psychologist is seldom able to use the entire population. For example, an experimenter at a large university could hardly be expected to convince every single enrolled student to take part in the "temperature-exam" study. To select the subjects for an experiment, psychologists therefore employ sampling techniques. Sampling is the attempt to select a group that accurately represents the entire population. Several sampling techniques exist. The selection of a particular sampling technique depends upon the purpose of the experiment and the availability of subjects.

Random Sampling

A random sample exists when the group selected from the population is chosen by drawing numbers "out of a hat" or by using a table of random numbers, where each person in the population has an equal chance of being selected. The experimenter continues to draw numbers (or names) until a large enough sample has been chosen.

Stratified Sampling

There may be subgroups within the population that should be represented in the experiment in order to accurately reflect the composition of the entire population. In such cases, the experimenter may choose a stratified sample, in which each subgroup is represented in the experiment according to the percentage of its members in the total population.

Matched Sampling

An experimenter may believe that individual subjects have certain characteristics that give them distinct advantages or disadvantages in the experimental situation. If such is the case, the experimenter will make sure that each group within a sample has its "fair share" of subjects with these characteristics. This technique is called matched sampling.

Choice of Sampling Method

The experimenter determining the groups for the "temperature-exam" study might use any one of the sampling techniques discussed above. A random sampling would be when all the members of the population are assigned a number and groups are chosen by drawing numbers until the low-temperature, high-temperature, and normal-temperature groups are determined.

But suppose that only sophomores and juniors are involved, and that the ratio of sophomores to juniors in the general population is 5 to 4. The experimenter might want to have the same ratio of sophomores to juniors in the sample. This would be stratified sampling.

Suppose the experimenter believes that each subject's IQ would play an important part in his or her test performance. In that case, the experimenter might make sure that each group of subjects is composed of equal numbers of people with superior IQs, average IQs, and so on. This would be matched sampling.

In some circumstances, an experimenter cannot use one of these sampling techniques and must use whatever subjects are available. This is sometimes called *accidental (convenience) sampling*. Here too, however, the experimenter tries to control for individual differences among subjects that could affect performance. This is done by randomly assigning the subjects to different groups.

Experimenter Bias

Psychologists try to eliminate bias by using appropriate

experimental and sampling techniques. They may, however, be unaware of unintentional biases that they have. These biases are classified under the general heading of experimenter bias.

The experimenter in the "temperature-exam" study could inadvertently indicate to the high-temperature or low-temperature subjects that they are not expected to do too well on the exam. Even a gesture or an offhanded remark to the subjects might be enough to introduce such bias into the experiment. Furthermore, the very design of the experiment may indicate experimenter bias. If the high room temperature were $100°F$ (not $86°F$) and the low temperature $36°F$ (not $50°F$), the experimenter might very well be accused of "forcing" the issue.

Other Psychological Methodologies

Some psychological information cannot be obtained by using the experimental method. Psychologists also use techniques such as naturalistic observation, clinical case histories, and testing and surveying as means for gathering information. These techniques may not be as precise as the experimental method is, but they do give psychologists additional ways in which to gather and analyze information.

Naturalistic Observation

Naturalistic observations are careful, unbiased examinations of events that occur in a basically unmanipulated environment. The psychologist does not control the circumstances in order to force or select a particular response from a subject. Instead, the psychologist conscientiously records whatever the subject does. For example, a psychologist who is interested in studying children at play might observe several children together in a playroom. Using a one-way mirror (or perhaps videotape equipment), the psychologist could then observe and record the children's activity without making her or his presence known. In this way, the psychologist could minimize the influence an "adult presence" might have on the children. The children could do as they wish, unless for some reason the psychologist halts their play.

Clinical Case Histories

The primary goal of a counseling or clinical psychologist is to help people overcome their personal problems. In the course of treating someone, a counseling or clinical psychologist may make a record of problems, insights, and techniques that were important in the treatment. Such reports are called clinical case histories. They are often studied by other psychologists because they may expose some factor that has general significance for the understanding of behavior. Usually, the information presented for the first time in a clinical case history is subject to skeptical questioning; more controlled investigation may take place before a clinical case history is accepted by other psychologists.

Suppose a five-year-old girl is brought to a psychologist because of her very aggressive behavior patterns, which have alarmed her parents and teachers. The psychologist suspects that the aggressive behavior is the result of frustration brought about by a recent change in the family's attitude toward the girl. To summarize and clarify this belief, the psychologist writes a clinical case history, describing in detail the girl's aggressive behavior and her family situation.

At the conclusion of the case history, the psychologist may suggest that the problem can be lessened with appropriate alterations of the family's behavior. However, the psychologist might also want to investigate the frustration-aggression relationship in a more systematic manner. Both the case history and other records might be useful to psychologists for future reference in the treatment of people with similar problems.

Tests and Surveys

Psychologists often obtain information about behavior by asking the subjects to respond to specially designed tests, surveys, interviews, and questionnaires. All of these provide stimuli to which the subjects react. Psychologists study these reactions in an attempt to find out more about a particular subject's or group's behavior.

A test or survey technique has been designed to investigate almost every aspect of behavior, including personality, intelligence, attitudes, and aptitudes. Tests and surveys have two basic advantages: they allow for the rapid collection of information, and they give the psychologist the ability to compare a subject's responses with those of thousands of others who have taken the same test. Tests and surveys have one serious disadvantage—a subject may purposely give misleading responses.

Much of the information obtained through the various psychological methodologies is analyzed by the use of statistics. Statistics is the discipline that deals with the collection, analysis, interpretation, and presentation of numerical data. The following section will discuss the statistical techniques most commonly used in psychological research and test interpretation.

Purposes of Statistics

Statistics has two major purposes in psychology: (1) to summarize or simplify the data that have been obtained; and (2) to permit descriptions or inferences to be made from these data.

Descriptive Statistics

Descriptive statistics provide simplified, or "shorthand," summaries of data. They are used to present the data collected in as concise a form as possible. In this chapter, frequency distributions, measures of central tendency, and measures of variability are some of the descriptive statistics discussed.

Inferential Statistics

Inferential statistics provide the means for evaluating relationships that exist within data obtained from a sample. Psychologists use inferential statistics when making predictions, often of the effect of some variable upon responses.

Symbols Used in Statistics

Several symbols are frequently used in statistical representations. Some of the most common are included in the following list:

$$
\begin{aligned}
N &= \text{number of scores} \\
X &= \text{score (or scores)} \\
M \text{ or } \overline{X} &= \text{the mean or average score} \\
d &= \text{the difference of a score from the mean} \\
\Sigma &= \text{sum of} \\
D &= \text{the difference in rank} \\
r \text{ or } \rho &= \text{correlation} \\
SD \text{ or } \sigma &= \text{standard deviation}
\end{aligned}
$$

These symbols can be used in combination. Thus, the formula

$$SD = \sqrt{\frac{\Sigma d^2}{N}}$$

would be read as: The standard deviation (SD) is equal to the square root of the sum (Σ) of the squared differences of the scores from the mean (d^2), divided by the number of scores (N).

Formulas Used in Statistics

There also are several formulas that are often used in psychological statistics. The following are the most common of these:

For calculating the mean:

$$M = \frac{\Sigma X}{N}$$

For calculating the standard deviation:

$$SD = \sqrt{\frac{\Sigma d^2}{N}}$$

For calculating the coefficient of correlation by the product-moment method:

$$r = \frac{\Sigma (d_x)(d_y)}{N (SD_x)(SD_y)}$$

For calculating the coefficient of correlation by the rank-difference method (where D represents a difference in rank for any one subject):

$$\rho = 1 - \frac{6(\Sigma D^2)}{N (N^2 - 1)}$$

Discussions of these formulas and examples of the use of each are presented later in this chapter.

Frequency Distributions

To be able to comprehend items of raw data, it is often necessary to arrange the data in a frequency distribution, which is a visual representation of how the scores are distributed. This is accomplished by dividing the measurement scale of the data into class intervals, which are portions of the scale determined by the investigator. Thus, each item of data will fall within one of the class intervals set up by the investigator.

Frequency Polygons

Frequency polygons are line graphs that represent a frequency distribution. An investigator studying the effects of room temperature on the performance of a task might plot a frequency polygon as in Figure 2.2.

Histograms

A histogram is a bar graph that represents a frequency distribution. The data presented above could also be plotted as a histogram, as in Figure 2.3.

Symmetry and Skew

Some frequency distributions have an equal number of scores (or other data) arranged in similar patterns on either side of the middle of the distribution. Such distributions are called symmetrical distributions. When the scores "bunch up" at one end of the distribution, the distribution is said to be skewed.

Distributions may be positively skewed or negatively skewed, depending on where the "bunching" occurs. *Positive skew* means that most scores are found at the lower end of the measurement scale used; *negative skew* means that the majority of scores are found at the upper end (higher values) of the measurement scale. The sketches in Figure 2.4 illustrate dis-

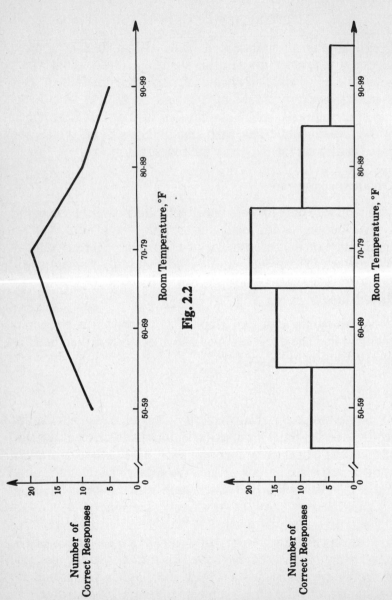

Fig. 2.2

Fig. 2.3

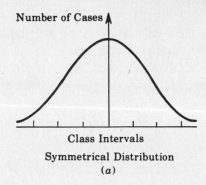

Symmetrical Distribution
(a)

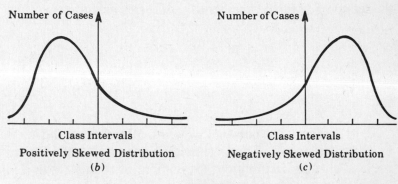

Positively Skewed Distribution   Negatively Skewed Distribution
(b)   (c)

Fig. 2.4

tributions that are symmetrical, positively skewed, and negatively skewed. (Note that the "tail" of a skewed distribution is found at the end of the distribution that gives the skewing its name: positive or negative.)

Measures of Central Tendency

A measure of central tendency is a statistical technique in which a single number is determined that best represents a group of numbers. Three different measures of central tendency are commonly used: the mean, the median, and the mode.

The Mean

The mean is the average score for a distribution of scores. It is determined by adding all the scores in the distribution and dividing by the number of scores. The formula for the mean is written as follows:

$$M = \frac{\Sigma X}{N}$$

Suppose you are given this set of scores: 14, 10, 12, 11, 15, 7, 8. To calculate the mean (M), you would divide the sum of the scores (ΣX) by the number of scores (N), as follows:

$$M = \frac{\Sigma X}{N} = \frac{77}{7} = 11 \; ans.$$

The Median

The median is the point below which 50 percent of the items in a distribution fall. Thus, the median is located at the fiftieth percentile of the distribution: the number of scores above it is equal to the number of scores below it. To determine the median one must list the scores in numerical order and locate the middle score in the series. (Note: When the distribution has an even number of scores, the median is equal to the average of the two middle scores.)

Suppose, for example, you are given this set of scores: 10, 8, 17, 4, 11, 8, 12. To determine the median, you would order the scores (4, 8, 8, 10, 11, 12, 17) and identify the middle score. In this case, the median is 10. (You may also want to calculate the mean for this distribution; it, too, is 10.)

The Mode

The mode is the score that occurs with the greatest frequency within a distribution. The mode is the only one of the three measures of central tendency that may have more than one value.

Examine again the distribution in the example above. The mode is 8. However, if one more score of 10 is placed in the distribution, it would become a bimodal distribution with modes of 8 and 10.

Measures of Variability (Dispersion)

Another characteristic of a distribution is its variability, or the dispersion of its scores. In other words, variability refers to whether the scores are clustered closely together or are spread out. Two measures of variability used commonly are the range and the standard deviation.

The Range

The range is an easily calculated measure of variability. To calculate the range, simply subtract the value of the lowest score from the value of the highest score. It should be noted that a range may give a misleading impression of a distribution in which all the scores but one are bunched closely together. If this single score's value is very different from the values of the other scores, the range may show great variability in the distribution when in fact there is very little variability. Using the distribution above (4, 8, 8, 10, 11, 12, 17), calculation of the range yields a value of 13 (17 − 4).

The Standard Deviation

The standard deviation is a more sensitive measure of variability than the range because it takes into consideration every score, rather than just the extreme scores. A basic formula for the standard deviation is as follows:

$$SD = \sqrt{\frac{\Sigma d^2}{N}}$$

Using the distribution of scores found above (4, 8, 8, 10, 11, 12, 17), calculation of the standard deviation would progress as follows:

Score	d (Difference from mean)	d^2
17	$10 - 17 = -7$	49
12	$10 - 12 = -2$	4
11	$10 - 11 = -1$	1
10	$10 - 10 = \ \ 0$	0
8	$10 - \ \ 8 = \ \ 2$	4
8	$10 - \ \ 8 = \ \ 2$	4
4	$10 - \ \ 4 = \ \ 6$	36

$\Sigma X = 70$

$N = 7$

$M = 10$

$\Sigma d^2 = 98$

$$SD = \sqrt{\frac{\Sigma d^2}{N}} = \sqrt{\frac{98}{7}} = \sqrt{14} = 3.742 \quad ans.$$

The Normal Probability Distribution

When many scores are collected and plotted on a graph, they often fall in a nearly symmetrical distribution called the normal curve. The normal curve is the graphic representation of the normal probability distribution, and an idealized version is shown in Figure 2.5.

The percentages shown are approximate, but do indicate that about 68 percent of any set of scores (or other numerically valued responses) will fall somewhere between the mean-plus-one standard deviation and the mean-minus-one standard deviation. Furthermore, 95 percent will fall between the plus-two and minus-two standard deviations from the mean.

Percentile Values

The normal curve (Figure 2.5) can be redrawn to show what percentage of the scores falls between each indicator of deviation from the mean, as in Figure 2.6.

It is then possible to determine the percentile values for a given score. For example, the mean score represents the fiftieth percentile (2 1/2 + 13 1/2 + 34 = 50). A score one standard deviation above the mean would be at the eighty-fourth percentile (2 1/2 + 13 1/2 + 34 + 34 = 84). A score one standard deviation below the mean would be at the sixteenth percentile

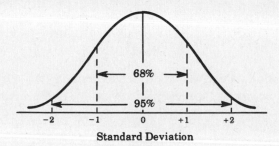

Standard Deviation

Fig. 2.5

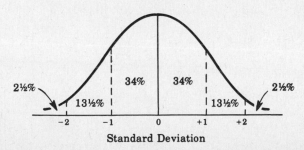

Standard Deviation

Fig. 2.6

(2 1/2 + 13 1/2 = 16). More detailed representations of the normal curve can be found in statistics textbooks.

Use of the Normal Probability Distribution

One of the most common uses of the normal probability distribution is in interpreting scores obtained from testing. If the mean and standard deviation of a distribution are known, a score obtained from one subject can be compared to the distribution.

If test results are distributed in a normal curve that has a mean of 500 and a standard deviation of 100, a score of 600 is in the eighty-fourth percentile. That is, the subject's test performance was better than the scores of 84 percent of the people who took the test. It is also possible to determine from the curve that 95 percent of the subjects who took the test had scores between 300 and 700.

Correlation

Correlation, which is sometimes expressed through a number called the *correlation coefficient*, refers to the relationship

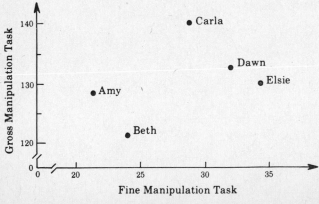

Fig. 2.7

between two variables. A correlation may be shown graphically by using what is called a *scattergram*, or *scatter diagram*. A correlation can also be represented numerically by calculating the coefficient of correlation.

A scatter diagram, such as the one in Figure 2.7, could be used to plot the results obtained from five subjects who performed both fine manipulation and gross manipulation tasks.

Calculation of the rank-difference correlation was conducted in the following manner:

Subject	Fine Manip.	Gross Manip.	Rank Fine	Rank Gross	D	D₂
Amy	21	128	5	4	1	1
Beth	24	121	4	5	−1	1
Carla	29	140	3	1	2	4
Dawn	32	133	2	2	0	0
Elsie	34	130	1	3	−2	4

$$\rho = 1 - \frac{6\,(\Sigma D^2)}{N(N^2-1)} = 1 - \frac{6(10)}{5(24)} = 1 - \frac{60}{120} = +.50$$

Numerical Values for Correlation

No matter which formula is used for calculating a coefficient of correlation, the numerical values obtained will range from 0 (no correlation) to +1.00 or −1.00. If the correlation is positive (+0.01 to +1.00), the value of one variable increases as the value of the other increases. When the correlation obtained is negative (−0.01 to −1.00), the value of one variable increases as the value of the other decreases. The larger the absolute value of the correlation (regardless of sign), the better the predictions that can be made.

The scatter diagram shown in Figure 2.7 and the correlation coefficient obtained above both show a positive correlation. In

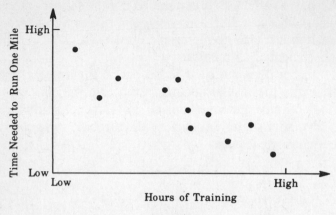

Fig. 2.8

general, the higher the value obtained for the fine manipulation task, the higher the value for the gross manipulation task. A negative correlation would be illustrated by the scatter diagram in Figure 2.8.

The relationship indicates that the greater the number of hours of training, the shorter the time needed to run one mile. The correlation coefficient obtained would be approximately –0.67.

The Concept of Contingency

The concept of contingency is important in understanding correlation. It is possible to calculate a fairly high positive coefficient of correlation (such as +0.75) that does not represent a meaningful relationship. This is because a correlation coefficient does not automatically indicate a contingent, or causal, relationship between the two variables studied. One should therefore use caution in interpreting the meaning of any correlation.

It would be possible, for example, to calculate a correlation coefficient that showed a positive correlation between the ever-increasing height for the world's record in pole vaulting and the ever-increasing number of telephones in service in the United States. The value would be positive, yet the possibility of a contingent (causal) relationship is very small. If there were a contingent relationship, the interpretation would have to be that because more telephones were used, the record went higher, or that because the record went higher, more telephones were used. Neither interpretation seems reasonable, and additional investigation would probably reveal other causes for both increases.

The Concept of Regression

In statistics, regression refers to the functional relation between two variables, and is expressed through a technique called *linear regression*. This leads to a value that allows us to see if we can use a previously obtained correlation coefficient of one variable to predict the values of a second variable.

Insurance companies use the concept of regression to establish their rates. Premiums for automobile insurance vary according to the age and sex of the driver. Previous correlational studies have shown, for example, that male drivers between the ages of 16 and 25 have more accidents than do other drivers. Consequently, the companies will predict that a client who is a male within that age range has a greater likelihood of having an accident than do other drivers. The company will therefore charge a greater premium to insure this particular client.

Significance

In comparing any two groups of scores, we usually find a difference between their means. Also, in correlating any two sets of measurements, we seldom get a correlation of 0, because of the operation of chance factors. The question is: When is the difference greater than what might be produced by chance?

Suppose that we are interested in finding out whether special coaching will result in higher scores on the SATs. In their last year of high school, half the members of the senior class are assigned to take a special review course in mathematics, while the rest of the class takes gym. Later, we compare the scores of the two groups on the SAT in mathematics and find that those who took the review course had a mean score of 600, while the other group had a mean score of 550. Is this difference significant?

We must answer this question in terms of probabilities: What is the probability that such a result could have occurred by chance? Is it 1 out of 2, 1 out of 5, 1 out of 1,000? Or is it somewhere between these numbers? Of course, the less likely it is that the results could have occurred by chance, the more convincing our conclusions.

Psychologists conventionally use a predetermined value (such as 1 in 100 or 1 in 20) to indicate whether the results of an experiment are accepted as statistically significant or were likely due to chance. These values are expressed in terms of probability (p). A $p < .05$ indicates the results could have occurred by chance less than five times out of one hundred or one in twenty. A $p < .01$ indicates that the results could have occurred by chance less than one time out of one hundred. The .01 level is obviously more stringent.

The choice of a significance level is arbitrary and usually depends on how willing the experimenter is to make an occasional error. Where a matter of life and death may be involved (as in testing parachutes), the researcher would select the most stringent criterion (perhaps one in one million!). The criterion is chosen before the experiment is begun, and there are a number of statistical tests that are used to determine whether the results meet the predetermined criterion, or level of significance.

CHAPTER 3

Physiological Psychology

Physical structure and glandular activity play an important part in determining the behavior of an individual. Understanding how physical structures influence behavior entails study of the individual components of the nervous system and how these components are arranged into systems and subsystems. Understanding how chemicals called hormones affect behavior entails a study of the endocrine systems of the body.

Much physiological information is gathered simply to increase our knowledge about bodily functions. Often, however, practical applications of this information can help psychologists predict or control behavior. Such knowledge has also benefited the medical profession by providing treatments for a wide variety of medical conditions.

This chapter examines some of the physiological bases of behavior and human functioning. First it looks at the structure of the nerve cell and its organization into the central and peripheral nervous systems that allow communication throughout the body. Then it considers the glandular systems that, through chemical regulation, affect a variety of human behaviors, including reaction to stress, level of energy, and sexual activity.

Elements of a Neuron

A neuron is the basic structural unit of the nevous system. It is a single cell made up of three basic elements: the cell body (which contains the nucleus), dendrites, and an axon. There are billions of neurons within the human body. The neuron fibers (dendrites and axons) are bunched together to form nerves, which carry signals throughout the body.

Cell Body

The cell body is the center of the neuron and serves to assimilate and make use of the nutrients that supply energy for neuron activity. Unlike the cell body of most other cells, a neuron's cell body has two different kinds of branches, or extensions. These are the many dendrites and the single axon that extend from the cell body.

Dendrites

The "receiving" portion of the neuron is formed by the many dendrites. These are usually short and thin and may number more than a thousand for a single cell.

The dendrites receive (or sense) signals in the form of transmitter substances coming from other nerve cells. If sufficient numbers of dendrites are excited, the signal is transmitted through the length of the cell as an impulse, or wave.

Axon

Each neuron has only a single axon, although the axon may

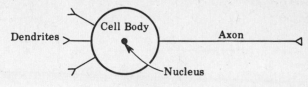

Fig. 3.1

have branches at its end. The axon serves to conduct the impulse away from the cell body. The axon then passes on the signal to the dendrites of the next neuron. Axons may vary in length from only several microns to several feet, depending upon the location of the particular cell.

While the entire neuron is covered by a cell membrane, many axons also are covered with a fatty substance called myelin. Myelinated axons will conduct impulses at a faster pace than will unmyelinated axons.

An easy way to picture a myelinated axon is to think of a string of somewhat irregular beads. The string is the axon, while the beads are the myelin. The signal seems to skip from gap to gap between the beads and progresses faster than a signal that flows smoothly through an unmyelinated axon.

Transmission of a Signal

Many factors are involved in signal transmission. Essentially, each signal travels the length of a cell and then crosses a gap to the next cell, where the process of transmission is repeated. Cells differ in their capacity to transmit and in the type of signal transmitted, but the basic process of all transmissions is the same.

Synapse

A signal originally reaches a cell when a transmitter substance that is secreted by the axon of one cell crosses a gap

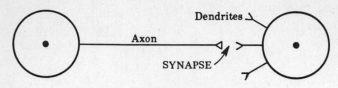

Fig. 3.2

between that axon and the dendrite of the next cell. This gap is called a synapse.

Synapses are one-way connections. Signals pass from axon to dendrite, but do not travel in the opposite direction. In most cases, the signals are received by the dendrites of the next cell, although occasionally cell bodies or axons receive messages across a synapse.

Imagine a fountain pen full of ink. When you pull the lever on the side of the pen, ink will squirt out and be absorbed by a piece of paper. The synapse works in a similar fashion. When the transmitter chemicals are released from the axon, they cross the gap and are absorbed by the dendrites. Just as the ink cannot be released by the paper and replaced in the pen, the transmitter chemicals are not released by the dendrite and cannot return to the axon.

Transmitter Substance

At the end of each axon there is a bulge, or knob, that holds the synaptic vesicles. As a signal reaches the end of the axon, these vesicles discharge a chemical called the neurotransmitter substance, which is received by the next cell at special receptor sites.

Graded Potential

Transmission across a synapse may be excitatory or inhibitory. The chemical transmitter substances (such as acetylcholine) either activate or constrain the firing of the next cell. The sum of excitation and inhibition is called the graded potential. When the messages transmitted across the various synapses leading to the next cell surpass that cell's threshold for firing, the neuron is activated and transmits a signal throughout its length.

All-or-None Principle

If the graded potential is sufficient to cause a neuron to fire, the signal will always travel the entire length of the cell. There is no possibility that a signal can deteriorate and "die" within the length of a single cell. Thus, the firing of the cell is described by what is called the all-or-none principle. Each neuron fires at a fixed intensity; that is, the intensity is the same for every firing of the cell.

Resting Potential

The membrane of a nerve cell is able to let in or keep out specific ions, or electrically charged molecules. This allows the cell to control and monitor many chemical and electrical reactions. Outside the cells, positive and negative ions are freely distributed in equal amounts, thus neutralizing each other's charge. Inside the cells, however, there are more negative than positive ions since the cell wall controls what ions enter and leave the cell.

In a resting state, the cell membrane of a neuron maintains a certain level of permeability (penetrability) such that the inside of the cell is polarized, having a slightly negative electrical charge when compared to the outside. This relationship is called the resting potential of the neuron and exists because positively charged sodium ions are kept out of the cell by the membrane, while positively charged potassium ions and negatively charged chloride and phosphate ions can get in. Depolarization represents the flow of sodium ions into the cell, which changes its relative polarity.

Action Potential

When the graded potential surpasses the neuron's threshold, the signal passes through the length of the cell as an action potential. The action potential travels much like a wave.

The permeability of the axon membrane nearest the cell body shows a swift change, and the electrical charges reverse so that the inside of the cell becomes positive and the outside negative. This is called depolarization.

Although there is a rapid repolarization of the activated region, the signal does not fade. Rather, the adjoining section of the axon depolarizes. This depolarization-repolarization sequence repeats itself, conducting the impulse through the length of the axon.

Envision someone lighting a nonfilter cigarette. If the match is held too far from the end, the cigarette will not light. Once the heat is sufficient, however, the cigarette starts to burn. Now suppose the person places the cigarette in an ashtray and ignores it while it continues to burn. Eventually, the cigarette will burn completely, without having to be relit.

A nerve signal operates in the same fashion. It does not fire unless the stimulus strength is sufficient; but once it is started, it goes through the entire length of the fiber. (Note: The axon has an advantage that the cigarette does not have: When the axon has completed its task, it can repolarize and fire again. The tobacco, on the other hand, turns to ash and cannot be reconstituted.)

Refractory Phase

The refractory phase is the period of time required for repolarization of the cell. Although this may be a very short period of time (less than a thousandth of a second in some cases), no signal can pass through the cell during the first part of the refractory phase, called the *absolute refractory period*. The remainder of the refractory phase, called the *relative refractory period,* is the time during which the cell can be activated once again, but only if the excitation is stronger than normal.

Signal Strength

The action potential is always of the same intensity for every firing of a particular neuron. The strength of a signal is thus dependent on factors other than the size of the action potential. Three variables appear to contribute to signal strength: (1) the frequency with which any one neuron is being fired, (2) the total number of neurons being fired by the signal, and (3) the particular route of the neurons being fired. In general, a greater frequency of firing and a greater number being fired makes for a greater intensity of signal. The route of the signal determines the particular type of stimulation that will be coded as a result of the signal.

Summary of Signal Transmission

Whether a signal goes through a neuron or not, then, is a function of several related properties. The input of both excitatory and inhibitory stimulation to the neuron is summated in the cell body. If the excitatory potential (called the graded potential) reaches a certain level, the neuron "fires," much like a rifle, carrying the signal along its length. The signal is then transmitted to the dendrite or to a body organ.

The actual firing of the neuron either occurs or it does not—

there is no intermediate level. This is called the all-or-none principle. Before the neuron fires, it is in a state called the resting potential. When it fires, an electrical charge, called an action potential, passes along its length.

In a resting state, the cell membrane has a certain level of permeability that keeps out positively charged sodium ions and lets in negatively charged chloride ions. Thus, the inside of the cell is slightly negative compared to the outside.

When the neuron is stimulated, the potential across the membrane is reduced. If this reduction in potential is great enough, a sudden change in membrane permeability occurs and the charges reverse; the outside is now slightly negative compared to the inside. This change affects the adjacent portion of the axon, and the process repeats itself along the entire length of the axon. This is the neural impulse, or action potential, which remains the same strength throughout the transmission.

A neuron always fires with exactly the same potential. Thus, the signal (or "message") transmitted does not depend on the size of the action potential. Instead, the strength of the signal depends on the frequency with which a particular neuron is fired and the number of neurons firing at a particular moment. The type of message caused by the signal is determined by the pathway of the firing neurons.

Arrangement of the Nervous System

The billions of neurons that make up the nervous system of the human body can be categorized into two divisions—the central nervous system (CNS) and the peripheral nervous system (PNS). Each has subdivisions that function in specialized ways.

The Central Nervous System

The central nervous system is composed of two major subdivisions, the brain and the spinal cord. These two parts are joined at the base of the brain so that there is a constant passage of signals to and from the brain and body.

The CNS is encased in protective bone, with the skull surrounding the brain and the backbone surrounding the spinal cord. Both parts receive sensory messages from the *afferent* (sensory) part of the peripheral nervous system and both can send signals to muscles and glands by connecting with the *efferent* (motor and autonomic) part of the peripheral nervous system.

In general, the spinal cord serves two major functions: (1) carrying impulses back and forth from body to brain or brain to body; and (2) controlling many reflexes. The brain controls many of the more sophisticated functions, including perception, memory, and voluntary movements, and many of the more basic functions such as breathing or swallowing. Brain signals may even modify actions that occur at the spinal-cord level.

Structure and Function of the Brain

Through evolution, the brain has developed three layers. The first two layers form what is called the "old brain." The third layer is called the "new brain." Most of the first layer now forms a central core for the brain and controls basic, rudimentary behaviors. The second layer contains the limbic system and exercises control over sequential activities and emotions. The third, most recently developed layer, is the cerebrum. The cerebrum controls higher mental processes.

Central Core

The central core, which is the layer of the brain that developed first, includes the medulla, thalamus, hypothalamus, and cerebellum; it has as its center the reticular activating system. The behaviors controlled by the central core include basic survival functions such as breathing, eating, drinking, arousal, coordination, regulation of temperature, and sexual activity.

Medulla. The medulla, or brain stem, is an extension of the spinal cord, located within the skull, at the base of the brain. It is involved in the control of our nonvoluntary responses, such as respiration, heart rate, and gastrointestinal functioning.

Thalamus. The thalamus comprises a group of cell bodies arranged in the shape of a football. It relays sensory information to the cortex (vision, hearing, touch, taste). The thalamus also regulates sleep and wakefulness in conjunction with the limbic system.

Reticular Activating System. The reticular activating system (RAS) consists of interconnected neurons that run throughout the thalamus and into the midbrain. While this system is still something of a mystery, it is believed that it serves as an arousal system for certain brain areas. Thus, it appears to play an important role in sleep and wakefulness, as well as in the organism's general state of attention and activity. Destruction of the RAS results in permanent unconsciousness, whereas electric stimulation of the system produces generalized cerebral activation.

Hypothalamus. The hypothalamus is a small area, about the size of a fingertip, located in the forebrain. It regulates the internal environment (heart rate, blood pressure, body temperature) and controls such basic drives as hunger, thirst, sex, and rage. It also influences the secretions of the pituitary gland, which we will discuss below.

Cerebellum. The cerebellum is responsible for motor coordination and balance. It is central to such activities as walking, threading a needle, and driving a car.

Limbic System

The second layer of the brain, the limbic system, surrounds the central core. It seems to function in a coordinated fashion

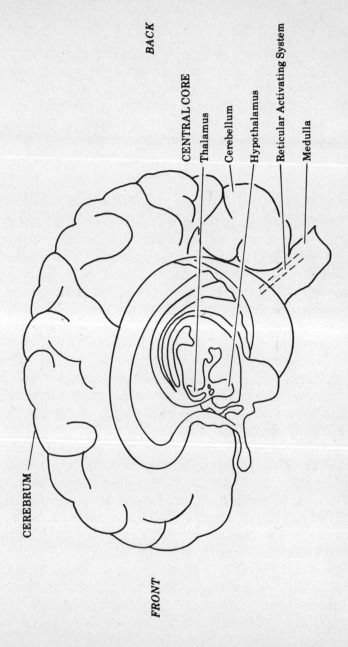

BACK

CENTRAL CORE

Thalamus

Cerebellum

Hypothalamus

Reticular Activating System

Medulla

CEREBRUM

FRONT

Fig. 3.3

with the hypothalamus, programming the sequences of activities necessary to satisfy the basic needs that the hypothalamus regulates. For example, feeding or mating are behaviors carried out in sequences unless damage has occurred to the limbic system. The limbic system apparently has a regulating function for emotional behaviors also. Damage in this area may produce unusual emotional patterns, such as inappropriate rage, or complete docility even when under attack.

Cerebrum

The third and most highly evolved layer of the brain, the cerebrum, is composed of two cerebral hemispheres. The outer layer of these hemispheres is called the cortex. The cerebrum is concerned with higher mental activities, such as thinking and reasoning. These complex mental skills are controlled by the cortex. Careful study of the cerebral hemispheres has allowed a labeling of specific areas and a "mapping" of many of their functions.

Central Fissure and Lateral Fissure. While all of the cortical surface of the brain is convoluted (wrinkled), two especially deep convolutions appear. The central fissure runs from the top middle of the brain toward the center side. The lateral fissure runs from the lower front of the brain toward the center side.

Cortical Lobes. Each cerebral hemisphere is divided into four lobes. The frontal lobe is in the area from the front of the central fissure all the way to the front of the lateral fissure. The parietal lobe goes from the rear of the central fissure to the center back of the brain. The occipital lobe is the lower back portion of the brain. The temporal lobe is the area from the front of the occipital lobe to the rear of the lateral fissure.

Localized Functions. A number of functions have been identified for different areas of the cerebral hemispheres. The motor area is found in the back portion of the frontal lobe cortex, just in front of the central fissure.

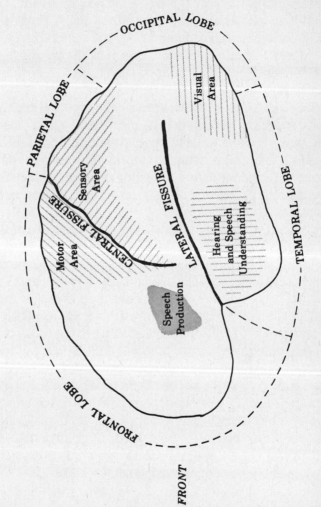

Fig. 3.4

Just to the rear of the central fissure, in the front of the parietal lobe, is the sensory area for tactile stimulation, or touch. Vision is located at the very back of the brain, in the occipital lobe. Hearing, speech understanding, and speech production are located near the lateral fissure. Much of the rest of the cortex remains unmapped, but it is believed that association and memory functions are located there.

Corpus Callosum. The corpus callosum is a thick band of fibers connecting the cerebral hemispheres. These fibers serve as the pathway for signals to travel from one side of the brain to the other. These fibers may be made temporarily nonfunctional by using a technique called spreading depression; they may also be permanently separated by surgical cutting, to prevent massive epileptic seizures.

Research evidence indicates that the two halves of the brain may operate independently. In general, such studies have shown that over 90 percent of the population is left-hemisphere dominated. (Note: Because of a crossing-over of control, the left hemisphere controls the functions of the right side of the body.)

"Split-brain" research has shown that language skills usually depend upon left-hemisphere functioning. Suppose a subject has had the corpus callosum severed and is shown the word "matchbox" so that "match" is transmitted to the right hemisphere and "box" to the left hemisphere. The subject will be able to report seeing only the word "box." When asked what kind of box, the subject may guess "shoebox," or "hatbox," only getting "matchbox" by chance. Of course, normally, both cerebral hemispheres act in unison since they are joined by the corpus callosum and by other connecting neuron pathways.

Electrical Stimulation of the Brain

Electrical stimulation of the brain (ESB) is accomplished by implanting electrodes into brain tissue and delivering mild electric shocks. Brain cells respond to such shocks much as they do to the electrical impulses that are constantly transmitted throughout the nervous system. Since the brain does not contain sensory receptors for pain, the shocks are not painful.

This technique has been used to determine what functions are affected when different areas of the brain are stimulated, and has helped with the mapping of the brain. ESB also has been shown to serve as a reinforcement or an aversive stimulus, depending upon where the electrode is placed, and experimental therapeutic uses have been investigated. Much more information regarding uses of ESB remains to be gathered, but ethical and practical problems may place limitations upon the extent of such study.

The Peripheral Nervous System

The peripheral nervous system (PNS) has two subdivisions: the *somatic system* (concerned with sensory and motor functions) and the *autonomic system* (which controls the functions of many glands and smooth-muscle organs). The somatic system, especially the sensory processes and perception, is treated in greater depth in Chapter 5.

The autonomic nervous system is further divided into the sympathetic and parasympathetic divisions. Although there are some exceptions, these divisions usually work in an antagonistic, or opposite, manner. An example of antagonistic functioning within the autonomic nervous system is the inhibition of bladder release caused by the sympathetic system, and the stimulation of bladder release caused by the parasympathetic system. Another illustration is the sympathetic system's inhibition of digestion and the parasympathetic system's facilitation of digestive processes. (Note: In extreme emotional situations, parasympathetic control may override sympathetic functioning, causing an involuntary discharge of the bladder.)

Sympathetic System

On either side of the thoracic and lumbar (middle) portions of the spinal cord, there are chains of nerve fibers and cell bodies that link the spinal cord to various visceral organs. These are the sympathetic chains. This system tends to act as a unit and is involved primarily with aroused, or excited, activity.

Parasympathetic System

The fibers of the parasympathetic system connect with many of the same visceral organs as the sympathetic system. These fibers originate in the cervical (top) and sacral (bottom) portions of the spinal cord. They tend to operate independently from the sympathetic system and are involved with quiet, recuperative functions.

The autonomic system is so named because many of its functions are automatic and self-regulating, continuing whether or not conscious thought is involved.

The Glandular Systems

The human body contains two sets of glands that are important for body functions—the exocrine glands and the endocrine glands. In general, *exocrine glands* (such as salivary glands or sweat glands) secrete fluids to the outer surfaces of the body, while the *endocrine glands,* discussed below, secrete hormones, or distinctive chemicals, that carry "messages" through the bloodstream to certain areas of the body.

The autonomic nervous system acts upon the endocrine glands, stimulating the glands to produce hormones. The hormones serve as chemical communicators, circulating throughout the body via the bloodstream but affecting only particular "key" organs. This endocrine system activity helps control growth, sexual behavior, level of energy, reaction to stress, and even the functioning of the nervous system itself.

Pituitary Gland

The pituitary gland has been described as the body's "master gland." Connected to the hypothalamus, the pituitary gland is a tiny organ, less than one-half inch in diameter, located below the base of the brain. The pituitary gland's connection with the brain provides an important interaction between the nervous system and the endocrine system. It is actually two glands in one, consisting of a posterior and an anterior lobe, each having very different functions.

Posterior Lobe

The posterior pituitary is structurally and functionally an extension of the hypothalamic area of the brain. It releases two hormones: oxytocin, which is important in childbirth, as well as in initiating the flow of milk through the nipples; and vasopressin or ADH, the antidiuretic hormone, which helps control the amount of water in the body.

Anterior Lobe

The anterior pituitary is considered essential for life. It secretes seven major hormones, three of which (the gonadotropic hormones) control the sex glands. The growth (somatotropic) hormone initiates the growth of an individual's body; too little of this hormone results in dwarfism, while too much growth hormone leads to gigantism. The other hormones are thyrotropin, which controls the thyroid gland; adrenocorticotropic hormone (ACTH), which triggers release of hormones in the cortex of the adrenal glands; and melanocyte-stimulating hormone, which causes the skin to darken. The secretions of the anterior pituitary are especially important because they also control the activity of other endocrine glands.

The Gonads

At the time of puberty, the anterior pituitary's production of gonadotropic hormones goes from an almost negligible amount to the high level found in adults. This hormone causes the gonads—*testes* in the male and *ovaries* in the female—to mature. These gonads can then produce the germ cells (sperm in the male, ova in the female) as well as the sex hormones (testosterone in males and estrogen and progesterone in females), which are responsible for development of the secondary sex characteristics that appear at the beginning of adolescence. In the male, there are changes such as the appearance of facial and body hair, deepening of the voice, development of the body musculature, and enlargement of the penis, prostate, and seminal vesicles. In the female, breast development, appearance of axillary and pubic hair, rounding of the body contours, and especially enlargement of the uterus and the onset of menstruation are signs of puberty.

Thyroid and Adrenal Glands

Two other endocrine glands provide good examples of the importance of the glandular system in the overall functioning of the body. The thyroid gland, located below the vocal cords and surrounding the front of the windpipe, is responsible for controlling the body's rate of metabolism. An adult with an underactive thyroid tends to be fat and sluggish, while someone with thyroid hyperactivity is thin and jumpy.

The adrenal glands, which rest on top of the kidneys, secrete adrenaline and noradrenaline, hormones that help the organism to prepare for emergencies and to cope with stress.

CHAPTER 4

Developmental Psychology

Developmental psychology is the study of how an individual grows and changes through the life span. As a group, developmental psychologists are concerned with the entire life span, including both prenatal (before birth) and postnatal (following birth) development. Any one psychologist may be interested in only a part of the life span, or in any one behavior throughout the life span. In other words, the study of developmental psychology may begin at the moment of conception and continue until death.

Child psychology places special emphasis on the childhood period, extending from birth through puberty, which takes place at age 12 or 13. Historically, this study has concentrated on physical development, but in the past 40 years child psychologists have made considerable progress in understanding the child's cognitive, emotional, and social development.

Adolescent psychology and adult developmental psychology focus on the periods from puberty (early adolescence), through a variety of young-adult and midlife transitions, into the conflicts and challenges of old age. While early psychologists and researchers believed that most psychosocial development ends by the completion of adolescence, we now recognize that the adult years are also marked by important stages of growth and development, with their own identifiable characteristics.

This chapter will summarize findings about all these stages of development in different areas, such as physical growth, cognitive development, social learning, and moral reasoning. We will begin by examining the evolutionary and genetic background of the human being.

Evolution refers to those changes in a species that occur very gradually over long time spans. Genetics is the study of the transfer of hereditary characteristics from one generation to another. Psychologists are interested in evolution and genetics because an organism's heritage may influence its behavior significantly. Both long-term evolutionary trends and short-term genetic changes can suggest to psychologists a good deal about the causes of behavior.

The Study of Evolution

Charles Darwin's *On the Origin of Species*, published in 1859, was the first theoretical study of evolution to be widely accepted by scientists. Although earlier theories were proposed, none of them had the scientific credibility Darwin brought to his theory as a result of his extensive travels and detailed notes comparing the development of animal species in different parts of the world, under different conditions.

Darwin proposed that the features of successive generations are modified through the evolutionary process. He believed that those traits that provide an organism a survival advantage are retained, while those that are disadvantageous gradually disappear over the course of evolution. Some traits or body structures, such as the human appendix (which was once important for digesting vegetation), may remain even after their purpose has long since disappeared. Two major concepts of Darwin's theory are adaptation and selection.

Adaptation

The adjustment that an organism makes to its environment is called adaptation. The result of adaptation is that individual members of the species survive and reproduce, keeping their genes in the pool of genes that determine future generations, although other, less dramatic functions are also served by adaptation.

Selection

Traits that allow a species to adjust to the environment are generally passed on from one generation to the next. Traits that are disadvantageous for survival are usually eliminated by natural selection. For example, the slowest-running tigers were gobbled up by their predators, generation after generation, allowing the faster-running tigers to survive and reproduce new generations of fast runners. The selection of characteristics has been summarized in the popular phrase "survival of the fittest." In his book, Darwin wrote about the natural selection of characteristics over long periods of time. Forced selection through selective breeding is also possible.

Ethology

An area of investigation related to evolution is ethology, or the study of behavior patterns, particularly of animals, in natural settings. Evidence gathered through naturalistic observation indicates that evolutionary processes modify both the physical and the behavioral attributes of organisms.

Physical Characteristics

Evolutionary adjustments include the development of physical traits, such as camouflage coloration, thick fur for warmth, and the development of a thumb that works in opposition to the other fingers of the hand. Perhaps the most dramatic example of a species' adjustment is the development of the human brain. The human brain has evolved into a structure that has tremendous capacity for sensory and motor functions, the translation of motivation and emotion, and a vast variety of learning skills.

It is particularly in their ability to learn and reason that humans surpass all other organisms. The evolution of a highly elaborated brain, with a massive cerebral cortex, apparently enables humans to demonstrate advanced thinking, learning, and memory skills. Humans are especially distinguished from other species in their ability to depict the world symbolically by using language. (See Chapter 11.)

Behavioral Characteristics

The evolution of adaptive behavioral characteristics is sometimes easier to illustrate in lower organisms than in humans. The patterns that have developed for different organisms often are *species-specific*; that is, the behavior pattern is common to all members of a species, and only to that species.

Modal Action Patterns (MAPs)

One frequently observed example of species-specific behavior is a modal action pattern (MAP). MAPs are stereotyped sequences of movement and are found in all members of a species. It has been suggested that the human facial expressions that accompany emotions are MAPs. Expressions such as smiling when happy are evidenced at a very early age. They follow essentially the same patterns for all human societies and are easily identified by observation.

A MAP is usually triggered by a *releaser stimulus*, or sign stimulus. When the releaser stimulus is present, the response can be expected; when it is absent, the response pattern is unlikely to occur. For example, a young herring gull will emit a pecking or gaping response at the sight of the releaser—the red spot on its parent's beak. Elaborate courtship rituals, such as the display movements of male birds, fish, and insects, are elicited by the presence of a member of the opposite sex.

Vacuum Activity

On occasion, MAPs appear in the absence of any observable releaser stimulus. It has been suggested that this may occur when the motivation level increases to the point where the organism cannot keep from acting. This kind of MAP responding is called vacuum activity.

Researchers have experimentally deprived starlings of the opportunity to catch flies. (The presence of a fly is considered to be the releaser stimulus.) The starlings will sometimes initiate an entire fly-catching pattern even though no flies are present. The starlings are thus engaged in vacuum activity.

Displacement and Redirection

In some cases, organisms may be confronted with two incompatible sets of releaser stimuli. Often, the organism will vacillate between the two MAPs usually elicited and instead may perform an irrelevant response—one that is appropriate to neither stimulus situation. This irrelevant responding is called displacement activity.

For example, observation has shown that herring gulls confronted with two stimuli—one that ordinarily triggers fighting and one that ordinarily triggers fleeing—may choose to initiate nest building. In this case, nest building is a displacement activity because it is not appropriate to either stimulus.

Even in the presence of only one releaser stimulus, similar irrelevant responding sometimes appears. This is called redirection: a response is elicited but it is inappropriate to the stimulus. Both displacement activity and redirection are somewhat comparable to the ego defense mechanism called displacement. (See Chapter 13.)

Habituation

MAPs are sometimes made in response to inappropriate stimuli. If such inappropriate stimuli are presented repeatedly, the organism eventually adjusts and no longer shows the MAP. This ability to adjust is called habituation. A starling raised in darkness may, when it is first released in a lighted environment, chase its own shadow in an attempt to find food. Before long, however, the bird will show habituation; it will no longer pursue its shadow.

Habituation might also occur in response to recurrent appropriate releaser stimuli, but this is unlikely to happen. The pattern probably will be rewarded and therefore be elicited again when the stimuli reappear.

Complex MAPs

Research on the migratory patterns of birds and on other, similar behavioral patterns indicates they are very similar to simple MAPs. However, it has been difficult to determine what releaser stimuli are involved and what specific responses comprise such complex MAPs.

Genetics

Genetics is the study of the biological transmission of characteristics from a parent to an offspring. This transmission takes place when the germ cells (a sperm from the male, an ovum from the female) unite during conception to form a zygote. The zygote is the single, original cell formed by the sperm and egg.

This cell then divides again and again to form a multicellular organism.

Chromosomes

In higher organisms, all cells except germ cells contain one set of chromosomes inherited from each parent. For example, human body cells usually contain 46 chromosomes, arranged in 23 pairs. Human germ cells contain only 23 single chromosomes. At conception, the egg and sperm are united into a single cell, the *zygote*, which then has the full complement of 46 chromosomes.

One particular pair of chromosomes determines the sex of the offspring. The sex-determining chromosomes are labeled X or Y. A complete female body cell (that is, not a germ cell) is designated as XX: its sex-determining chromosome is made up of two X chromosomes. A male body cell is designated as XY: its sex-determining pair is made up of one X chromosome and one Y. When the body forms germ cells, these chromosome pairs split. Thus, all female germ cells (eggs, or ova) carry the X designation, whereas only half the male germ cells (sperm) carry the X chromosome while the other half carry the Y chromosome. Determination of sex is thus dependent on the sperm cell that fertilizes the egg.

Genes

All chromosomes contain genes. Genes are found in a long molecule called deoxyribonucleic acid (DNA), which combines with a protein structure to become organized into chromosomes.

Genes are the basic units of hereditary transmission. They are paired, just as the chromosomes that hold them are paired. The genes hold "information" for the production of proteins; this information determines the way in which the organism will develop.

Mutations

Sometimes, a spontaneous or sudden change occurs in the DNA. The result of this is that the cell does not replicate itself exactly. The resultant change is called a mutation. Mutations are permanent and frequently produce a radical and harmful effect on human offspring.

Crossing-Over

The genetic code is also not duplicated exactly in the offspring when genes that were previously linked become unlinked or linked with a different set of genes. This is called crossing-over. Crossing-over alters the set of characteristics found in the offspring and, consequently, the pattern that is passed on to succeeding generations.

Genetic Influences

Once the zygote is formed, the presence or absence of various genes determines whether or not a particular characteristic will be observed in the offspring. In some cases, a characteristic of an offspring is determined by only one or two genes. In other cases, many genes may work together to control some aspect of the offspring's development.

The diversity of characteristics determined by genes includes skin color, eye color, hair color, height and weight tendencies, internal organ development, and the possibilities for birth defects. Only anatomical and physiological characteristics can be passed through heredity to succeeding generations, while the parents' learned characteristics cannot be inherited.

Dominant and Recessive Genes

Each pair of genes controls specific activities of development. The members of the pair are not always alike. If the paired

```
       FATHER
       N      a
      ┌──────────
MOTHER  N │ NN    Na      N = normal skin coloring (dominant)
        a │ Na    aa      a = albino skin coloring (recessive)
```

Fig. 4.1

genes are not alike, one of the pair (the dominant gene) will act as a controller, while the other (the recessive gene) will not affect the process of development. Recessive characteristics appear in an offspring only when both members of the gene pair are recessive.

Skin color, for example, may be either normal (which is dominant) or albino (which is recessive). The offspring will be albino only if both parents transmit that trait in the germ cells that form the zygote. It is possible for both parents to have normal skin coloring and still produce an albino child, as Figure 4.1 shows. Although both parents show normal skin coloring, one of four conceptions could be albino (*aa*).

Birth Defects

Some birth defects result from a defective gene. Other birth defects are the result of a disruption of the pregnancy by some environmental agent, such as drugs or disease.

With advances in research, physicians and psychologists have been able to assist many couples with genetic counseling. Working with medical doctors and biologists, psychologists can estimate before or during pregnancy the probability that difficulties will arise. In many cases, this has helped alleviate anxiety for the couple or at least let the couple anticipate a potential problem.

Twins

Twins are of two types: identical and fraternal.

Identical Twins

Identical twins have the same hereditary pattern because they are the result of a single conception. In the process of cell division, the initial cell cleavage (division) may produce a complete separation, and two offspring will develop. Each identical twin has the same genetic characteristics as the other.

Fraternal Twins

Fraternal twins develop from separate conceptions. Their genetic characteristics are no more alike than those of any other siblings. They are twins only because they develop and are born at about the same time.

The probability of fraternal twins (or any other siblings) having exactly the same genetic characteristics is exceedingly small. The chances of both parents exactly repeating the same combination of chromosomes are $2^{23} \times 2^{23}$, or about 1 in 70 trillion.

Selective Breeding

Recognizing that hereditary characteristics influence the offspring in a pronounced manner, it is reasonable to consider trying to mate parents in combinations that will produce favorable offspring. Such a procedure is called selective breeding. It has been demonstrated successfully for many different organisms, including pedigreed dogs and cattle.

Humans have developed a number of social and moral restrictions that keep them from using the same principles to breed "better" humans. However, a kind of selectivity is practiced by humans who will breed only with members of a particular race, religion or social class. The science of "improving" the human species through selective mating, called *eugenics*, has never taken hold simply because few people are willing to say what human characteristics ought to be encouraged and what human characteristics ought to be discouraged through selective breeding.

The Relationship of Heredity and Environment

Early researchers tried to determine how hereditary or environmental events produced atypical offspring. While such research continues, a more recent trend has been to investigate how heredity and environment affect the development of offspring with ordinary characteristics.

Studies of hereditary influences on behavior have been grouped under the heading "behavioral genetics." Disputes in behavioral genetics have arisen especially around the development of personality and intelligence in humans. While some researchers have stressed the importance of hereditary influences on these aspects of behavior, others have emphasized environmental effects. This dispute, often referred to as the nature-nurture controversy, or the nativist-environmentalist controversy, is not easily resolved. Attempts to quantify the influence of heredity versus the environment have led to varying and often contradictory results.

Certain hereditary effects, such as the sex of the child or some birth defects, cannot be denied. However, much of the research relating hereditary variables to personality or intelligence is subject to differing interpretations. It is reasonable to conclude that both heredity and environment interact to influence such traits, and that trying to attribute percentages of effect to either is not meaningful.

Stages of Physical Development

Physical development, or maturation, may influence a human's behavior profoundly. Developmental psychologists therefore study both prenatal and postnatal development, from the moment of conception, when a person's hereditary patterns are set, until death. Any one developmental psychologist may study only a part of the entire age span or focus on a particular behavior throughout the life span.

Environmental variables are very important in determining the way in which a human will develop. During the prenatal stages, environmental influences such as drugs, smoking, or disease may slow down development. Postnatal environmental influences—such as home setting, parental attitudes, nutrition, and disease—may also affect development. The stages of development and growth usually appear in a set sequence, but variations in the time of their appearance are inevitable, and may be influenced by the prenatal or postnatal environment.

Prenatal Stages of Development

The three stages of prenatal development are the germinal, embryonic, and fetal stages.

Germinal Stage

During the first two weeks following conception, in what is called the germinal stage, the zygote (fertilized cell) begins the process of cell division, or *mitosis*. During this time, the cells are not yet attached directly to the mother. That physical attachment occurs at about the end of the second week, and marks the beginning of the embryonic stage.

Embryonic Stage

During the next four weeks, until approximately the end of

the sixth week, the group of cells is called an embryo. The process of cell division and diversification continues during this period. By the completion of the embryonic stage, sufficient development has taken place that the basic physical features of the baby-to-be can be recognized.

Fetal Stage

During the remaining 32 weeks of pregnancy (assuming a full-term pregnancy of 38 weeks), the baby-to-be is called a fetus. By the end of this period, the fetus is between 18 and 21 inches in length and about seven pounds in weight.

Postnatal Stages of Development

Postnatal development extends from the moment of birth to death, and is usually divided into five stages: infancy, early childhood, later childhood, adolescence, and adulthood. Along with the spurts of physical development, there are comparable patterns of growth in cognitive and social learning. While all children progress through basically the same growth pattern, the age for completion of each stage may differ considerably from child to child. Such variations are referred to as individual differences. An extreme variation, such as reaching puberty at age 7 or age 17, shows just how much difference can exist. In addition, there is a significant difference in growth rates between females and males. In general, until adolescence, females' physical development outpaces that of males.

Infancy

Beginning at the moment of birth, infancy extends to about age two. During this period, there is a continued rapid growth rate and the development of motor and perceptual skills. By age two, the child's weight is approximately triple what it was at birth. The end of infancy is not marked by a particular event, but rather is designated as the point at which the child has established relative independence as a result of motor, social, and cognitive growth.

Early Childhood

The early childhood stage extends from age two until about age six. Motor, cognitive, and social development continue at a fairly rapid pace. The end of this period is marked by the fact that all basic skills seem well established. At the end of infancy, a child can walk or run, stand or sit, and generally move about independently. During the next four years, motor development continues so that by age six, the child has the capability for much more proficient movements, such as jumping, hopping, skipping, catching, balancing or tiptoeing. While further competence can be expected to develop, basic skills are solidified fairly well by this time.

Later Childhood

This period extends until the child reaches puberty. The time for the onset of puberty varies considerably, but typically it occurs at about age 12 or 13 for girls, and about one-half year later for boys. Just before the actual beginning of puberty, there often is a period of rapid physical growth, called the prepubertal growth spurt.

Adolescence and Adulthood

Adolescence extends from the onset of puberty until about age 19. The end of adolescence is marked by the relative completion of growth and the attainment of an adult body configuration. From the end of adolescence until death, a person is considered an adult. Adolescence and adulthood will be discussed in detail later in this chapter.

Growth Trends

Two growth trends occur almost universally in developing children: the cephalo-caudal trend and the proximo-distal trend.

Cephalo-Caudal Trend

In general, the growth of the head end of the body can be expected to progress more rapidly than the growth of the lower portions of the body. This is true during both the prenatal and postnatal stages. A newborn child's head will seem disproportionately large if compared to the head of an adolescent or adult. The ratio of head size to body size is about 1 to 4 for a newborn. As the lower portions "catch up," the adult ratio is approximately 1 to 8.

Proximo-Distal Trend

In general, the growth and motor development of the central portions of the body progress more rapidly than the growth and motor development of the extremities. Observation of the development of a child's arm and hand movements will show that initial attempts to reach for objects are gross movements of the entire arm. Only later does development allow independent use of the hand and fingers in a very sophisticated manner. Again, this trend is true for both the prenatal and postnatal stages of development.

Individual Differences

There are general standards that seem to apply to the growth and development of all humans, but one very important point must be kept in mind: Any one person will have a unique growth pattern that may not fit exactly into the stages outlined above. This variation of growth rate (and cognitive and social development) is referred to as individual differences. Psychologists must be careful to recognize that each person's development must be treated as a unique case.

Methods of Study

The standard methods of psychological investigation described in Chapter 2 are used by developmental psychologists. In addition, developmental psychologists have come up with some specialized techniques for investigations in their field.

Longitudinal Investigations

Longitudinal investigations are studies conducted over a fairly long period of time, using the same subjects throughout. These subjects may be used for any investigation in which age is the independent variable.

Longitudinal investigations have certain advantages. Using them, it is possible to study the development of behavior within a single individual and to observe the effects of early experiences upon later behavior. Furthermore, because only one subject group is used throughout, the investigator can be sure that its hereditary patterns and experiences will be constant, and not extraneous variables.

For example, an investigator has identified two groups of children. By age five, one of these groups has had extensive exposure to educational toys, while the other group has not. Trying to determine what effects these experiences have on motor-skills capabilities, the investigator begins a two-year longitudinal study of the motor skills of both groups. Such a study could determine the cumulative effects of the preschool experiences.

Longitudinal investigations also have some disadvantages. The length of time involved may lead to a fairly high expense, a fairly high dropout rate among subjects, or the possibility that by the time the study is completed, the problem being investigated may no longer be of interest.

Cross-Sectional Investigations

Cross-sectional investigations can be conducted rapidly. Using subjects in different age groupings, the investigator studies how age, the independent variable, affects behavior. These studies tend to be less expensive than longitudinal studies, but they lack the precision of experiential and hereditary control. The dropout rate of subjects can be expected to be low.

Consider, for instance, the longitudinal investigation of the effect of educational toys on motor development mentioned above. In a parallel cross-sectional study, the psychologist might select children at ages three, five, and seven and subject them to the same tests of motor skills. The assumption is that the measured behaviors are age-related indicators and can lead to age-related predictions. For example, we can assume that in two years the typical three-year-old will be responding as the typical five-year-old responds now.

Retrospective Studies

Another method frequently used to collect developmental data is the retrospective study. Parents or other significant adults (such as teachers) are asked to recollect events from some individual's past. Sometimes, these recollected reports are compared with information available from other sources (such as school records or medical records). Quite frequently, the recollection of the adult is found to be inaccurate or incomplete, often creating a version of the past that is more favorable than what actually occurred. These distortions are not necessarily deliberate, but may represent instead mistakes of memory.

Often a retrospective study is used because it is the only information-gathering method available. Psychologists who use this method, however, must take into account the possibility that a person's recollections or memories are distorted or incomplete.

Developmental Scales

Developmental scales report the average, or "typical," behavior for children at different ages. The scales are constructed from data collected by observing a large number of children and can be used as a basis for comparisons. For example, a longitudinal study of exceptionally bright children compared their growth and performance records with those of "typical" children to determine where similarities and differences existed.

Readiness and Critical Periods

As a special part of some investigations, developmental psychologists may try to determine when (or if) an individual is capable of learning a particular response. Two concepts have resulted from such studies: readiness and critical periods.

Readiness implies that appropriate development must have occurred before the learning can take place. Once the necessary level has been reached, the capability remains.

Critical periods also implies that appropriate development must have occurred before learning can take place, but in addition states that there is a cutoff point or time limitation that ends the period of capability or receptivity.

Readiness can be illustrated by a child's ability to walk. A one-month-old child simply does not have sufficient motor skills or physical growth to be able to walk. However, at a later date (often at about 12 months) the child reaches readiness for this behavior. In other words, the child has gained the ability to learn to walk. At any time thereafter the child can actually learn to walk.

A critical period can be illustrated by imprinting, which occurs early in the life of certain organisms (for example, duck-

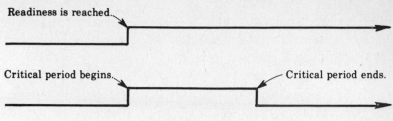

Readiness is reached.

Critical period begins.

Critical period ends.

Fig. 4.2

lings or chicks). Imprinting appears as a combined following and attachment response generated by moving objects in the environment. Generally, the moving object is the mother, although many other moving stimuli have been used successfully to demonstrate imprinting. If having a moving object in the environment does not occur during this critical period, imprinting becomes almost impossible. In other words, after the critical period is over, the duckling or chick loses the ability to learn the imprinting response.

The lines in Figure 4.2 represent the difference between readiness and critical periods.

Deprivation and Enrichment

Many children receive what can be called "normal" amounts of stimulation or opportunity. In some cases, the level may vary considerably, and the effects of this variation may be observed.

Deprivation conditions exist when the level of stimulation or opportunity is significantly reduced. The usual result from a prolonged deprivation condition will be a level of accomplishment significantly below normal. Obviously, because of ethical considerations, this kind of condition cannot be tested experimentally on humans. It can be observed only if it has occurred in some natural circumstance. Research using lower organisms has helped provide information about the effects of deprivation.

Enrichment occurs when stimulation or opportunity is considerably above normal levels. In general, enrichment seems to produce beneficial results in terms of the development of motor, cognitive or social skills.

Physical (Motor) Development

Several different aspects of physical development are studied by psychologists. Some of these, such as height and weight and other physical characteristics, provide information that may then be correlated with behaviors. For example, what is the relationship between a subject's weight-height ratio and his or her performance on an agility test?

Psychologists also study other aspects of physical development, including the sequence of motor skills, sensory processing, and perceptual development. These may include studies relating to the progressive learning of eye-hand coordination, the development of sensory abilities or the improvement of perceptual learning.

One of the most widely studied motor skills is walking. A typical development sequence for a child's first 12 to 14 months would be:

1. chin up   6. stand holding on
2. chest up   7. crawl
3. sit with support   8. walk when led
4. sit alone   9. walk alone
5. stand with help

This would not complete the sequence, however. Continuing development would result in the child's ability to jump, negotiate sharp turns, tiptoe, hop, skip, and go up and down stairs without difficulty.

The development of motor skills is very much tied in with the development of sensory processes, perceptual skills, cognitive skills, and social learning. Sensory processes convert the physical energy of the environment into new impulses. Perceptual skills interpret these sensations and make the environment understandable to the child who is physically attempting to negotiate it. Cognitive skills and social characteristics allow communication, interpretation, and reinforcement of motor behavior so that movement skills may continue to become more sophisticated.

Research testing shape constancy (see Chapter 5) has shown that babies only eight weeks old are able to recognize and respond to the shapes of objects even when the objects are placed in new and different positions. The skill becomes more advanced as the child grows older, and it is eventually accompanied by the ability to label shapes correctly. This kind of sequence is very important to our understanding of the development of perceptual skills.

Cognitive Development: Piaget's Theory

Sequences of cognitive development can be identified in a manner similar to that used for physical development. *Jean Piaget* (1896–1980), a Swiss psychologist, proposed a series of cognitive development stages that has been widely accepted. Piaget's theory not only accounts for the ways in which new thought processes are developed but also explains the child's processes of thinking.

Adaptation

Central to his formulation is the principle of *adaptation*. To Piaget, intelligence is an aspect of adaptation to one's environment. In its simplest sense, adaptation is an equilibrium between the organism's behavior and the environment. It involves two complementary processes: assimilation and accommodation.

Assimilation refers to incorporating new information from the environment and dealing with it by using existing responses or old habits. *Accommodation* refers to changing one's habitual way of responding or acquiring new responses in order to deal with new information; in other words, one modifies one's concepts so that they are in line with a new reality.

Suppose a young boy is given a rubber ball for the first time. He has no experience with this kind of toy. He responds to it first by biting it, because this is his usual way of dealing with round objects such as apples or plums. He is thus assimilating it; that is, he is trying to deal with the new object by using the old responses.

After a while, the child drops the ball, and he sees that it bounces back up. He will probably drop it again and after a while deliberately bounce it up and down. He has learned a new way of dealing with this object and has modified his behavior to meet the demands of the environment. This behavior is an example of accommodation.

Between these two processes, assimilation and accommodation, the child learns to adapt, establishing an equilibrium between behavior and environment as well as integrating aspects of the environment into his existing concepts. Piaget suggested that intelligence develops in a sequence of stages that is related to age. In each stage, a person acquires new mental abilities that set the limits of what can be learned during that period. Although the order in which the stages appear is invariant—that is, it is the same for all children—Piaget believed that the age at which one enters each stage depends on one's native abilities and the quality of one's environment.

There are four major stages of development: the sensorimotor stage, the preoperational period, the period of concrete operations, and the period of formal operations.

Sensorimotor Stage

According to Piaget, the sensorimotor stage lasts from birth to about age two. Starting from a complete egocentrism and a failure to distinguish between self and outer reality, the child progresses to an understanding of sensations, develops perceptual skills, begins to understand cause-and-effect relationships, and creates intentional and anticipatory behaviors.

Object Permanence

During this stage, the child comes to understand the concept of object permanence—that something continues to exist even when it cannot be directly observed. For example, the sun is there, although it is blocked from view by the clouds. Or, more significantly, the child begins to understand that when the parent is not present, he or she can return shortly.

Egocentrism

During the sensorimotor stage, the child's attitude toward the world is characterized by egocentrism, the belief that nothing exists outside oneself and that one is the cause of all actions. The egocentric child is unable to put himself or herself in another's place or to understand another person's position. Thus, according to Piaget, the child who pesters his or her mother after she has said that she doesn't feel well and wishes to be left alone is immature, not perverse.

Preoperational Stage

During the preoperational stage, which lasts from about age two until seven, the child shows considerable progress in the ability to represent things by language, drawings or symbolic play. Early conceptualization and prelogical reasoning (that is, reasoning that is partly intuitive and partly logical but is still lacking some important logical processes) develop.

The period includes two substages: the preconceptual and the intuitive.

Preconceptual Substage

At the preconceptual substage the child learns how to deal with objects and events symbolically through play (for example, by making a block stand for a house or two sticks for an airplane) or through early attempts at drawing. The child has the ability to represent things by using language but is still egocentric. For example, Piaget noted that a child might make up a word such as "stocks" for socks and stockings and assume that everyone knows what is meant. This stage is called preconceptual, because children do not yet have the full ability to understand concepts, such as that of "classes" of things, although this is beginning to develop.

Intuitive Substage

In the intuitive substage, which begins around the age of four, children are able to use the principle of classes—organizing related items (such as clothing) into groups—and their thinking, on the whole, is more logical. But there are still certain weaknesses to their logical thinking.

The child may, for example, have difficulty dealing with the results of *transformations*. A girl is shown two identical drinking glasses filled to the same level with juice and is asked to say whether there is the same amount to drink in the two glasses. After she recognizes that they contain equal amounts, the juice from one glass is poured, in her presence, into another glass that is taller and thinner, so that the juice now reaches a higher level. Most four-year-olds say that the tall, narrow glass contains more juice. They cannot deal with transformations, and they base their judgment on appearance rather than on reasoning. Similarly, if shown two frames, each containing eight circles, with one frame containing larger circles than the other, and asked, "Which box has more circles?" a young child will point to the box with the larger circles. Again, appearance wins out over reason.

Concrete Operational Stage

From age seven until age eleven, the concrete operational stage, the child's thoughts are characterized by logic, the understanding of relationships, and the development of coordinated series of ideas. During the period of concrete operations, the child develops the ability to use logic beyond immediate perception. What is most important during this stage is that the child's thinking becomes less egocentric, less biased in favor of immediate perception, and more in accord with the logic of reason and applied thought. Piaget asserted that most of our knowledge about reality comes from within by the force of our own logic.

Conservation

Given the same transformation problems during this stage, children judge equality with the aid of reason. When shown two glasses of juice, the girl no longer judges only on the basis of appearance; she begins to reason that if the two glasses held the same amount as before, and if nothing was added or taken away during the pouring, then both glass still have the same amount of juice, even if it doesn't appear to be true. The child has learned the principle of conservation—that if nothing is added to or taken away from an amount, it remains the same. Conservation of substance is discovered around the age of seven or eight; conservation of weight around nine or ten; conservation of volume at eleven or twelve.

Seriation and Classification

Seriation and classification are two other important concrete operations. Seriation consists of arranging elements according to increasing or decreasing size; classification involves putting things that are alike together. Both of these operations become more sophisticated between the ages of about seven to twelve, as the child's concrete-thinking abilities mature.

Formal Operational Stage

From eleven years until adulthood, during the formal operational stage, the child's thoughts progress to incorporate formal rules of logic. Abstract concepts become understandable, and the child can generalize from one situation to another. The child shows interest in the future and can use theories or hypotheses to propose what might happen.

Suppose, for instance, a child is asked to describe the concept of heating the house. The child in the sensorimotor stage would only react with, "It's hot," or "It's cold." A child in the preoperational stage might respond by saying, "Mom or Dad can change it with the dial." A child in the concrete operational stage might understand the relationship of the thermostat and the temperature level, but this understanding would be based upon the concrete operation of actually turning the thermostat dial. At the formal operational level, the child could hypothesize relationships involving different kinds of thermostats or heating devices without necessarily having such objects available.

Piaget's theories stress the sequence of events in cognitive development. The ages are suggested as average or typical, but not necessarily binding. This emphasis on sequence tends also to underplay the amount of cognitive development, which is usually studied as a part of intelligence (see Chapters 11 and 12).

Language Skills

Development of language appears to be primarily a matter of a sequence and selective learning. All children have the potential for learning any language, and for some time are able to generate any required sounds. A child of the Asian race and a child of the Caucasian race can generate the same basic sounds in infancy and early childhood, but lose some of these sound abilities when they are not reinforced in early language learning because the sound is not part of the language the child is learning. The sequence of language development is the same from culture to culture (and from one language-speaking population to another); only the specific language contents are different. (See Chapter 11 for more information on the development of language.)

Social Development

Comparable to physical and cognitive skills, social characteristics have been studied in terms of sequences of development.

Attachment and Detachment

Two aspects that appear to be important in social development are the growth of attachments and the display of independence (or detachment).

Attachment seems to develop in the first six months of life. Probably based upon various reward conditions, the child develops a relationship with the parents or other significant people, such as brothers and sisters.

In the second six months of the first year, the child has developed sufficient physical abilities to be able to move about in the environment. Coincident with this, the child begins to show detachment, or independence. Frequently, a display of such independence is first made only when a reassuring adult is nearby to reduce any potential fears.

Peer-Group Influence

A major facet of social development, which also appears to be sequential, is the attachment to or influence of peers, or age-mates. In general, it has been found that as the child grows older, his or her values are more and more determined by what is acceptable to peers and are less influenced by the values of older persons.

Sex (Gender) Roles

What is considered a "typical" or "acceptable" gender role seems to change with each succeeding generation. Some types of behavior are traditionally labeled "masculine" or "feminine," but the identification of gender roles changes constantly. Physiological differences obviously exist, but appropriate roles are in many cases determined not by physiological differences but by social influences. Consider, for example, that women today routinely perform many jobs that were once thought only appropriate for men because of the presumed "delicacy" of women: police officer; bus, taxi, and truck driver; mail carrier; astronaut. On the other hand, a gender stereotype such as "Men are the warriors" has persisted largely unchallenged for a much longer period of time.

Aggression and Cooperation

The development of aggressive and cooperative characteristics seems to occur in much the same way as the development of other behaviors. Opportunities for the child to express or practice such behaviors, models for him or her to imitate, and reinforcement given for responding all play a role in determining how and when these characteristics are developed.

Many of the previously mentioned variables—physical growth, attachment, peer-group influences and establishment of gender roles—may contribute to the pattern that emerges. Research has paid particular attention to the possible effects of modeling (see Chapter 9) on the development of aggression.

Moral Development: Kohlberg's Theory

Moral development often is studied as a part of social development. Learning what is considered to be right and wrong (which is obviously a function of the society in which the child is living), seems to go through a sequence comparable to the other aspects of social, cognitive, and physical development.

Three levels of moral development have been identified by psychologist *Lawrence Kohlberg,* whose theory continues to be prominent today.

1. *Preconventional* (Ages 4 to 10). The child behaves appropriately because of fear of punishment or the chance to receive a reward, but does not recognize any higher principle.

2. *Morality of Conventional Role Conformity* (Ages 10 to 13). In this stage, which Kohlberg calls conventional reasoning, other people's expectations of conformity are the basis for judgment and conventional conformity.

3. *Morality of Autonomous Moral Principles* (Age 13, or not until young adulthood, or never). This last level is one of self-accepted values, in which appropriate behavior is determined by abstract principles rather than by convention or by rewards and punishment.

A very young child might say it is wrong to steal from a store because you might get caught and punished. In the second level, the child might feel stealing is acceptable because "everybody" does it; if the child does believe stealing is wrong, it would be because "good" people do not do things like that. In the third level of moral development, the child comes to the conclusion that stealing is wrong because it was contrary to the principles of honesty and fairness.

Puberty and Adolescence

Adolescence is traditionally divided into three parts: puberty (early adolescence); middle adolescence; and late adolescence, the transitional period to adulthood. While there is much continuity in development over these periods, each has characteristic stresses and problems of its own.

Puberty is the period of life that links childhood and adolescence. While it occurs simultaneously with the early period of adolescence, and the two terms are used interchangeably with some degree of freedom, puberty describes more the physical period of development, while adolescence is used more to describe a psychological period.

Puberty

While there is no specific age that clearly marks the beginning of puberty, some general norms have been established. Boys enter puberty between the ages of twelve and fourteen and a half, while girls enter this period slightly earlier, between about ten and thirteen years old. If we consider the hallmark of puberty to be sexual maturity, then these figures are basically accurate.

A number of factors have been identified as important forces during puberty. Social constraints, which check and stifle the burgeoning forces of sexuality, may become objects of rebellion. In the school, where the pubescent spends a large portion of time, teachers and other personnel may be viewed as oppressors, encouraging, by their mere presence, rebellion and rage. This is also a period of sexual awakening, and often of sexual confusion, that is met with ambivalent reactions by both sexes.

Psychologists have identified three key challenges as central to the pubescent's growth: (1) the challenges posed by the biological changes of puberty; (2) the challenges posed by entry into a new social system, the junior high school; and (3) the challenges derived from the sudden entry into a new role status (as a member of the adolescent subculture).

Physiological Changes in Puberty

Physiological characteristics of puberty include menarche, the first menstruation, for the girl and reproductive potency, the presence of sperm in the semen, for the boy. Just as significant is the appearance of the secondary sex characteristics, which for boys are: pubic hair, facial hair, deepening of the voice, heavy muscular development, and angular body build. For the girl, the secondary sex characteristics are: breasts, triangular pubic hair patterns, and more subcutaneous fat, giving the rounded body contour. While these physical changes are the clearest signs of puberty, there are also marked psychological changes—changes in attitudes, interests, emotions, and cognitive ability—that become the crux of the adolescent experience.

Changes in Attitudes and Interests

The many physical changes of puberty are accompanied by changes in attitudes and interests that are either the direct or indirect result of the rapid physical growth and sexual development typical of this period. The reactions a pubescent receives from his or her peer group are often influenced by the manifestations of these secondary sex characteristics. The size of a girl's breasts may help or hinder her popularity with the boys; she might become the object of jokes, an outcast or she might become an object of admiration, respect, and lust pursued by the socially prestigious older boys. Likewise, a boy's lack of facial and body hair may place him at a disadvantage in comparison with his more hirsute peers who equate facial and body hair with virility.

Important but sometimes subtle relationships exist between pubescents' physical maturity, social standing, and their resultant behavior and performance with their peers. Although the physical reality of this period is not the only element that exerts a profound influence, it is a highly significant aspect of the early adolescent's experience and must be recognized as such.

Adolescence

Adolescence extends over a period of many years, from puberty until approximately nineteen years of age. After puberty, during the middle period of adolescence, there may be open conflict with the family, with the school or with society in general: much of the "storm and stress" associated with all of adolescence is actually based on this period.

Views of Adolescence

Erik Erikson provides a rich and detailed description of the adolescent period. Adolescents, he argues, are largely concerned with what they appear to be in the eyes of others and with trying to find an occupation suitable to their skills. According to Erikson, the "search for identity" is the major motivating and organizing force in this period.

In trying to find themselves, to develop a sense of identity different from all others, adolescents try out various roles. There are two dangers to this stage: role confusion (being unsure of who one really is) and assuming a negative identity such as that of a juvenile delinquent or substance abuser. Thus, Erikson calls the crisis of adolescence one of *identity versus role confusion* (also called the identity crisis).

Another view of adolescence, one developed during the early 1960s, approaches this period as a time of painful growing in which the individual is beset by numerous conflicts, doubts, and difficulties in adjustment. The more contemporary view, on the other hand, de-emphasizes the "storm and stress" conception of adolescence, and emphasizes the stabilizing, goal-directed aspects of adolescent development. Psychologists have found, for example, that the youth of the 1980s have returned to the patterns of hard work and goal-directed behavior that characterized youth of the 1940s. Recent surveys have confirmed that young people today are job oriented, less active politically, and more personally ambitious than their contemporaries of ten years ago.

Cognitive Growth

The formal operational thinking described by Piaget continues to develop during the adolescent years. Adolescents are capable of abstract thinking and of more realistic planning for the future. They not only plan for themselves, but may also plan to change society. Much interest in social concerns characterizes the adolescent's thinking.

Social Behavior

During the adolescent years, as the young person begins to establish his or her own identity outside the nuclear family, important new social roles are explored and tested. These roles are increasingly, though not exclusively, defined by the peer group, and include to a large degree the beginnings of what will ultimately emerge as an adult sexual lifestyle. Most people have their first sexual experiences (not necessarily intercourse) during their adolescent years. These experiences constitute an influential part of adolescent socialization, which is integral to sound psychological adjustment.

Sex and the Adolescent

It is during adolescence that dating and sexual behavior become important forces in a person's socialization. One of the most important tasks of this period is learning courtship behavior. This behavior, which we would generally call dating, becomes the basis for later, permanent attachments.

One of the chief developmental tasks of the dating period, and of dating behavior in general, is to define, clarify, and strengthen one's sexual or gender identity. The complex psychological adjustments to the new physical demands imposed by the body pose conflicts for many young people. At the very point in life where sexuality becomes a compelling force, parental disapproval and the risk of pregnancy encourage the limitation or postponement of sexual activity. Adolescents must learn to express their sexuality in rewarding yet responsible ways.

Adolescent Alcohol and Drug Abuse

One of the more refractory problems facing society today is the widespread misuse of drugs and alcohol by adolescents. Beginning in the mid-seventies, and continuing through the late eighties, alcohol emerged as the single most abused drug in the adolescent culture. It is estimated that there are over three million teen-age alcoholics today, most of whom are enrolled in schools. No one knows exactly why this is, but it may represent an ironic adolescent rebellion against the prevailing adult acceptance of marijuana.

The manifest symptoms of alcohol abuse among teenagers are as evident or more evident than the symptoms of drug abuse, which at times may be obscure. The adolescent problem-drinker is likely to have a high absentee rate, may appear intoxicated in class, and will invariably fall behind in schoolwork.

Adulthood

There are several unique developmental challenges associated with the adult years. While childhood is a period of foundation learning (both emotionally and cognitively) and adolescence is an experimental, transitional period in which new social behaviors are explored and new perceptions integrated into an image of self, adulthood, by far the longest period, comprises many vastly different challenges. During these years the individual takes on major new roles and develops new responsibilities.

These new roles and responsibilities touch many different areas of life, posing many personal decisions. Should I marry, have children, raise a family, or remain single and committed to values outside family life, such as religious or political commitment, personal growth and education, creative endeavors, or making money? The challenges of the world of work are also dominant. A career, or job, or vocational (or nonvocational) lifestyle is established during these years. Growth and development in interpersonal relationships, along with a new social recognition, also emerge.

Because the adult's life expectancy has increased greatly—and along with longer life the promise of healthy physical functioning—the vocational options available to the adult have changed dramatically. For example, a 50-year-old police officer, retiring from the force after 25 years, could learn an entire new field and devote almost as many years to the new field as he or she gave to the first one. Career options are, therefore, a vital element in the new challenges of this period.

Then, of course, there are the challenges of working together to make a marriage work, of raising a family, of dealing with the economic realities of life. Finally, there are what to many prove the two most difficult problems of adulthood: poor health and retirement. It is a time of awareness of one's own ever-approaching death, of seeing one's contemporaries die, and of losing those whom we love.

Stages and Challenges of Adulthood

Eric Erikson's Stages

Erikson, who conceptualizes the life process through eight stages, called the "Eight Ages of Man," designates three stages as particular to the adult years. Each stage, in his system, is understood in light of the developmental challenge that predominates in that period.

1. *Intimacy versus Isolation.* Immediately following the adolescent period, in which a sense of identity is acquired, the young adult is ready for intimacy and has the capacity to commit

himself or herself to permanent relationships. The individual who is not able to achieve intimacy during this period, who finds himself or herself cut off from others, suffers from a deep sense of isolation.

2. *Generativity versus Stagnation.* In young and middle adulthood, the conflict is between the drive to provide for future generations, directly or indirectly, and the tendency to become overabsorbed in self, unable to foster growth. In its broader sense, according to Erikson, generativity refers not only to bringing children into the world, but also to the varied forms of creativity associated with mature adult living.

3. *Integrity versus Despair.* The goals of this stage, mature adulthood, sum up what is perhaps the highest point of human development. At the same time they help us see how the development of a successful individual is not only compatible with, but also contributes to, the perpetuation of the species: specifically, by contributing new ideas and advancements to human civilization.

Daniel Levinson's Stages

Daniel Levinson, a psychologist who has devoted himself to studying the adult years, particularly men's, has used different categories to chronicle human adulthood.

1. *Preadulthood* (Birth to about age 22). During this stage, a person develops from the highly dependent lifestyle of childhood and adolescence to the beginnings of a more independent, responsible adult life.

2. *Early Adult Transition* (About age 17 to 22). In this stage between the late teens and early 20s, falling between and overlapping preadulthood and early adulthood, a person reworks and improves relationships with family and important others to form for him- or herself a place in the adult world.

3. *Early Adulthood* (About age 21 to 45). This is the period in which we form a family, establish a career, and develop the

adult lifestyle (both socially and economically) that will probably be with us for the rest of our lives.

4. *Midlife Transition* (Ages 40 to 45). This is the end of early adulthood and the beginning of middle adulthood. There are often many conflicts during this period.

5. *Middle Adulthood* (Ages 40 to 65).

6. *Late Adulthood Transition* (Ages 60 to 65). This stage links middle and late adulthood and is part of both.

7. *Late Adulthood* (Ages 60 to 65 on).

Current Trends in Adult Living

Several outstanding social, economic, and demographic factors have brought about major changes in the lives of middle-aged and older adults in our contemporary American society. First, we know that the percentage of the population aged 60 and over rose from less than 4 percent in 1830 to 18 percent in 1986. Middle-aged persons, between 45 and 65, now constitute about 20 percent of the population. In other words, between these two age groups, we are speaking about 38 percent of all Americans. Moreover, about 50 percent of the American work force are women, many of them between 45 and 65.

There have also been dramatic changes in the timing of the family cycle over the past few decades. Children leave home at an earlier age, and at the same time, the life span has lengthened because of the advances in medicine and the growing availability of health care. These changes have led to an extended postparental interval in which the husband and wife are the only members remaining in the household.

Other recent trends include delayed marriage, premarital cohabitation, an increase in single-parent households, and delayed entry into parenthood. Some of these trends are directly attributable to the changing role of women and the increased number of women in the work force. Others are reflections of attitudes and values that have accrued since the mid- to late-

1960s, beginning with the "hippie" movement, with its philosophy of sexual liberation, and including the Vietnam war protest movement. Still other changes are economic, as many young couples confront the difficulties of marrying or having children in their early twenties—a time reserved by many for higher education or career preparation.

CHAPTER 5

Sensation and Perception

In this chapter we examine how people sense the world around them (sensation) and process this information (perception). It is important to recognize that humans have many more sensory processes than are usually attributed to them. Many descriptions of human sensory processes detail the "basic five" senses, but it is probably more appropriate to recognize a "basic seven" and then to realize that each of these seems to have subcategories. The seven designations are: vision, hearing, taste, smell, skin or touch, kinesthesis, and balance.

Sensory information is processed according to certain regulating principles and constancies of perception. Sometimes, however, stimuli can be interpreted incorrectly, giving rise to illusions. Unusual perceptual experiences discussed here include hallucinations and extrasensory perception (ESP).

Sensation

Sensation is the process by which stimuli are detected, identified, and gauged. Sensation merely reveals or conveys information, while perception is the interpretation of information.

The Basic Sensory Process

No matter which sensation is being described, a certain sequence of events appears necessary for the sense to operate. First, some stimulus appropriate to that sense must be present in sufficient strength to initiate reception. The signal is picked up by a receptor (a nerve ending specialized for such a task) and transmitted through the sensory (or somatic) peripheral nervous system to the brain. The signal activates a particular part of the brain that records the signal as a sensation. It is not until the signal has reached the brain that sensation occurs.

Location of Receptors

Most sensory receptors are located in relatively protected positions within the body. (All but some skin receptors are at some distance from the surface of the body and are therefore difficult to damage.) Receptors for vision, for example, are not on the surface of the eye, but rather at the back of the eyeball, well guarded by the eyeball itself and by surrounding tissue, bone, and hair.

Range of Reception

Each sensory process is limited in its range of reception. A human's sensory capabilities are generally quite good, although they are sometimes surpassed by other animals' capabilities. Stimuli occurring outside an organism's range of reception are not recorded by the organism. For example, although they are close to the range that can be sensed, ultraviolet and infrared light rays cannot be seen by humans unless some special device is used to transform the rays into the visible range. Human vision is limited to the visible spectrum.

Thresholds

As mentioned above, stimulation must be of sufficient strength for reception to occur. The level of strength necessary for reception is called a threshold. A distinction is made between thresholds for revealing the presence or absence of a stimulus (absolute threshold) and those for detecting a change in the value of a stimulus (difference threshold).

Absolute Threshold

The absolute threshold is the minimum value of stimulus intensity that will elicit a response from an observer. This can be the faintest sound one hears or the dimmest light one sees. Since this value varies under different observation conditions, psychologists consider an intensity detected by a subject 50 percent of the time as the absolute threshold. (This percentage has been accepted arbitrarily.) Figure 5.1 shows how the value for an absolute threshold is determined.

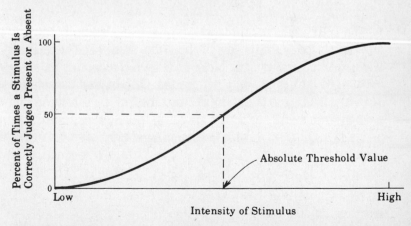

Fig. 5.1

Difference Threshold

The difference threshold is the minimum change in a stimulus value that can be detected as a change. This is often called the *just-noticeable difference (j.n.d.)*, or the smallest difference between two stimuli that can be detected.

Sensory Adaptation

On occasion, stimulation is at an unusual level compared to normal circumstances. In many of these cases, humans are able to make adjustments and adopt a pattern of behavior that allows them to cope with the new level of stimulation. This process of coping is called sensory adaptation.

Sensory adaptation occurs when there is a prolonged sensory signal that is accommodated over time into the background of our experience. For example, when you first enter a house where bread is baking or coffee brewing, the smell is quite noticeable—it is a prominent sensory experience. But after a short time, you get "used to it"—your sensory processes adapt—and it is no longer noticed unless pointed out.

Transduction

To fully understand reception of sensory stimuli, one more term must be introduced. When the stimulus (mechanical, chemical, radiant, etc.) is picked up by the receptor, its energy is changed into an action potential that then begins the sequence of events leading to the brain's registration of the sensation. This change from energy to action potential is called the transduction of the signal. Of course, the incoming energy level must be at least at the absolute threshold value before transduction can occur.

Detection Theory

Early theories of sensory reception maintained that each stimulus must have some minimum, unchanging value for its absolute threshold and some constant amount or ratio of change for its difference threshold. Later work has shown that such concepts are relatively naive. Absolute threshold values and difference thresholds may vary, depending upon a number of conditions. Three conditions have been studied extensively and appear to be most important: motivation, probability of the stimulus, and extraneous variables.

Motivation

Research in this area has suggested that certain payoffs or costs can affect a person's judgments regarding the presence or absence of a stimulus or any change of stimulus level. Evidence indicates that threshold values differ depending upon motivation, with greater or lesser sensitivity resulting.

Suppose, for example, that immediately following breakfast, you get into your car and set out to take some clothes to the dry cleaner. As you drive, you would be relatively unconcerned with whether or not you notice a restaurant sign, but your response to the dry cleaner's sign would be important. If you notice it, you can complete your chore; if you miss it, you might spend a lot of additional time and energy driving around trying to find the right place. Thus, your sensitivity to the dry cleaner's sign might be very acute, while your threshold for other advertising signs might be much higher. Motivation is discussed in greater detail in Chapter 7.

Probability of Stimulus

Past experience will often provide information regarding the likelihood that a stimulus will occur again in the future. With likelihood high, the subject can be expected to detect the stimulus, whereas a very small likelihood may mean the subject will devote energies to other stimuli and miss this particular one. A threshold therefore varies with the probability of stimulus occurrence.

Extraneous Stimuli

We are often in situations where many stimuli are present. Some of these stimuli may be very important to us; others may be extraneous, or irrelevant to our goals. These extraneous stimuli are frequently called "noise." Excesses in noise may raise threshold values by making it more difficult to detect the appropriate stimulus.

What is considered noise in one circumstance may not be in another. A cheering crowd may be expected and appreciated at a baseball game but judged inappropriate and distracting by a golfer in a tournament. The golfer's ability to detect stimuli (such as the flight path of a ball or the "break" of a green) may vary with the amount of interference created by the crowd.

Types of Sensory Processes

Vision

The most thoroughly researched sensory process is vision. This probably resulted because the visual apparatus is relatively accessible and because early philosophers believed vision to be the "dominant" sense.

The chain of visual reception follows the basic sensory sequence described above. Light energies (specifically visible light, a relatively small part of the total electromagnetic spectrum, which also includes radio waves and x-rays that we cannot see) enter the eye by passing through the cornea, pupil, and lens. There they are picked up by the visual receptors located at the back of the eyeball, in the retina. Here, these energies are transduced into action potentials and are transmitted via the optic nerve to the visual region of the brain, where they are registered and interpreted as sight. The image is brought to the retina in an upside-down position but is transformed to an upright position by the brain.

The Retina

The retina is a light-sensitive surface located at the back of each eyeball. It contains two kinds of receptors, called cones and rods, that transduce the physical energy of light into action potentials.

Cones. Cones are receptors that function primarily in daylight or in highly illuminated environments. They are concentrated toward the center of the eye, particularly in the fovea, an area directly across from the lens where maximum visual acuity occurs. The cones provide the receptors for color vision.

Rods. Rods are receptors that function in dim light. They are found throughout the retina except in the fovea. When looking at a dim star, it is sometimes easier to focus by tilting the head a little to the side. This is because cones do not operate in dim light conditions and so the stimulus must be brought into focus on rod receptors, which are located more in the periphery of the retina.

The Blind Spot. One place in each retina contains no receptors at all. This is called the blind spot, an opening in the retina where the optic nerve exits to the brain. In general, because of the dual operation of the eyes, and because through past visual experiences we have learned to compensate for this, the blind spot of the visual field is not readily apparent.

Color Vision. Color vision is a function of the cones. Research has shown that not all cones receive all colors. The most popular explanation of the difference among cones is the *trichromatic theory of color vision.* Essentially, the trichromatic theory says some cones are most sensitive to reds, some to greens, and a third group to blues. The color received is a result of how many of each of these receptors are activated by a given stimulus.

Properties of Light

The color (or hue) of the stimulus, the intensity of the light source, and the saturation of the stimulus are all properties of light stimuli.

Color, or hue. Color is determined by the wavelength of the light. Humans are able to see colors ranging from reds (the longest visible wavelengths) to blues (the shortest) and any wavelengths between. This range of color vision has been named the visible spectrum.

Intensity. Intensity is the amount of physical energy produced by a light source. The viewer's reaction to this intensity is usually labeled as the brightness of the light.

Saturation. Saturation is determined by the variety of wavelengths in a light source. A pure spectral color is said to be completely saturated. When a color is composed of light of many wavelengths, the saturation is decreased; in other words, the color becomes "washed out."

Visual Dysfunctions

Several fairly common visual dysfunctions exist. Obviously, the most severe is total blindness, which often results from traumatic damage to nervous tissue.

Nearsightedness, farsightedness, and astigmatism are dysfunctions in which the rays being received are not focused properly on the retina. *Nearsightedness* (also called *myopia*) is a condition where the eye focuses well on things that are close by but not on things that are far away, which appear blurry. *Farsightedness* is the opposite, where such closeup activities as reading a book are hindered by blurry vision. *Astigmatism* is a condition that prevents the focusing of a sharp image, either near or far. Correction by use of glasses or contact lenses is often possible.

Color blindness occurs when particular cones are either missing or malfunctioning. The most common color blindness is an inability to recognize reds and greens. Much less common are inaccuracies in receiving blues or yellows, or total color blindness, where no color reception exists.

In general, color blindness is not correctable. Individuals with red-green color blindness must rely on position and brightness cues to determine if a traffic light is red or green. (Placing the green lens above the red, as a highway system in Canada once did, would confuse the position cues for color-blind drivers, and might create a hazard.)

Hearing

Hearing (also called *audition*) is an organism's ability to receive mechanical energy in the form of sound waves. The sound waves are generated when a source is made to vibrate, resulting in compression and expansion of adjacent molecules. The repeated compression and expansion is carried by some medium to the hearing receptors. Most frequently, the transmission medium is air molecules, although sounds can pass through other gases, liquids, and solids.

The reception and registration of sound waves follows the basic sensory sequence described earlier.

The *outer ear* "traps" the sound waves and funnels them to the eardrum. The *middle ear* contains three small bones, the *malleus, incus,* and *stapes,* which transfer the vibrations from the eardrum to a second membrane, called the *oval window.*

The *inner ear* contains the *cochlea,* a snail-like structure filled with fluid and hairlike receptors that transduce the mechanical energy into an action potential.

From the cochlea, the signals are transmitted through the

auditory nerve to the *auditory cortex* of the brain, where the actual registration of the sound takes place.

Properties of Sound Waves

The two most distinguishing characteristics of a sound wave are its frequency and amplitude.

Frequency, the number of sound waves per second, determines the pitch a listener hears. The greater the number of waves per second, the higher the pitch.

Amplitude represents the amount of energy in each wave as measured by the height of the wave. Amplitude determines the intensity of the sound—that is, how loud it will be.

Auditory Localization

In many instances, the receiver (the person or animal hearing the sound) is interested not only in how the stimulus sounds, but from where the stimulus is coming. Identifying the direction of the sound source is called auditory localization. Basically, localization depends on the discrepancy between the time one ear receives the sound and the time the other ear receives it. When the sound source is exactly equidistant from both ears, the receiver may have to rely upon some other sensory process (for example, vision) or turn the head slightly to create a time differential in order to determine direction.

To demonstrate the difficulty in determining the location of auditory stimuli that arrive at both ears simultaneously, do the following. Sit with your eyes closed and have someone sound a noise source directly in front or directly in back of you. Try to point to the location of the source. You may find you are unable to determine where the source is located unless you either open your eyes or turn your head.

Auditory Dysfunctions

The most severe auditory dysfunction is total deafness. Other hearing dysfunctions are mild losses throughout the hearing range, or partial dysfunctions in which only a segment of the range cannot be heard. Damage to the conductive mechanisms or the nerves involved may be the cause of such losses.

The Chemical Senses: Smell and Taste

Smell (*olfaction*) and taste (*gustation*) are sensory processes that receive stimulus energy in the form of chemical substances. Comparable to the other senses, the receptors transduce these energies into action potentials, which are relayed to specialized areas of the brain to be recorded as odors or tastes.

Smell

The receptors for smell are hair cells located in the membranes of each nasal passage (the olfactory epithelium). Human receptors are quite sensitive to certain odors but relatively insensitive to changes in the concentration of an odor.

Taste

Taste receptors are specialized cells with hairlike endings grouped together into taste buds. They are found mostly on the tongue. Research has shown that taste receptors can be classified into sweet, sour, salty or bitter, with each type most sensitive to only one of these stimuli.

Flavor

The combination of taste and smell results in flavor. This is probably a result of the two types of receptors being sensitive to very similar chemical stimuli. An interesting experiment demonstrated how important odor reception is to flavor. A subject was blindfolded and had the nasal passages completely blocked. Different foods, such as an onion, a potato, and an apple were chopped into similar-sized pieces and fed to the subject one at a time. In this condition, the subject was unable to differentiate among the foods. However, once the nasal blocks were removed, the subject made rapid distinctions. (This is an easy experiment to try for yourself.)

Smell and Taste Dysfunctions

Unless some kind of nervous-tissue damage occurs, dysfunctions of the chemical senses are likely to be rather mild. They may occur, for example, when a person has a bad hay fever attack or perhaps burns the tongue.

The Skin Senses

The skin (touch) senses provide sensory experiences from receptors found in the skin. Four varieties of reception are identified: heat, cold, pressure, and pain. These receptors are not distributed evenly throughout the body. Certain areas, such as the face and hands, have many more receptors than do other areas such as the back. The receptors consist of free nerve endings, Pacinian and Meissner corpuscles, and hair follicles.

Temperature

The receptors responsible for sensing temperature are free nerve endings, which send signals of cold and hot to the brain. Although different points on the skin may be more sensitive to cold or warmth, it has not been shown that these receptors are specific to either of the temperatures; rather they are of similar structure to other skin receptors that cannot differentiate changes in temperature.

Pressure

Receptors responsible for sensing pressure or touch are the Pacinian corpuscles, found in the muscles and internal organs as well as under the skin. In hairy parts of the body, the sense of touch is registered by means of nerve fibers called basket nerve endings, which are wrapped around the shaft of hair, making it very sensitive, even to a breeze blowing over the skin.

The Meissner corpuscles provide a sense of touch in areas of the body where there is no hair, or where the hair follicles are scant, such as the palms of the hand or the sole of the foot. The free nerve endings, which provide almost all skin sense signals, come into play in areas of the skin where there are neither hair follicles nor corpuscles.

Pain

Pain is received primarily by free nerve endings, which branch throughout the dermis and epidermis. These receptors are present in all areas of the body but are more closely packed in some areas than in others, making those areas more sensitive.

The Kinesthetic Senses

Kinesthetic receptors are located in muscles, joints, and tendons. They provide information about the activity and position of the body. This, in turn, aids with coordination.

Which receptors are activated depends upon the direction and angle of movement. The signals from the kinesthetic receptors are registered and interpreted in the brain, just as with the other senses.

Balance

Balance (the *vestibular* sense) has receptors located in the vestibular areas of the inner ear, next to the hearing apparatus. There are two main types of structures: the semicircular canals and otolith organs.

Semicircular Canals

The three semicircular canals are at approximately right angles to each other. These canals are filled with a liquid, which moves as the head rotates in any direction, just as the colored liquid in a leveler moves as the leveler is tipped. Small hair cells in the canals are stimulated as the liquid moves over them, and signals are then transmitted through the vestibular nerve to the brain stem.

Otolith Organs

The otolith organs work in a similar way but are responsible for sensing positions of the head rather than these rotations, which are sensed by the canals. They are important when we are at rest and our head tilts, such as when we fall asleep in a train or in a boring movie. The interaction between these two types of vestibular sense organs provides a total sense of balance or equilibrium.

Vestibular Dysfunctions

Dysfunctions of balance may lead to vertigo or nystagmus (involuntary oscillation of the eyeballs). These dysfunctions can frequently be overcome by relying on other sensory processes. A trip to a fun house can show how maintaining an upright position may sometimes be quite difficult. When visual cues make the relationship between floor and walls appear to be different from what it really is, a person may have to rely upon kinesthetic, touch or vestibular cues. It is easy to demonstrate the complex interactions of these sensory processes by trying to stand on one foot, first with your eyes open and your head in an upright position, then with your eyes closed and your head tilted forward.

Perception

Perception is the process by which a person interprets sensory stimuli. The sensory processes merely report about the stimulus environment; perception translates these sensory messages into understandable forms.

Perception appears for the most part to be a function of experience (although many aspects of perception are developmentally the same for all children, as discussed in Chapter 4). Suppose you were flying in an airplane, several thousand feet above the ground, on a clear day. The cars, roads, houses, and trees below would appear doll sized or smaller (sensation), but you would realize they were normal sized (perception). Research evidence indicates that a subject whose perceptual experience is restricted or eliminated will be unable to develop normal perceptual reactions. Furthermore, a subject who cannot or is not permitted to interact with the stimulus environment will not show normal perceptual development.

Two types of factors influence perception: external (stimulus) cues and internal (personal) cues. Both internal and external cues affect the way in which a subject will pay attention to, or attend to, a stimulus. A subject must pay at least some attention to a stimulus in order for perception to occur.

External Cues in Perception

External cues develop from the properties of a stimulus or groups of stimuli. Interest in the effects of external stimuli on perceptual development arose during the early years of Gestalt psychology. The Gestalt psychologists realized that stimuli provided the start for more than just sensation. They stated that the totality of a stimulus situation was more than the sum of its separate aspects.

Consider, for example, the following nonsensical jumble: "fiuoynacdaersiht, s'tiaelcarim!" Rearranged, these letters read: "if you can read this, it's a miracle!" However, you have to have the correct arrangement and spacing of letters to appreciate the meaning. In other words, the whole of a situation is more than its parts. The stimulus components, in and of themselves, do not always allow someone to understand or interpret the stimulus environment.

Figure-Ground Relationship

The relationship between the main or featured stimulus and any surrounding stimuli is called the figure-ground relationship. In general, this relationship determines how distinct the main stimulus (the figure) will be within the total context (the ground).

Much perceptual research is done with vision, but a figure-ground relationship can also be illustrated by listening to music. The melody represents the figure and harmony provides the ground. If one or both of these are varied, as by altering the rhythm, volume, or instrumentation, the figure-ground relationship may change.

Figure-ground relationships are called *unstable* if the figure can sometimes be perceived as the ground and the ground can sometimes be perceived as the figure. For example, Figure 5.2 can be perceived as either a dark X on a light background or a light X on a dark background. Figures may also be described as *ambiguous* if they can be "correctly" interpreted in more than one way. In Figure 5.3 it is impossible to tell whether the X is on the front or the back of the box.

Fig. 5.2

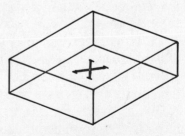

Fig. 5.3

Intensity

Research has shown that, in general, the more intense a stimulus, the more likely it is that a subject will pay attention to it. However, extremely high values may be painful or harmful.

For example, as a general rule the louder a noise, the more likely it is to be heard (and thus recognized and interpreted). However, extremely loud levels may cause distortion or even do damage to one's hearing. Musicians using electric amplification are frequently warned of this possibility.

Contrast

A stimulus that differs noticeably from the others surrounding it (by virtue either of its quality or its quantity) is more likely to be noticed than is a stimulus that is similar to the stimuli surrounding it. This is the principle of contrast. A man who is five feet ten inches tall appears very short in the company of basketball players who are six feet four inches tall and over, but when he stands next to several men who are five feet five inches tall, he appears very tall. The context in this example is provided by other people—the tall basketball players in the first case, the shorter men in the other. This is an example of size contrast.

The principle of contrast is reversed when *camouflage* is desired. Soldiers may wear clothing that "blends in" with the surrounding environment, and highway police may drive unmarked cars so that they will not be easily seen by speeders. In general, a person who does not want to be noticed will try to blend into the environment, thus minimizing contrast.

Continuity

Continuity refers to the uninterrupted "flow" of a stimulus. A subject is likely to perceive a stimulus situation as a combination of regular or continuous stimuli rather than as a combination of irregular or discontinuous stimuli.

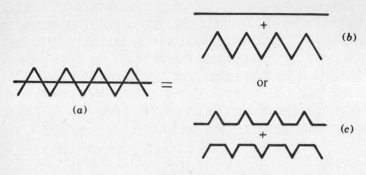

Fig. 5.4

In Figure 5.4, drawing (*a*) is usually perceived as the combination of a straight line and an "accordion" line, as in drawing (*b*) rather than as the combination of two "sawtooth" lines in drawing (*c*).

Grouping

The placement or arrangement of stimuli can affect how we attend to and understand them. Grouped stimuli appear together in time or space, especially in some rhythmical pattern or arrangement. Such grouping helps the subject to apprehend the stimuli and organize them into an understandable form. For example, in Figure 5.5, the Xs are easiest to count accurately when they are arranged in groups as in drawing (*b*).

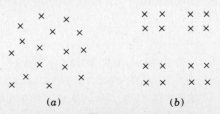

Fig. 5.5

The main principles of perceptual grouping include proximity, similarity, continuity, and common fate. All of these principles illustrate the Gestalt belief that the whole is more than the sum of its parts. In other words, how we perceive an object or a group of objects depends on the way in which the brain organizes the various parts of the stimulus pattern.

Proximity: Groups tend to be formed from elements that are close to each other.

Similarity: Groups tend to be formed from elements that are similar in size, shape, color or appearance.

Continuity: If all elements in a set of stimuli go in the same direction, they are perceived as part of the same group. For example, given the numbers 2, 4, 6, and 8, if you were asked which number came next, you would probably say 10.

Common Fate: Objects that move together in the same direction and at the same rate are seen as part of a single form or unit. They are bound together by what Gestalt psychologists call common fate. This tendency to see moving elements as belonging together enables us to enjoy the sight of marchers stepping in unison.

Closure

Closure is most easily defined as the filling in of gaps in information. A subject receives "incomplete" information, but enough so that it is possible to "finish" the stimulus. (A person's ability to show closure depends on previous knowledge of what is appropriate, of course.) Television game shows often make use of the principle of closure. Incomplete phrases, pictures or musical themes are presented to a contestant, who must quickly complete the cue in order to win a prize.

Closure is illustrated in Figure 5.6. We perceive the three drawings as a triangle (*a*), a square (*b*), and a circle (*c*) by "completing" the shapes.

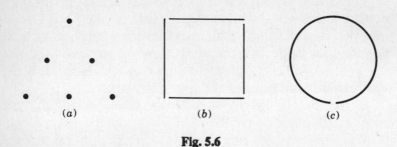

Fig. 5.6

Real and Apparent Movement

One of the most compelling stimulus properties is movement. Subjects are more apt to respond to moving stimuli than to those that are static. Furthermore, some stimuli that actually are static can be presented in such a way as to create apparent movement.

A movie illustrates apparent movement. A quick examination of motion-picture film reveals a series of still images. Only the rapid, coordinated presentation of these images will give the viewer the impression of movement.

(Note: Movement can also be implied by sound, such as in a stereo demonstration record where the train noise seems to move across the room, from one speaker to the other.)

Perceptual Constancies

The stimulus we receive from any one object may change as the position or condition of the object changes. Our retinal images of objects change in size and shape as the objects come nearer or as we change our position with respect to them, and we register changes in object brightness and color under different lighting conditions. Yet, we perceive our world as stable and unchanging. It is an important attribute of our perceptual system that certain aspects of our environment are perceived as constant no matter under what conditions we view them. This phenomenon is called perceptual constancy.

Size Constancy

Research has indicated that subjects perceive size, shape, and color constancies. Imagine throwing a model plane so that it moves away from you, loops, and returns toward you. The retinal image you receive is of an object that first grows smaller and then seems to increase in size. However, you perceive that the actual size of the plane remains constant throughout the flight. This is an example of size constancy.

Shape Constancy

Consider, too, that as you move away from a dinner plate on a table, the image on the retina of each of your eyes will become less and less like a circle and more like an oval. Despite such stimulus changes, a person will perceive that the object itself has not changed; that is, the plate will still be perceived as a circular object. This effect is called shape constancy.

Color Constancy

The ability to perceive the brightness or color of an object as the same despite varying degrees of illumination is referred to as brightness constancy. Although there is considerable difference in illumination between day and night, we see snow as white whether the sun is shining on it or it is dark outside. We see a black cat as black whether it is sleeping in a dark alley at night or stretched out in the bright sunlight. Again, context helps us out; that is, the blackness or whiteness is relative to the background of the visual field. A red dress photographs redder at twilight, because a camera reflects color in an absolute way, and at twilight the light spectrum narrows. But when we actually look at the red dress directly, it appears to us to be the same color whether we see it in broad daylight or at twilight. The effect is due to color constancy.

Monocular Depth Cues

In visual perception, some of the most important stimulus properties provide depth cues. If these cues can be accurately perceived by one eye alone, they are called monocular depth cues. Examples of monocular depth cues are interposition, perspective, texture gradient, and shadows.

Interposition

Interposition occurs when one object appears to "block out" part of another object in the visual field. Interposition provides information about the size, distance, and location of the various stimulus objects.

Perspective and Texture Gradient

Perspective and texture gradient often operate together to provide information about three-dimensionality. Perspective is the apparent "drawing together" of parallel lines as they recede into the distance. Texture gradient is the change in the distinctiveness of the texture of the stimulus, from noticeable or coarse when it is nearby to smooth or fine in the distance. Both cues provide an understanding of the visual field.

Shadows

Shadows also offer cues that aid in the perception of three dimensions. The distance, height, and shape of an object may be made more intelligible when shadow cues are present.

Retinal Disparity

Retinal disparity refers to the fact that the visual images on the retina of the two eyes at any one moment are never exactly the same. This results from the physical separation of the two eyes in the head. The two disparate images provide a binocular depth cue because the brain is able to "blend" them so that you see just one image, which carries information about depth and three-dimensionality.

Stereoscopic viewers rely upon retinal disparity to provide the impression of three dimensions. A pair of two-dimensional pictures is viewed through special lenses. Each picture sends a slightly different image to each retina. The brain then combines these images into what appears to be a three-dimensional view.

Internal Cues in Perception

Internal cues appear to be a function of a subject's cognitive processes. For example, the motivation of a subject, a subject's past experience or the expectations of a subject at a given time may all act as internal cues.

Motivation

Perception is frequently influenced by the motivation of the subject. This may result from the subject's physiological condition or from social experience. A subject may have learned to give special attention to stimuli that reinforce or satisfy the motive condition. If the subject is never motivated to perceive a certain stimulus (that is, if perception of that stimulus has not been rewarded), the subject will tend to ignore the stimulus.

Experiments have shown that our needs, motives, interests, and values influence our perception. In one experiment, when subjects were shown a series of ambiguous pictures, those who were hungry tended to report seeing more food-related objects than those who were not hungry. In another study, it was found that poor children tended to overestimate the size of coins to a greater degree than did rich children, demonstrating what the experimenters believed was the relationship between the value of an object to the perceiver and its perceived size.

Past Experience

Previous learning can make a subject anticipate the meaning of future stimulus situations. Such anticipations may be correct or incorrect. Laboratory experiments, using ambiguous stimuli, have shown that if a person is told in advance that he or she will be shown particular objects, this information influences his or her perception of the material. When presented with an image very briefly, a subject will tend to see what he or she believes is being presented.

Set

Set is defined as a temporary tendency (or expectancy) to respond in a certain fashion. This tendency may change as the subject is confronted with different instructions or rewards. Read the following sentence: "If Frieda follows Fred frantically, Fred flees fleetingly!" How many f's do you count? If you counted eight, your set was accurate. If you counted only seven, you probably were caught by the first-letter set and missed the f in the word "if."

Unusual Perceptual Experiences

Illusions

Sometimes stimuli can be interpreted incorrectly. Some stimuli exist in a configuration that almost always leads to incorrect perception. When this occurs, the perception is described as an illusion.

The famous Müeller-Lyer illusion (Fig. 5.7) shows how stimulus cues may lead to perceptual misunderstanding. Lines A and B are exactly the same length, but line A appears shorter than line B.

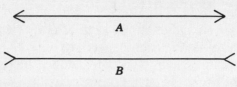

Fig. 5.7

(Note: Illusions are often confused in everyday speech with hallucinations, which are perceptions of "stimuli" that actually do not exist.)

Subliminal Perception

Several years ago, an attempt was made to create advertisements that would be presented at stimulus values just below the conscious threshold. The idea was that the person would receive the advertising message without being aware of the stimulation. Such unconscious perception is called subliminal perception. Most subliminal advertising campaigns have since been abandoned because of difficulties in establishing threshold values. Research has shown, however, that subliminal perception can occur; that is, you can perceive something without consciously being aware of it.

Extremes of Sensory Load

Sensory deprivation (very little stimulation) or *sensory overload* (a great amount of stimulation) may exceed a person's "normal" capabilities for sensory adaptation. When this happens, unusual patterns of responding (such as hallucinations) may result. It seems that people are unable to continue to correctly interpret the stimulus environment if extreme sensory overload or extreme sensory deprivation is maintained over a prolonged period of time.

Extrasensory Perception (ESP)

Our senses are quite limited as to what they can and cannot perceive. The eyes, for example, can see only a small portion of the total electromagnetic spectrum, and the ears can hear only a fraction of the sounds in our environment. Extrasensory perception is considered the ability to sense beyond these normal limitations; for instance, being able to receive messages generated without the intervention of words or body language. Research in this area is still in rather primitive form and is very controversial, without any acceptable proof at this time that there is such a thing as extrasensory perception.

Extrasensory perception (ESP) is said to have occurred when a correct interpretation or manipulation of the environment has taken place without any information being provided by regular sensory processes. Several varieties of ESP have been studied, including telepathy, precognition, clairvoyance, and psychokinesis.

Telepathy is the transfer of thought from one person to another without the aid of usual sensory channels. *Precognition* refers to the ability to anticipate future events. *Clairvoyance* is the ability to discern information that could not have been received by regular sensations. *Psychokinesis* is the capacity for making objects move by using only thought processes. As mentioned above, there is no accepted evidence, at this point, for any of these ESP phenomena.

CHAPTER 6

States of Consciousness

Consciousness is the term for those internal mental experiences of which a person is aware. There may be an interaction between these mental experiences and the physiological processes of the body, but the definition of consciousness is limited to those internal characteristics that make up a person's mental experiences.

Several consciousnesses appear to exist for any one person. Not only is there a sleeping consciousness and a waking consciousness, but there are other areas of consciousness not accessible to routine observation. Split-brain research, for example, indicates a left-hemisphere consciousness that is separate from the right-hemisphere consciousness. Furthermore, research in abnormal personality patterns has revealed rare cases of multiple personalities; that is, individuals with more than one distinct set of personality characteristics accompanied by independent sets of conscious processes.

This chapter considers the nature of consciousness and looks at some of the internal and external forces that act on it: biofeed-

back, meditation, sleep rhythms and stages, dreams, hypnosis, brain surgery, and psychoactive drugs.

Characteristics of Consciousness

Many types of consciousness may be experienced by an individual. A few examples are: thoughts or ideas, feelings, sensations and perceptions, and dreams. It appears that consciousness is a function of brain activity and that each individual may have several consciousnesses.

Differentiation of Consciousnesses

Consciousness appears to be an active brain process. When the brain is functioning normally, conscious processes may occur. Because the brain functions during sleep, dreams are included in the category of conscious processes. Someone who is unconscious (as perhaps in a coma) does not appear to have comparable brain functioning.

By using a device called an electroencephalogram (EEG), psychologists have been able to monitor and record the electrical activity in certain parts of the brain. The type of electrical activity observed *may* vary as the subject's state of consciousness changes, but different states of consciousness do not *necessarily* show markedly different types of electrical activity in the brain.

Consider your recollection of waking events as opposed to your recollection of dreams. The electrical activity of the brain is very similar for both states of consciousness, yet dreams often include illogical, dramatic or vivid mental experiences that differ very much from mental experiences in a waking state. You may dream of flying by flapping your arms, but such a mental experience would not fit into your waking consciousness.

Limitations of Consciousness

Consciousness is not always working at full capacity, and can be limited by a number of different factors. Each limitation impedes a person's normal perception of the world and responses to the environment. Limitations of consciousness can be documented in at least three ways:

Disruption of Brain Processes

If brain processes are disrupted or destroyed, conscious processes may be likewise upset or eliminated. Consciousness is a function of the brain, and therefore depends on the appropriate operation of the brain.

Expansion of Consciousness

A second limitation is found even when all brain functioning is normal. Similar to the way attention can affect perception (see Chapter 5), consciousness is limited to the person's capacity to receive and process information. Certain behaviors, such as meditation, or certain drugs, such as LSD, seem to affect the limitations of consciousness, producing so-called expansion of consciousness. However, even these appear to have limits.

Environmental Conditions

Environmental conditions may alter conscious processes. Interruption, conditions of fatigue, ecstasy, or sensory deprivation or overload represent examples of interferences that might place limitations upon a person's consciousness.

Internal Influences on Consciousness

Consciousness may be influenced by both internal states and external stimuli. Internal influences on consciousness may be the result of purposeful or nonpurposeful behavior on the part of an individual.

Social Learning

Control of consciousness may be the purposeful act of an individual. Quite frequently, however, the decision to think or act in a certain manner is a function of the social restrictions or social perceptions a person has learned through past experience in a particular society—learned in the family, through training, or by the influences of mass media of communication. Most simply stated, social learning may lead to the facilitation or inhibition of conscious processes. That is, learning may "encourage" or "discourage" certain kinds of mental experiences in a person's consciousness. For example, if a well-trained botanist and a well-trained geologist hike through a forest together, it is very likely that each would have a distinctly different consciousness of the experience. While their experience would be shared, what each takes from the experience and processes in his or her consciousness would be different.

Certain social standards may influence a person's consciousness and thus influence the person's behavior. For example, people who condemn a rich man for making use of tax loopholes may themselves make use of tax loopholes whenever they are able. The fact that such behavior is inconsistent may be blocked from consciousness by social learning.

Biofeedback

Biofeedback is a technique by which people can observe measurements of bodily processes that are otherwise unobservable. Individuals are then able to find ways to regulate processes such as heart rate or blood pressure, which are usually thought of as involuntary physiological responses. Quite frequently, this is accomplished by using a monitoring device that indicates the status of the otherwise "hidden" variable. For example, a blood pressure meter can be connected to a loudspeaker that emits a loud beeping noise as the pressure increases and a soft tone as the pressure decreases. As the person learns to control the bodily process, it is reflected by a change in the signal. In other words, the feedback provides information that helps the person focus conscious processes so as to manipulate the bodily activities.

Evidence indicates that migraine headaches may result from excessive blood flow in the brain area. To overcome this, biofeedback techniques have been used to teach people how to adjust their blood flow so that more blood goes to other parts of the body, thus decreasing the headache symptoms. A monitoring device helps the person to learn conscious control of blood flow to the brain area.

Meditation

Meditation techniques are used to try to "focus" conscious processes in a manner unlike that used in everyday circumstances. Two types of meditation are used frequently, concentrative meditation and opening-up meditation.

Concentrative Meditation

Concentrative meditation limits conscious attention to a specific object or sound; the goal is to narrow attention to that direction only and to block out other stimuli coming from the environment. The result of concentrative meditation is supposed to be improved clarity of thought.

Opening-up Meditation

Opening-up meditation tries to develop continuous attention to everything that is happening. The technique is supposed to produce a broad understanding of the total environment.

Both techniques will produce changed states of consciousness for some users. Many meditators claim profound benefits from meditation, including increased understanding of the self and the relationship of the self to the environment. Sometimes meditation is accompanied by changes in physiological processes, such as those described for biofeedback.

Sleep

Some of the most widely studied groups of conscious processes are those that occur during sleep. The use of an electroencephalograph (EEG) makes it possible for psychologists to study the sleeper's brain activity while it is occurring. Another important device used in the study of sleep is the electrooculograph (EOG), which records the movements of the eye when the eyelids are closed. It measures the visual pursuit activity— movement of the eyeball as if following an object—taking place while a person is asleep.

Extensive research has shown that several variables are quite significant in studying sleep.

Circadian Rhythms

Circadian rhythms are the cyclical patterns of the "biological clock" each individual has or develops. Studies demonstrate that this biological clock operates in a regular, rhythmical fashion. The clock develops as a person becomes accustomed to particular environmental circumstances, resulting in daily rhythms of behaviors such as hunger, body temperature, hormonal flow, and sleep. These rhythms usually match the 24 hour day, although research has shown that a person placed in an environment where time cues are eliminated may establish a rhythm on a shorter or longer cycle.

A person whose sleep patterns are upset may require a period of adjustment (often several days to several weeks) before a new, workable sleep pattern establishes itself. Or, a traveler who has crossed several time zones in a short time (as in transoceanic jet flights) will experience tiredness and hunger at the "wrong times." The circadian rhythms the traveler has established in one time zone will not fit into the time cues of another time zone. It may take several days for the traveler's circadian rhythms to readjust to the new time zone.

Sleep Rhythms

Sleep not only occurs at rhythmical times during a twenty-four-hour day, but also shows rhythmical patterns within the sleeping period. Research has identified four different stages of sleep, or depths of sleep, by recording changes in EEG frequencies and magnitudes. A person may move through this four-stage cycle several times during one night's sleep.

The description of each stage is based on the kind of wave activity shown by the EEG. In general, stage 1 sleep is characterized by alpha brain waves (a rhythm of approximately 8 to 12 cycles per second). Stage 2 includes continued alpha activity, together with occasional spindles (bursts of 14-cycle-per-second activity), while in stage 3, high-amplitude waves of 1 to 4 cycles per second are characteristic, along with some delta waves (1 to 2 cycles per second). Finally, stage 4 shows almost exclusive delta-wave activity, of 1 to 3 cycles per second.

REM Sleep

In addition to isolating four stages of sleep, psychologists have distinguished between two basic types of sleep: periods in which the sleeping subject shows rapid eye movements (REM sleep) and periods in which there is no rapid eye movement (non-REM sleep).

The average four-stage sleeping cycle lasts 80 to 90 minutes. After the first cycle is complete, each stage 1 sleeping period seems to be accompanied by REM activity. Most dreaming appears to occur during these stage 1 REM sleeping periods, while little dreaming is found in stages 2, 3 or 4.

Ironically, during the dreaming state, the brain waves are similar to those that are associated with waking states. Even though it is difficult for an individual to be awakened during this period of sleep (as anyone who has had a dream interrupted knows), the EEG wave patterns during dream time look like those of the state of wakefulness. For this reason, dream sleep (the REM period) is often called paradoxical sleep because the subject's heart rate, respiration rate, and EEG patterns closely resemble those observed when the subject is awake.

But while these electrical patterns mimic wakefulness, the chemistry of the body is entirely different during dream sleep. Nerve transmitters which normally allow us to move about are all disabled during dream sleep, leaving the dreamer virtually paralyzed. And it's a good thing, too. If the muscles of the body that allow us to stand and move our limbs did not remain paralyzed during dream sleep, there would be considerable danger that individuals would hurt themselves or others by acting out their dreams in real life.

Observation of a sleeping person usually allows easy identification of the REM-sleep periods. A sleeper who is awakened during this period will very likely report dreaming. (This is a very simple experiment to try at home, provided you can find a cooperative observer or sleeper.) Research has shown that sleepers awakened during REM sleep will report dreaming about 80 percent of the time, whereas sleepers awakened from non-REM sleep will report dreaming only about 15 percent of the time.

As we noted in Chapter 3 in discussing brain structures, the reticular activating system, a network of neurons around the thalamus and midbrain, is believed to play in important role in sleep and wakefulness. This system appears to be controlled by two sleep centers, located in the medulla and pons, which together are responsible for inducing sleep.

Dreams

Dreams appear to be a part of almost everyone's experience, although some people are much more capable of recalling dreams than are others. Some research has suggested that dreams serve a recuperative function. If REM sleep is not allowed to occur for several sleeping periods in a row, irritability, anxiety, and even hallucinations may result.

During a typical night's sleep, these dream periods recur four to six times at intervals of about 90 minutes. A full night's sleep is characterized by a several repeated movements through stages 1 to 4, with recurrences of this REM period each time. In other words, each of us dreams several times each night with fairly regular frequency. Alcohol and drugs cut down on this dreaming: when a person withdraws from these substances, a side effect is sleep full of often nightmarish dreams.

Interestingly, sleepwalking and sleeptalking do not usually occur during REM sleep and do not seem to coordinate with dreams that are remembered upon awakening.

External Influences on Consciousness

External stimuli may influence an individual's consciousness in many ways. Hypnosis, surgery, and drugs all fall within this category of external influences on consciousness.

Hypnosis

Dramatic demonstrations of the external control of consciousness often can be provided by hypnosis. A hypnotized individual accepts the hypnotist's directions, showing increased suggestibility. The hypnotist may be able to restrict or direct the subject's attention. Furthermore, a hypnotized subject may experience a distorted perception of reality or show pronounced relaxation or alertness, depending upon the hypnotist's instructions. Very deep hypnotic states may approach a level of mystical experience.

Placed in a fairly deep hypnotic state, a subject may follow the hypnotist's suggestions and talk about certain topics, experience certain motivations such as thirst, or perform somewhat unusual responses. Hypnosis is often thought of as a party or stage display; however, scientific uses include modification of pain thresholds and applications in psychotherapy.

In spite of the endorsement of hypnosis by the medical and psychological establishments, there is considerable debate regarding the nature of the hypnotic state. On the one hand, there is the traditional view that the behavior associated with hypnosis requires an altered state of consciousness. On the other hand, a growing number of psychologists feel that the behavior of the hypnotized subject may be interpreted as merely a form of conscious role enactment in response to cues from the hypnotist. Hypnotized subjects may be responding to complex situational cues in the same way that student volunteers in an experiment try to guess the purpose of the experiment so that they can enact their role as they believe the experimenter wants them to.

Not all people are equally susceptible to hypnosis: 5 to 10 percent of the population cannot be hypnotized at all, while a like percentage can reach very deep hypnotic trances. However, the effects of hypnosis tend to be similar for most people between these extremes.

Surgery

Consciousness may be affected by certain types of brain surgery. The most obvious example of this is the split-brain procedure, which separates the functioning of the two hemispheres entirely by dividing the corpus callosum. (See Chapter 3.) The separated hemispheres show individualized consciousnesses and, in some cases, respond differently to the same stimulus.

It is not possible to predict all the effects that might be produced by brain surgery. Changes in emotional reactions, memory skills, or perceptual understandings have been demonstrated by testing patients before and after surgery. However, mapping of the brain is not yet complete enough for consistently accurate predictions to be made.

The case of Phineas Gage is renowned in psychology as one of the first documented examples of the effects of brain tissue destruction upon conscious processes. In 1848, Gage was struck in a work accident by a piece of pipe that entered his eye socket and exited through the front top portion of his skull. He lived, but lost the brain tissue in the region of his frontal lobe. Very noticeable changes in his behavior were noted, especially in his emotional reactions to certain events. The loss of brain tissue apparently changed his way of responding, while all other variables remained relatively the same.

Psychoactive Drugs

Psychoactive drugs are those that can cause subjective, psychological changes in a person's consciousness. These include alcohol, narcotic drugs, hallucinogens, stimulants, antidepressants, sedatives, marijuana, and many more.

Frequently, psychologists try to distinguish between individuals who merely use such drugs and those who become reliant upon them. Relying upon such a drug when there is no reason to do so is termed drug abuse. Psychologists prefer the concepts of use and abuse rather than describing someone as an addict, because a person may be a habitual user of one or more of these drugs and not be either psychologically or physiologically addicted.

Alcohol

Alcohol, a depressant, is the most widely used of all the psychoactive drugs. When taken in sufficient quantity (which varies from one individual to the next), alcohol can depress aspects of central nervous system functioning, causing conscious reactions that are noticeably different from those produced in a nonalcoholic state.

The flirtatiousness of people at a cocktail party may be the result of the depression of certain brain activity by alcohol. Continued drinking may lead to continued changes in brain activity, with the result that the previously cheerful "life of the party" may become hostile, lose motor coordination, and possibly pass out.

Marijuana

Smoking or eating marijuana may produce a psychoactive drug effect. Quite often, the marijuana "high" is a state of elation, in which the user claims an enrichment of sensory experiences.

Research into marijuana use has shown that the effects produced may be a function not only of the amount and characteristics of the marijuana used, but also of the expectations of the user. Motivation, past experience, and many other variables may create effects greater or lesser than those expected from the properties of the marijuana itself.

Expectations sometimes produce remarkable effects. People who think they are drinking alcohol or smoking marijuana have been known to get "drunk" when actually drinking cola or "high" when actually smoking oregano. The social setting, a person's beliefs, and many additional factors contribute to such behavior.

Prescription Drugs

It is surprising to some that many prescription drugs are listed as psychoactive drugs. However, many of these drugs do produce a changed state of consciousness; in fact, this is often the effect that is sought when the drug is prescribed. Included in this category are drugs such as amphetamines, barbiturates, and many drugs, such as tranquilizers, prescribed in the course of psychiatric treatment.

The legal use of drugs has led to the development of a separate scientific discipline, called psychopharmacology, that investigates the psychological effects of drugs. It must be recognized that although these drugs have legal and appropriate uses, they can be abused and drug dependency may develop.

One difficulty with psychiatric drugs is that both physician and patient may become too dependent upon their use. A physician may prescribe them as "cure-alls," using them indiscriminately rather than carefully analyzing a patient's symptoms and considering other treatments. The patient comes to expect the drug-produced result and, in cases where the drug is being used to control behaviors or emotions, abandons efforts at self-control and relies on the drug effect instead. It should be recognized that psychological effects can also be produced by common, or nonprescription drugs. For example, a person could become caught up in a repetitive stimulant-sedative cycle, using caffeine or nicotine as the stimulant and "sleeping pills" as the sedative. Because tolerance levels build, more and more of each drug becomes necessary.

Narcotic Drugs

Narcotic drugs are used frequently as painkillers. However, abuse of narcotic drugs such as morphine or heroin has become widespread. Initial misuse of narcotics commonly occurs for social reasons, but repeated dosages lead to a physiological dependence that continues to increase. The dependence has two aspects: the need for larger doses to prevent withdrawal symptoms (which can be quite severe), and the need for larger doses to produce the euphoric effect.

Hallucinogenic Drugs

Hallucinogenic (or psychedelic) drugs are so named because a major feature of their use is the production of hallucinations. These drugs, such as LSD or mescaline, are available legally only in controlled circumstances such as medical research.

One characteristic of hallucinogens is that the effect produced by their use cannot be predicted reliably. It is even difficult to predict whether the resultant initial experiences will be "favorable" or "unfavorable." Many individuals have used LSD with a positive result (particularly a feeling of increased sensory awareness), but some have experienced "bad trips," with pronounced anxiety, loss of coordination, and unpleasant hallucinations. Some claims of repeated "flashbacks" of such hallucinations—recurrences months or even years later—have also been reported.

CHAPTER 7

Motivation

Motivation may be defined as those conditions that initiate, guide, and maintain behaviors, usually until some goal is reached or the response has been blocked. The word motive comes from the Latin movere, which means "to move" or "to activate." Literally, then, a motive is whatever moves one to action. Psychologists differ in their views of the nature of motivation and therefore define the term in different ways. While most definitions reflect the fact that motivated behavior has three aspects—an energizing aspect, a directional aspect and a persistance aspect—some stress one aspect more than the other. Motivation, it is agreed by all, plays a central part in all behaviors.

Motives can be unlearned, such as the drive to obtain food and water, or acquired, such as the motive to form friendships, or they can be a combination of learned and unlearned, such as maternal behavior.

This chapter discusses these different kinds of motives and shows how each influences behavior. It then describes four types of conflict situations studied by psychologists. Finally, it looks at the main theories of motivation—humanistic, psychoanalytic, social learning, and activation-arousal.

The Motivation Cycle

Some motives appear in cycles. The cycle of motivation follows a three-part repetitive chain: (1) a need or drive builds; (2) instrumental responses are made as attempts to reach some goal to satisfy the need; and (3) once the goal has been reached, relief from the need follows. Often, the relief is only temporary, and the cycle may start again.

An obvious illustration of the motivation cycle is the sequence of hunger, finding and eating food, temporary relief, hunger again, and so on. The repetitive nature of the motivation cycle can be shown for many different motive conditions, and the time span for the cycle may vary.

Variables Affecting the Motivation Cycle

While the motivation cycle itself seems rather simple, it may be altered or modified by several types of variables.

Assessment of Motivation

The strength and quality of a motive condition may be estimated in one of two ways. First, strength can sometimes be estimated by determining how long it has been since the motive was last satisfied. This period of time represents the deprivation the person is experiencing. Parents of a very young child, for example, are able to estimate how hungry their child is by knowing how long it has been since the child was last fed. In experiments, psychologists may manipulate deprivation in order to influence a subject's motive condition.

A second means of estimating the strength of motivation is to observe particular behaviors and infer from them a subject's motive condition. This method depends on naturalistic observation, and requires that the observer has had some previous knowledge that associates a certain kind of behavior with a particular motive condition. For example, parents may estimate a child's hunger by observing certain behaviors (such as crying) that are associated with hunger.

Adaptation of Response

Many motives promote nonproductive responses, which do not serve the instrumental purpose of leading to a goal. In many cases, a person will have to make a behavioral adjustment so that different instrumental responses are made and the cycle can be completed. A young child, for example, may find that banging on the table with a spoon or shouting at a parent does not serve to get the parent to bring food. The child may have to adjust his or her behavior, perhaps by learning to ask politely for food, in order to satisfy the motive condition.

Goal Specificity

Not all goals are viewed as equally desirable. A person who appears to prefer a certain goal over others, even when the others would satisfy the motive condition adequately, is exhibiting goal specificity. For example, parents feeding a very young child may find that the child expresses preferences very noticeably, even when communication by language has not yet developed. The child may spit out the carrots but gulp down all the green beans.

General Principles of Motivation

It is difficult to determine just how many different types of motives exist. It is sometimes impossible to make a simple distinction between unlearned motive conditions and learned motive conditions. Furthermore, it is sometimes impossible to determine the origins of motives. Despite these difficulties, certain principles seem to apply to many, if not all, motive conditions.

Instinct, Need, and Drive

Instinct, need, and drive are three terms used to describe motive conditions.

An *instinct* is defined as an innate condition that regularly provokes a specific, complex response from all members of a certain species when a distinctive stimulus pattern is presented.

A *need* is sometimes described as a deficit or imbalance. A need may be physiological (such as a need for warmth) or psychological (such as a need for achievement).

A *drive* is either the state resulting from the physiological need or a general wish to achieve some goal.

Classification of Motives

Human motives may be categorized in several different ways. Each of these categories will be discussed in the text that follows.

Classification 1. Primary or Secondary Motives

Primary (Unlearned) Motives: Motives that are unlearned, such as the drives to obtain whatever the body needs to survive (air, food, water)

Secondary (Learned) Motives: Motives that are learned, or acquired; they vary from person to person as a result of social needs, such as the motive of acquiring wealth

Classification 2. Physiological, Social, or Effectance Motives

Physiological Motives: Motives that are derived from bodily needs and are, therefore, inborn

Social Motives: Motives that are learned as a consequence of associating with other human beings, such as the motive to form friendships with one's peers

Effectance Motives: Motives that originate in the desire to increase one's ability to deal with the environment, such as the motive to explore unknown territory

Classification 3. Combination Motives (Learned and Unlearned), such as sex, maternal behavior, and contact comfort

Functional Autonomy

Some responses to a motive condition may persist even after the original motive condition ceases to exist. In such a case, the response itself becomes a motive. This is called functional autonomy.

Ask almost any "confirmed" smoker if smoking was enjoyable when it was first started. The answer you will probably get is no. Very few people start smoking because they find it truly pleasurable. Rather, they smoke at first because it brings social approval of some kind. However, smoking becomes self-motivating, in that the addiction to nicotine serves as a physiological need—so much so that the individual eventually may smoke even when it is socially disapproved.

Relation of Motivation to Performance

Even common sense tells us that there is a relationship between a person's motivation and performance. This relationship, however, is not always predictable. A person who is

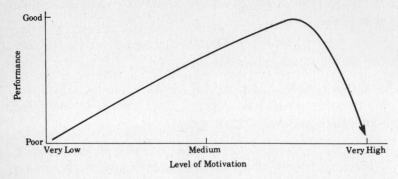

Fig. 7.1

completely indifferent to a task, who finds it boring or irrelevant, may not perform the task well. But, likewise, a person who considers a task too important may also perform poorly. The general relationship of motivation to performance is shown by the graph in Figure 7.1.

The exact maximum level of motivation that will yield the best performance will vary from task to task, but the general research finding is that performance will be poorer if the motivation level is lower or higher than an ideal point.

Students are familiar with the effects of motivation on performance. The student who does not care at all about a course often does poorly. The student who cares, but keeps it under control, does well. The student who cares too much (and "clutches") may also do poorly.

Unlearned Motives

Some unlearned motives are called *survival* or *physiological motives* because they must be satisfied if an organism is to continue to live. The list of survival motives is short: hunger, thirst, the need for air, the need to maintain body temperature, the need to relieve fatigue, and the need to eliminate body waste products. The responses that satisfy these motives are eating, drinking, breathing, sheltering, sleeping, and eliminating.

One additional motive condition, that of pain, also appears to be unlearned, and can be considered a survival motive. Pain enables a person to avoid dangerous situations and to prosper better in an environment filled with potential harms.

Homeostasis

The most basic motives of an organism are to maintain a life supporting equilibrium. This involves maintaining a stable internal environment, which requires a normal body temperature, a proper balance of water and salt in the body cells, a normal blood-sugar level, and so on. This tendency toward maintaining a balanced state is called homeostasis.

Our bodies are equipped with regulatory mechanisms that help maintain equilibrium. When there are slight deviations in body temperature, they are corrected automatically. When we get too hot, for example, the blood vessels near the skin dilate, permitting heat to escape, and the sweat glands excrete perspiration to cool off our bodies. Similar devices help us maintain other kinds of equilibrium, such as the oxygen-carbon dioxide level in the blood, blood-sugar concentration, and acidity of the blood.

Certain imbalances, however, cannot be handled by the automatic devices alone. In that case, a drive is aroused, and the organism becomes activated to restore equilibrium. For instance, if we get too hot, we try to find a cooler spot or seek some other way to cool off and return to a balanced state. If we are hungry, we become active in the direction of seeking food, and tension continues within the system until food is found and the need is satisfied. It is in this way that homeostasis is obtained—that equilibrium is restored.

A typical weight-reduction diet makes use of the body's tendency to make homeostatic adjustments. When individuals who are overweight reduce their food intake, they create an energy deficit. To make up for this deficit, the body will burn stored fats. This, in turn, will lower the weight and thus make the diet successful. (Note: You are always on some kind of diet. The question is, is the diet a good one or a bad one for you?)

Response Variability

Satisfaction of the survival motives is essential, but the type of satisfaction may vary from person to person and from time to time. The amount of variability differs depending upon which motive is being discussed, but all show some flexibility in terms of what responses and goals will complete the motivation cycle.

Someone living in the Northeast, for example, would recognize a need for some type of shelter at least during part of the year. Maintaining body temperature simply could not be done unless shelter were available. The response that would satisfy this need might range from living in a tent with an insulated sleeping bag to living in a 30-room mansion. Many motives, besides the need to maintain body temperature, would influence the choice of shelter.

Learned Motives

Learned motives are often called *acquired motives* or *social motives* because they develop (that is, they are learned or acquired) from social and environmental interactions. In many societies, these become the predominant motives because survival needs are satisfied readily and easily.

Learned motives generally develop as a result of societal rewards and punishments and include motive conditions such as the need for achievement, the need for friendship or affiliation, the need for dominance and social superiority, and the need for relief from anxiety. While these are not as directly related to survival as food or sleep, all of these may become very important as determinants of our behaviors.

It should be kept in mind that the list of learned motives given in this section is incomplete. A complete list of all learned motives would be exceedingly long. Several additional learned motives that have been studied are play, aggression, and autonomy.

Need for Achievement

One of the most extensively researched of learned motives is the need for achievement, sometimes called *nAch*. Individuals who seek a very high standard of performance for themselves have probably internalized achievement as a personal goal. However, they probably developed their need to achieve because of the social approval of success or the punishment of failure.

Much research on achievement needs has been conducted by using the Thematic Apperception Test (TAT) or some similar projective task. (See Chapter 14.) A person taking such a test is confronted with ambiguous pictures and is asked to describe them or tell stories about them. These stories or descriptions are supposed to reveal the subject's need for achievement. Responses are scored in accordance with the number of achievement-related themes that the responses contain. Such themes include striving for a goal or showing concern for success and failure. A person high in nAch might describe the main character as ambitious, facing challenges or planning for the future. The rationale behind this test is that in inventing a story for the picture, people reveal a lot more about themselves than they realize.

Early training seems to play a significant role in the level of a person's achievement drive. In one study, individuals who were rated high in nAch were found to have mothers who demanded considerable independence early in life; they were expected to do things for themselves—to earn their own spending money and choose their own clothes. Usually when parents are achievement oriented, their children are likely to follow in their footsteps. However, when parents are so sure of themselves and their opinions that their children dare not express a contrary view, the children may be unable to act independently and may, therefore, have a low achievement drive.

Most of these studies have been conducted with male subjects, although recent investigations have tried to identify achievement and fear-of-success motivations in women as well. In an early investigation of sex differences in attitudes toward achievement, male subjects were asked to respond to a statement describing a male who was the top student in his medical school class, and female subjects were asked to respond to a statement describing a female who was at the top of her medical school class. Almost all males responded favorably to the top male student; that is, they said the man's achievements would result in positive aftereffects. By contrast, the majority of the females indicated that the woman's success would lead to difficulties, particularly loss of femininity or social rejection. Subsequent research has called this result into question, but this technique for studying achievement motivation continues to be used.

Affiliation

The motive to associate with others or maintain social contacts, which we call affiliation, is found almost universally in human societies and is also characteristic of many animals. All higher animals and human beings demonstrate some affiliation by their dependence in infancy on their mothers (or caretakers) for the satisfaction of their basic needs. As they mature, they depend less on their parents for their physical needs but nevertheless turn to them for emotional support, assistance, and approval.

Harry Harlow's experiments with monkeys showed that infant monkeys raised with substitute mothers, some of which only fed them while others offered them only contact comfort, ran to the mothers that offered contact comfort whenever a frightening stimulus was introduced. Similar behavior is characteristic of young children. As children grow older, they seek affiliation with other people, in part because their strong need for approval requires the presence of others. This behavior reaches a peak during adolescence, when relationships with peers often become stronger than relationships with parents.

Relief from Anxiety

People are most likely to show affiliation behavior when they are in stressful situations and looking for relief from their anxiety. Stanley Schachter found, in a series of experiments, that a state of anxiety leads to an increased desire to be with others, especially others who are able to reduce the level of anxiety.

His subjects were female college students, enrolled in an introductory psychology course, who had volunteered to participate in psychological experiments in order to get extra credit. They were tested in groups of five to eight. The students, who did not know each other, were told by a man wearing a white lab coat, who was introduced as "Dr. Zilstein," that they would get a series of painful electric shocks.

They were asked to wait for ten minutes until the equipment was ready and were given the choice of waiting either alone or with other students in the same situation. Sixty-three percent of the students chose to wait with others, as compared with only 33 percent of a control group of subjects who were told that the shocks would be mild or painless. Thus, students who had been placed in a high-anxiety situation preferred to be in the company of other equally anxious people. This suggests that many individuals are less afraid when they can face a stressful situation with another person.

Aggression

Psychologists are in strong disagreement as to whether aggression is unlearned or learned. Furthermore, aggression is defined in several different ways, depending on the theoretical view of the person defining it.

The Freudian, or psychoanalytic, view is that aggression is an underlying urge that demands expression, either directly or indirectly. Aggression can become a problem when it cannot be expressed in socially acceptable ways—as in contact sports or debate.

The ethological viewpoint, discussed by Konrad Lorenz, is based on studies with animals. Aggression is basically considered the "fighting instinct." Lorenz feels that aggression functions to preserve the species as well as the individual, serving the vital functions of protecting one's territory against invasion, of defending the young, and of engaging in contests to select the strongest specimens for reproduction.

The social-learning theory suggests that aggression is a learned behavior, influenced particularly by observing the behavior of others, either directly or indirectly. Social learning theory also proposes that frustration always leads to aggression and that whenever aggression occurs, some form of frustration is responsible. Frustration is defined as the blocking of a desired goal, and aggression as the behavior intended to injure another person. If a person cannot injure the frustrating agent, he or she can displace the aggression from its original target to a more convenient target.

Effectance Motives

In addition to motives stemming from physiological needs and motives that are social in nature, there are also motives that impel us to interact with our environment and to realize our potential. Psychologists differ about the origin of these motives; some regard them as innate tendencies to seek stimulation and satisfaction, while others insist that these motives are acquired as a result of learning. There is a lack of agreement also as to what to call this group of motives. Among the names given are stimulus motives, psychological motives, and activity motives. We shall refer to them as effectance motives.

This term, coined by psychologist Robert White, suggests that individuals are motivated by a desire to function as effectively as they can in their environment—in other words, to become competent. When these effectance motives are satisfied, they increase one's competence to deal with the environment. In this group are the drives for stimulation, exploration and manipulation, self-actualization, and cognitive consistency, which is discussed in Chapter 17. We shall look at the other three here.

Stimulation

Stimulation needs refer to the levels and types of sensory or perceptual activity an individual requires. The need for stimulation appears to be both unlearned and learned. Stimulation needs include motives such as the need for activity, the need for variety, and the need to satisfy curiosity.

The need for stimulation is present very early in life and continues throughout the life span. Experiments have demonstrated that if people are placed in environments where there is no stimulation, they experience what is called sensory deprivation. The effects of this deprivation include decreased mental performance and, sometimes, severe psychological disturbances, such as hallucinations.

Too much stimulation can also be damaging. Some psychologists have been very concerned about the effects of highly stimulating educational television shows on children.

The psychologists suspect that such shows create a subsequent need for very high levels of stimulation in children who watch these programs; this is especially apparent when those children are presented with less stimulating educational materials requiring patience and perseverance. Although the psychologists realize that a minimal (unlearned) level of stimulation is essential if learning is to occur, they fear that the pre-school-age child will come to expect a learned level that cannot be duplicated or maintained in the school setting.

Exploration and Manipulation

Curiosity seems to be a characteristic of animals as well as humans. Rats will learn a maze without receiving any overt reinforcement, apparently just for the opportunity to explore some additional pathways.

Self-Actualization

This motive can be defined as the drive to discover our selves and to fulfill our potential—to be all that we can be. When this need is met, according to the humanistic psychologist Abraham Maslow, we feel a sense of happiness and well-being. Carl Rogers, Rollo May, Gordon Allport, and Erich Fromm all agree that self-actualization is an unlearned, uniquely human drive that impels us to action.

Combination Motives

Psychologists have found that some motives, called combination motives, result from the combined effect of unlearned and learned attitudes and behaviors. Other motives cannot be classified as either learned or unlearned; that is, their origins remain in debate.

Sex

Sex is probably the best example of a combination motive. Some aspects of sexual development and sexual response, such as onset of puberty or the amount of time needed for recovery between one ejaculation and the next, are physiologically determined. Other aspects of sexuality, such as standards of attractiveness or acceptable sexual practices, are a function of social learning. As a result, any one individual's sexual motivation results from a combination of physiological and social influences. (Note: Sex is not classified as a survival motive. Survival of the species depends upon sexual activity, but survival of an individual does not.)

Maternal Behavior

Maternal behavior is another combination motive. In many animals it is entirely instinctual and unlearned. In higher animals (such as monkeys and humans), however, it is learned behavior.

Like the sexual drive, maternal behavior is important for the survival of the species. The maternal behavior of animals includes four essential activities: nest building, cleaning, retrieving the young, and nursing. In animals, it is clearly an unlearned drive and a very strong one, since its basis is physiological. It is initiated by the secretion of the pituitary hormone prolactin during pregnancy, which also stimulates the mammary glands to produce milk after childbirth.

Among primates, maternal behavior appears to be learned, at least in part. Harry Harlow, an American psychologist, has conducted several important studies of maternal behavior in monkeys. He separated young monkeys from their mothers at birth and raised them in isolation. These monkeys later refused to mate, and when they were artificially inseminated, they ignored their young and repulsed their infants' attempts to make contact with them. Often, they behaved brutally to them, pushing the infants' faces to the floor, biting them, pounding them, and almost killing them. However, when they became pregnant a second time, their maternal behavior improved. This improvement, Harlow claims, demonstrates the influence of earlier experience (the previous parenting) on maternal behavior.

Among humans, maternal behavior is not as clearly biologically based as it is in many other animals, since it is not found in all women. Many women do not nurse their infants, do not show affection to them, and may even physically abuse them or abandon them. Human mothers who inflict severe physical punishment on their offspring are often found to have been beaten by their own parents. Thus, in both primates and humans, the mother's response to her offspring depends on her experiences as a child.

Contact Comfort

Contact comfort is one motive whose origins have remained in debate. Contact comfort is the apparent need of the young to have soft, warm, cuddly things to which they may cling. It is still impossible to state definitively whether this need is an unlearned, inborn reaction or the result of associating such stimuli with other rewarding activities, such as feeding.

A "special" blanket or stuffed animal may provide a young child with contact comfort. The reasons why the blanket or animal are so special, however, are not yet clearly defined. It is possible this motive also influences some adult behavior.

Conflict

More than one motive condition may be operating at any given moment. Sometimes the motive conditions are compatible with each other, but at other times they may be incompatible. Psychologists call this latter situation a conflict.

Conflict occurs whenever we are faced with a choice that involves the simultaneous occurrence of one or more competing motives or goals. Four different types of conflict situations have been described and studied: the approach-approach conflict, the avoidance-avoidance conflict, the approach-avoidance conflict, and the double approach-avoidance conflict.

Approach-Approach Conflict

One of the milder and more easily resolved conflicts is the approach-approach conflict, a situation in which a person must choose between two or more positively valued persons or objects. A conflict arises because only one of several possible positive responses can be chosen.

Suppose you are in a restaurant where dessert is included in the price of the dinner. You can choose only one dessert from the list of chocolate parfait, lemon meringue pie, strawberry shortcake, and hot fudge sundae. If you like more than one of the desserts listed, you are experiencing an approach-approach conflict.

Avoidance-Avoidance Conflict

An avoidance-avoidance conflict exists when a person is confronted with a choice between two or more unpleasant alternatives. For instance, in making up her program, Sally finds that the only courses still open are two that she dislikes—math and science—and she must choose between them. Behavior in this type of conflict situation is usually characterized by vacillation; that is, the individual approaches first one goal, then the other. The nearer one gets to each alternative, the stronger is the avoidance response. As Sally is about to decide on math, she shudders at the thought of working out all those equations, and the avoidance motive becomes stronger.

If the strength of one avoidance response is increased, the

person withdraws from the more disliked or feared situation and overcomes the conflict. If Sally hears, for example, that the new science teacher is particularly strict and gives low grades, she may resolve her conflict by choosing math instead. If both alternatives remain equally unpleasant, however, the individual may attempt to withdraw from the situation—either literally, by running away, or figuratively, by daydreaming—instead of facing up to the situation. This type of situation is resolved when one alternative becomes more positive than the other. Sally, for example, chooses to take math when she learns that her best friend, who is good in math, will be in that class.

Approach-Avoidance Conflict

An approach-avoidance conflict occurs when a person is confronted with a single goal that has both positive and negative qualities. This is a difficult conflict to resolve and tends to evoke a great deal of anxiety.

Ellen does not like the shape of her nose and believes that if she had plastic surgery, she would look beautiful. At the same time, she has a very low tolerance for pain, and she has been told that this kind of surgery involves a lot of post-operative pain. In the psychological laboratory, where a model of this type of conflict has been set up, rats have been trained to run an alley for a food reward. As they approach the food, they are given an electric shock. The rats' behavior is characterized by continued vacillation: first approaching the goal and then avoiding it. Humans, unlike rats, can think out the consequences of situations and make evaluations. The relative strengths of these opposing qualities must be weighed before a resolution can be reached.

Double Approach-Avoidance Conflict

Often, two goals have both good points and bad points. A young woman must choose between taking a good job or going to graduate school. If she takes the job, she will make a good deal of money now but will never get a master's degree, which she values. If she goes to school instead, she will obtain a degree but will forfeit an excellent salary for at least two years. This is known as a double approach-avoidance conflict, a situation in which there is more than one stimulus and each has both positive and negative values.

In life, most conflicts fall into this category, since most of our choices have both positive and negative features. Suppose someone who is on a weight-reduction diet is confronted with the menu described earlier. This person would see any one choice of dessert as both positive (how good it would taste) and negative (how many calories it has). The menu would thus create a double approach-avoidance conflict for the dieter. Unfortunately, there is rarely a totally satisfactory solution to this type of conflict, because each alternative has disadvantages that the person would like to avoid. When one finally makes a decision, he or she is likely to feel some regret afterward.

Theories of Motivation

Four well-known theories of motivation that attempt to explain motive conditions are humanistic theory, psychoanalytic theory, social-learning theory, and activation-arousal theory.

Humanistic Theory

The humanistic theory of motivation, as suggested by the psychologist Abraham Maslow, proposes a hierarchy of needs. This hierarchy lists human needs in an ascending order, indicating higher levels of development and growth. A simplified summary of this hierarchy, from lower to higher needs, is as follows: (1) physiological needs (survival motives); (2) safety needs (security motives); (3) belongingness needs (affiliation and acceptance needs); (4) esteem needs (status and achievement motives); and (5) self-actualization needs (to become what one is capable of becoming).

Each level of needs must be at least partially satisfied before the next will become important to an individual. The humanistic psychologist sees self-actualization as the ultimate goal of every person.

Psychoanalytic Theory

Sigmund Freud is given credit for psychoanalytic theory. Freud viewed motivation as largely unconscious and frequently an expression of aggressive or sexual desires. These might be expressed openly or in some symbolic form such as dreams or "slips of the tongue." (See Chapters 13 and 16 for a more thorough treatment of psychoanalytic theory.)

Social-Learning Theory

Social-learning theorists propose previous learning as the major source of motivation. The success or failure of particular responses leads to an understanding of what will produce positive or negative consequences and a desire to repeat successful behaviors.

Personal experience is not mandatory for social learning to occur; learning by observing some other person succeed or fail at a task may be sufficient to produce motive conditions. This is called modeling. Moreover, rewards or punishments may be either external or internal.

Activation-Arousal Theory

Activation-arousal theory proposes that any organism has a typical, normal, appropriate level of arousal and that behavior will be directed toward trying to maintain that level. This means that if environmental stimulation is too high, behaviors will occur in an effort to reduce arousal; if stimulation is too low, an increase of arousal will be sought.

A possible explanation of why a person might seek the anxiety-arousal of a sport such as sky diving may be found in this theory. The person may typically have a high level of arousal and use activities such as sky diving to keep arousal near or at this norm.

CHAPTER 8

Emotion

Emotion is a complex state, generally characterized by a heightened state of arousal and personal feelings. An emotion may be defined as a strong feeling accompanied by characteristic physiological activity of the internal organs (the physiological response). Emotions are very closely tied to motives. As a matter of fact, the two words share the same Latin root, movere, "to move." Both emotion and motivation move, or impel, the organism to action.

Psychologists recognize basic types of emotions such as fear, anger, and pleasure. This chapter looks at these basic emotions, considers how emotions are indentified and expressed, and discusses some general theories of emotion.

General Characteristics of Emotion

In one sense, emotions may be viewed as basic biological reactions. Although there is no clear understanding of *how* our neurological system formulates emotions, there is certainly a physiological basis for our emotions, in the sense that our brain appears to be "hardwired" to experience emotions. The limbic system, a part of the brain, has been identified as central in the origin of emotion. We also know that if the frontal lobe of the brain is removed (either surgically or by accident) or impaired (by a tumor), our basic emotional makeup may change dramatically. Likewise, aggression, sexuality, and fear may be heightened by tumors in other parts of the brain.

The judgment of emotional expression, however, is largely a subjective matter. This is true both for the person experiencing the emotion and for someone else who is judging that person's experience.

Stimulus Identification

Because so much subjectivity may be involved in judging someone else's emotions, it is usually necessary to identify the stimulus that generated the response in order to make an accurate evaluation of the emotion being expressed. Suppose, for example, you were looking at a picture of a 35-year-old man. You can see only his head, neck, and shoulders, and tears streaming down his cheeks. Are the man's tears an emotional response? And if so, what emotion do they represent? If the man is chopping onions, this probably is not an emotional response. If the response is emotional, however, it may be a reaction to a sad event or to a very happy one. Without seeing the stimulus, it is often difficult to tell the type of emotion that is being expressed.

Emotion as a Response

The concept of emotion as arousal and feeling implies that emotions are responses to the provoking stimuli. However, this internalized reaction may serve as only the first part of a chain of events that leads to an externalized (observable) response. In other words, emotion may become a stimulus for further responding.

Emotion as a Motivator

The internal reactions a person experiences may provoke additional responding. When this occurs, emotion serves as a motivator. The entire chain of reaction becomes: (1) an emotion-producing stimulus leading to (2) an emotional response (internal); (3) this emotion acts as a motivating stimulus, which results in (4) an expression of emotion (external).

When emotion is considered as a motivator, the same principles discussed for motivation (see Chapter 7) apply to emotion. Particularly, the relationship between the level of emotional state and performance will follow the inverted-U pattern as was illustrated in Figure 7.1.

Indicators of Emotion

There are three different indicators of emotion that are frequently used to identify the emotion expressed and the level of arousal and feeling being experienced. These are the personal reports of the person, the observed behaviors of that person, and evidence of physiological reactions accompanying the emotion.

Personal Reports

While outward response may not reveal a person's feelings or arousal, that person may choose to express an emotion by speaking or writing about it.

Observed Behaviors

Gestures, postures, facial expressions, movements, and other such responses may be used to help understand the emotion being expressed.

Physiological Indicators

Changes in heart rate, breathing pattern, blood pressure, pupil size, EEG pattern or galvanic skin response (GSR) are measures often interpreted as indicators of emotions.

Imagine a professional golfer preparing to tee off in a very important play-off match. Stopped by a reporter and asked, "How do you feel?" the golfer might respond, "Okay. Relaxed," or "Scared to death." This personal report might be confirmed or contradicted by observations made by the reporter: Is the golfer smiling or frowning, breathing normally or flushed and sweaty? The reporter might interpret all these indicators— spoken, observed, and physiological—and then decide how the golfer actually does feel.

Anthropomorphism and Parsimony

Two cautions about observing emotions should be kept in mind. First, one should not interpret too strictly the behaviors of lower organisms in terms of human emotions. Attributing human characteristics to a lower organism is called anthropomorphism. It should be avoided, especially when some other explanation of the organism's behavior is sufficient. When a dog is given food, it will often wag its tail. While there is some evolutionary evidence that such behaviors are the equivalent of the human's expression of happiness, and serve the purpose of communicating to other dogs that things are "safe," it is probably more appropriate to say that the dog is responding with its species-specific tail-wagging behavior than to say that the dog is feeling "happy."

The second caution about observing emotional behavior is that if a simple, or parsimonious, explanation is adequate for a given situation, one should use it in preference to a larger, more complicated explanation. This is the principle of parsimony.

Economy of explanation is desirable, however, only if the explanation is as good as or better than the more complicated alternative. Recall the discussion of sensation in Chapter 5. The sensing of a stimulus can be explained as a function of three major factors: motivation, probability of the stimulus, and "noise." The sensing of a stimulus can also be explained, however, by the single factor of threshold value. In this case, the latter (parsimonious) explanation is not as good as the more detailed explanation.

Basic Types of Emotions

Most languages contain many words and descriptive phrases associated with emotions. However, three basic types of emotions are recognized: fear, anger, and pleasure.

Fear

Fear is the reaction to a stimulus; anxiety is the state of apprehension that comes from anticipating a (not yet present) stimulus. The response to fear may be doubt, dread, dismay, or even horror; the fear-provoking stimulus might be described as frightening, alarming, or terrifying. Fear responses might motivate further behavior, such as escape, attack or panic. (Anxiety is likely to generate avoidance responses, provoked by stimuli described as worrisome or disturbing)

Fear-producing stimuli seem to change in importance as a person grows older. What is sudden, unexpected, and perhaps frightening to a child may not be at all fear-provoking to an adolescent or an adult. On the other hand, some fear-producing stimuli that affect adolescents and adults, particularly in social situations, may not provoke fear in a young child. A two-year-old in a nursery might have little worry about burping in front of the other children. However, an adolescent with a little gas might dread just such an event occurring in front of his or her peers.

Anger

The emotional reaction of anger may vary from being modestly "worked up" to being bitter, enraged or infuriated. Such reactions are provoked by displeasing or frustrating stimuli. Of course, as with other emotions, these reactions may serve to initiate additional responding, perhaps in the form of hostility, aggression, or regression (to an earlier level of functioning).

Pleasure

Pleasure ranges from simple reactions of delight or fun to ecstatic experiences of love. In general, pleasure reactions are generated by the presence of a favorable goal which is approachable. Expressions of pleasure may take such diverse forms as smiling, laughing, hugging and kissing.

Variations and Combinations

It appears to be possible to describe most other emotional situations as either variations of or combinations of these three basic emotions. The intent is not to limit the richness of our vocabulary in representing emotional circumstances, but rather to simplify explanation of how and why emotions occur. It is easy, for example, to think of how an exasperated person behaves. The upset and disgust, accompanied perhaps by bullying or blustering behavior, may be the result of anger (from some frustration), fear (of exposure of social inadequacy) or pleasure (derived from getting someone else to "give in").

Expression of Emotions

An emotion is an internal event, but it may in turn provoke external evidence of itself in the form of responses. These external responses vary, depending upon a number of factors including mode of expression, previous experience, and age.

Modes of Emotional Expression

Personal reports, observable behaviors, and physiological indicators all can provide information on the emotion a person is experiencing. However, contradictions may appear between what a person says he or she feels and what the physical signs of emotion reveal. For example, a person may verbally report one type of emotion when body position, gestures, and other reactions indicate some other emotion.

Previous Experience

One of the most influential factors in the expression of emotions is past experience. Typically, any given society or subculture develops stereotyped reactions that are deemed appropriate for certain emotion-producing situations. While these may vary considerably from one group to another, certain reactions (such as smiling when happy or crying when sad) appear to be quite universal.

One very important aspect of previous experience appears to be the opportunity to observe some meaningful model. Quite frequently, emotional expressions will imitate those shown by a model, especially if the model is seen as an important or significant person. However, the facial expressions associated with many emotions appear to be unlearned—not dependent on modeling—since they are the same across cultures and, from historical evidence in art, appear to have been the same throughout history.

Age Differences

Children display their emotions more frequently and more openly than adults do, but their emotional reactions are usually very brief. In adolescence, emotional reactions are more prolonged and may interfere with daily functioning and performance. Adolescents tend to brood about their emotional problems. During adolescence and young adulthood, emotions reach their peak, and as many parents can confirm, the emotions of the adolescent seem to be very volatile, ranging from extreme joy and excitement on the one hand to sudden outbursts of anger and moods of depression on the other.

The emotional experiences a person undergoes seem to exert a cumulative effect— through learning and experience—so that noticeable changes seem to take place as a person grows older. Several patterns appear to be quite general. An older person is likely to show more restraint or control in the expression of emotions. Along with this, there is a tendency for the emotional expressions that do occur to be more verbal and less physical. Furthermore, as a person grows older, one can expect her or him to show increasing complexity and differentiation of emotional states.

For example, a young child is very likely to show fear often, possibly by crying or withdrawing. Adults, on the other hand, have learned to try to hide their fear reactions and put up a "good front." Correspondingly, the young child will be much more likely to strike out physically when angered. The angry adult is more likely to speak out or gesture rather than strike.

Special Topics in Emotions

Research on emotions has led to practical applications of certain findings and to explanations of special problems.

Lie Detection

One practical application of the study of emotions has been the attempt to develop dependable lie-detection techniques. Research has substantiated that emotion-producing situations can often be detected by measuring physiological responses such as heart rate, respiration rate or galvanic skin resistance (GSR), even when personal reports or observed behaviors do not give any indication of an emotion.

The theory of lie detection depends on the thesis that a person who is telling a lie is in an emotion-producing situation. Thus, physiological indicators of emotion can be used to judge whether or not a person is telling the truth. Interpretations of the results from such tests must be made very carefully because many factors other than lying may be producing emotion. Indeed, research studies have so far not been able to establish distinct patterns of physiological indicators associated with precise emotional states.

Somatoform (Psychosomatic) Disorders

Physical illnesses brought about by psychological causes are called somatoform or psychosomatic disorders. The symptoms of physical illness are present, but there are no accompanying physical causes. The extent or severity of a somatoform disorder may range from a mild headache to severe paralysis, depending upon the provoking stimulus. A touch of nausea before a big exam may be psychosomatic in nature. The pressure of business may produce excessive stomach acidity and eventually ulcers. The need to attract or maintain attention may generate skin rash. All of these and many similar symptoms might be psychosomatic in origin. (Note: These reactions could also be the result of flu, malfunctioning glands, and an allergy, respectively. It is necessary to determine the cause before making any decision.)

Theories of Emotion

The earliest attempts to explain emotions were the Charles Darwin book *The Expression of Emotions in Animals and Man*, the James-Lange theory and the Cannon-Bard theory.

Darwin's Position

Charles Darwin, in his book, suggests that human emotions evolved as an adaptive mechanism over the course of the evolutionary process. Darwin contrasted the apparent emotive expressions of animals with the development of emotions in humans. He studied and recorded the emotional expressions of infants and children, and concluded that emotions ultimately serve our welfare by providing signals to others and intensifying our bonding with other people, allowing a group cohesiveness and social functioning.

The James-Lange Theory

The James-Lange theory is named for two individuals (William James, an American psychologist, and Carl Lange, a Danish psychologist) who independently developed the same basic idea at about the same time. The theory proposes that certain stimuli produce bodily changes that, in turn, generate felt emotions. First, this theory suggests, we see a mad dog; next, we respond internally (fast heartbeat, heavy breathing, sweating) and may run; and then, because our body is so keyed up, we feel the emotion of fear. This theory thus suggests that the physiological reaction comes first, then the emotion follows.

The Cannon-Bard Theory

A later theory, the Cannon-Bard theory of emotion, states that the feared object is seen and the bodily reaction and emotional responses are triggered simultaneously. This theory proposes that a stimulus is received by the cortex, is recognized as emotion-producing, and a return signal is sent to activate lower brain centers in the hypothalamus and limbic system. From this portion of the brain, signals are then sent out simultaneously to both external muscles and internal organs and back to the cortex. The muscles and organs make the physiological reactions to the emotion, while the cortex perceives the signal as the emotion. Thus, the theory proposes that physiological and psychological reactions occur at the same time.

Cognitive and Attribution Theories

More recent investigations into emotions have stressed the interaction of cognitive (intellectual) and physiological (bodily) influences. These theories emphasize the influence that thought processes can have on the emotion being felt by a person. Physiological arousal alone is not seen as the sole determinant of emotion, and a person's appraisal and labeling of a situation have a great effect on the emotion the person experiences. Cognitive and attribution theories place emphasis on an individual's ability to perceive cause-and-effect relationships between various situations and emotional experiences.

For example, a person might explain depression as a result of not sleeping enough, not being able to visit with close friends or not getting a raise when one was expected. In each case, the symptoms might be very similar, but the emotion is attributed to quite different causes.

On occasion, a sharp difference may exist between a person's first interpretation of an emotional event and what has been called the secondary appraisal. Secondary appraisal usually occurs some time after the initial emotion-producing event. The person may attribute the emotion to some cause completely different from what was first proposed.

Activation Theory

Activation theory emphasizes the role of the brain's reticular activating system (RAS) during emotional arousal. The RAS can be activated either by sensory stimulation or by the cortex itself—that is, by one's physiological state or by one's thoughts.

The organism's state of arousal varies from a minimum, as in sleep, rising to higher levels during various waking states, to a maximum in intense excitement. Emotional expression is part of one's pattern of arousal. Behavioral efficiency is at its peak when emotional arousal is at intermediate magnitudes.

In other words, some stimulation that raises the arousal level from its minimum, or sleep, level is essential for efficient performance; and moderate levels of stimulation, when a person is awake and attentive, are most effective for learning and responding. Too high a level of arousal, as in a state of extreme anger (what is sometimes called blind rage), will prevent an individual from using reason or logic in responding to a situation or in trying to solve a problem.

CHAPTER 9

Principles of Learning

Psychologists are concerned with learning and particularly with the different factors that influence acquisition, retention, and use of learned responses.

In this chapter we discuss some of the basic principles of learning. We begin by examining the classical conditioning paradigm, in which the pairing of stimuli produces learned responses. Next we look at operant conditioning, in which the consequences of a person's responses determine what is learned. Finally, we consider learning by modeling, or observing, the behavior of another person.

Some of the variables that affect the acquisition of new materials and the memory of those materials as measured by later retention will be discussed in the next chapter.

Definition of Learning

Learning is defined as a relatively permanent change in behavior that occurs as a result of experience. This definition implies there is acquisition of a response and retention of that response once it has become a part of an organism's behavior.

Learning and Maturation

The definition of learning given above stresses the effect of experience. The definition does not mean to diminish the importance of physical maturation; indeed, physical development may be a necessary condition for learning to occur. However, physical development alone is not sufficient; for learning to take place, an organism must also have experience.

For example, children around six months old have not developed sufficiently to be able to speak a language. Only when they are older can they begin to learn to speak. However, in the absence of the right kinds of experience—including appropriate models, practice, and reinforcement—even a much older child (such as an adolescent) will not learn to speak a particular language.

Learning-Performance Distinction

Learning and performance are not necessarily the same. A person's observable behavior (performance) will not always reveal what the person has learned. A young child who gets lost in a large crowd at a sports stadium may cry but be unwilling to talk. A callous observer might react by saying, "The kid doesn't even know his name." Actually, the child may have committed to memory his name, address, and telephone number. However, the child may additionally have been taught not to speak to strangers, and this latter learning may keep him from responding to questions he knows how to answer.

Classical Conditioning

Classical conditioning is a process in which an organism

learns to respond in a particular way to a stimulus that previously did not produce the response. This stimulus, which was once "neutral," becomes response-producing because it is paired (or associated) with another stimulus that does produce the response.

Classical conditioning also is called respondent conditioning or Pavlovian conditioning. The term *respondent* implies that the learned response is elicited involuntarily from the subject rather than produced by the subject in a voluntary (or operant) manner.

The term *Pavlovian conditioning* gives credit to the Russian physiologist Ivan Pavlov (1849–1936), the first person to investigate classical conditioning extensively. Pavlov devoted over 30 years of his career to the study of this type of learning.

Today, psychologists like Robert Rescorla view classical conditioning from a broader perspective. They see this type of conditioning as the organism's learning about the relations among events in its environment, which allows in turn for more effective function. An individual makes connections (technically, *associations*) among the many events occurring simultaneously and develops response strategies to deal with these. They object to the simplicity of the Pavlovian model, while acknowledging the breakthrough this model provided in understanding human and animal behaviors.

The Classical Conditioning Paradigm

A stimulus that is originally neutral and comes to be response-producing is called a *conditioned stimulus* (abbreviated as CS). The stimulus that produces the response on the first trial and each trial after is called the *unconditioned stimulus* (UCS).

The response elicited by the UCS is called the *unconditioned response* (UCR). Eventually, the same type of response will occur at the presentation of the CS: this response is called the

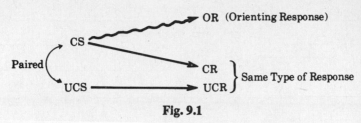

Fig. 9.1

conditioned response (CR). A diagram representing classical conditioning appears in Figure 9.1, above.

The *orienting response* (OR) indicated in Figure 9.1 often occurs on the first few trials. The subject responds by determining where the stimulus comes from or what stimuli are presented.

In his original investigation, Pavlov used dogs as subjects. He found that presentation of meat powder (UCS) would cause the dogs to salivate (UCR). Pavlov then paired the ringing of a bell (CS) with the presentation of meat powder. After several pairings, the dogs salivated at the sound of the bell (CR). The OR in this situation occurred in the first few trials, when the dogs turned their heads in an attempt to determine where the bell was located.

Interstimulus Interval

A paired CS and UCS may occur exactly together, or there may be a time interval between them. The time between the onset of the CS and the onset of the UCS is called the interstimulus interval (ISI). The word *contiguity* is used to describe this relationship between the presentation of the CS and the UCS.

The Pavlovian experiment described above may be conducted with several different kinds of contiguity relationships:

Simultaneous: The bell and the meat powder are presented at exactly the same time.

Delayed: The bell comes on first and remains on until the meat powder is presented.

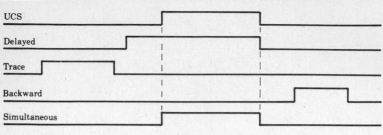

Fig. 9.2

Trace: The bell comes on and goes off before the meat powder is presented.

Backward: The meat powder is presented before the bell is rung.

Temporal: The bell is never rung. The CS in this situation would be a constant time period, such as five minutes. (The meat powder would be presented every five minutes.)

Figure 9.2 illustrates the relationship between the UCS and the CS in each ISI relationship.

Extinction (in Classical Conditioning)

Extinction in classical conditioning is the procedure of presenting the CS alone (without the UCS) for repeated trials. The word extinction is also used to refer to the result of such a procedure, in which the CR returns to its original (preconditioning) level.

In Pavlov's experiment, extinction was produced by repeatedly sounding the bell without presenting the meat powder. Eventually, the dogs stopped salivating at the sound of the bell. That is, the CR (salivating) returned to its original, preconditioning level.

Extinction as a Measure of Response Strength

Resistance to extinction is one measure of the strength of a

CR. In general, it is felt that the greater the resistance to extinction, the greater the strength of the established CR. In the absence of the UCS, a "strong" CR would persist for many trials in which only the CS was presented. A "weak" CR, on the other hand, would be extinct after a few trials in which only the CS was presented.

Asymptote

Repeated presentations of the paired CS and UCS often produce a CR that approaches a maximum strength. This "leveling off" of CR strength near some maximum is called the asymptote or asymptotic value of the response strength.

Effect of Partial Reinforcement on Extinction

Partial reinforcement occurs when the CS is paired with the UCS on some, but not all, of the trials. A partial reinforcement situation is described in terms of a percentage; for example, if the CS is paired with the UCS on half the trials, the subject experiences 50 percent reinforcement.

Research has shown that a CR acquired under partial reinforcement conditions is more resistant to extinction than is a response established under continuous (100 percent) reinforcement. This finding is called the *partial reinforcement effect* (PRE).

Suppose, for example, two dogs are conditioned to make the salivation response at the sound of the bell. One dog is trained in a continuous reinforcement situation, while the other hears the bell on every trial, but is presented meat powder on only some of the trials. The CR of the latter dog would be more resistant to extinction than would be the CR of the first dog.

Robert Rescorla and others suggest that these different reinforcement conditions provide the organism with unequal amounts of information, thereby allowing for different interpretations of environmental events. From this point of view the true power of reinforcement it is not based strictly on the idea that a stimulus leads to a response-reinforcement pattern. Rather, this contemporary interpretation suggests that a stimulus sets off a chain of information (reinforcement following response) that affects the ways the organism continues to act and respond.

Several theories have been proposed as explanations of the PRE. No one theory has gained general acceptance, but the general finding still holds: partial reinforcement results in greater resistance to CR extinction.

Spontaneous Recovery

Imagine a situation in which a CR appears to be extinguished. If, following a period of rest, the CS is again presented (alone, with no UCS present), the CR will sometimes reappear. This is called spontaneous recovery of the response. The strength of the CR will not be as great as it was originally, before extinction, but partial recovery of the CR will occur.

Suppose the CR of one of Pavlov's dogs was extinguished and the dog was kept out of the experimental setting for several days. If the dog was then placed again in the experimental setting, it would salivate (CR) at the sound of the bell (CS). Evidence of salivation under these circumstances would indicate spontaneous recovery of the dog's CR.

Stimulus Generalization

Stimulus generalization is demonstrated when a CR is made not only to the original CS, but to other stimuli that are similar to the original CS.

Primary Stimulus Generalization

Stimulus generalization that is based on the physical properties of a stimulus is called primary stimulus generalization. One of Pavlov's dogs, for example, might salivate both to a bell and to a similar-sounding chime. Humans may show comparable primary stimulus generalization by responding to a variety of automobile horns, all of which may sound similar.

Secondary Stimulus Generalization

Human beings, who have a command of language and other symbols, are able to show another form of stimulus generalization, called secondary stimulus generalization. A human CR may be given not only to the original CS, but to other stimuli that are judged similar not because they have the same physical properties but because they have the same meaning as the original CS. Thus, humans may respond in the same way to a variety of similar stimuli, such as the following:

Raise = Rays: When spoken, the same sounds yield primary stimulus generalization. The response is to a physical property: the sounds themselves.

Lift = Raise: Secondary stimulus generalization is demonstrated, based upon the context and word meaning.

Lift = Elevator: Secondary stimulus generalization also is demonstrated if one is familiar with the British use of the word "lift."

Stimulus Differentiation (Discrimination)

A subject who gives the CR to a particular CS but does not respond to similar stimuli shows differentiation. Historically, *discrimination* was the term used for this process.

Concept of a Continuum

A subject who responds to the original CS only, and not to any other stimuli, shows complete stimulus differentiation. If the subject gives the CR indiscriminately to all stimuli, complete stimulus generalization has occurred. These two extremes can be seen as the ends of a continuum; responses to some—but not just one stimulus or all stimuli—represent the middle points between these two poles.

Pavlov's dogs would have shown complete stimulus generalization if they had salivated to any noise. If, on the other hand, the dogs had responded to the original bell but no other similar sounds, they would have shown complete differentiation.

To illustrate stimulus generalization and differentiation, suppose the line in Figure 9.3 represents all the possible shades of blue. To the right, the blue becomes paler and paler until it is white; to the left, the blue becomes darker and darker until it is black. Now, suppose a person has been conditioned to respond to the color blue. The lines of the figure illustrate three possible response patterns based on the principles outlined above.

Pavlov showed that when dogs are forced to make choices (that is, to differentiate) between two stimuli that are very similar, they sometimes show signs of confusion and distress. Pavlov called this phenomenon experimental neurosis.

Response Generalization

Response generalization occurs when a subject gives not only the original response, but other, similar responses to the original CS. In other words, one stimulus elicits an entire class of equivalent responses. For example, a group of people are shown a new product that they admire. Their responses might include exclamations such as "Fantastic!" or "Gorgeous!" or "Wonderful!" or "Magnificent!" These exclamations illustrate response generalization in that they are equivalent responses given to a single stimulus.

Higher-Order Conditioning

When the strength of the CR is near its maximum value, the CS that elicits the CR may take the role of a UCS. A new pairing

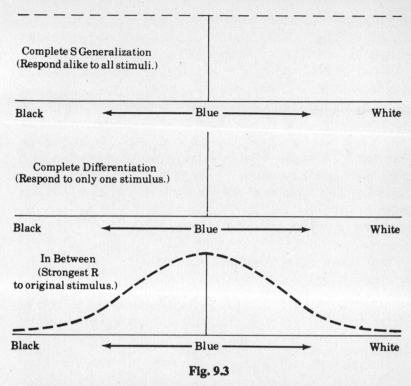

Fig. 9.3

could then be established, in which a new CS would be paired with the well-established CS without presenting the UCS. Repeated presentation would lead to the elicitation of the same type of CR by presentation of the new CS alone. This is called higher-order conditioning.

Assume that Pavlov's pairing of the ringing bell and the meat powder had been presented many times, until the dogs' salivation response was very well established. Subsequently, pairing a new sound, say a tapping noise, with the bell might lead to higher-order conditioning, even though the meat powder was no longer presented. After repeated tap-bell pairings, a salivation response would be elicited by the tapping noise alone.

Higher-order conditioning is sometimes used when the pairing of the original CS with the UCS may produce difficulties because of distraction or incompatibility; it is then hoped that the CR can be produced by the second CS. The first CS–UCS pairing allows the eventual desired conditioning.

It should be noted that each new-CS–old-CS pairing is both a conditioning trial for the new CS–CR attachment and an extinction trial for the old CS–CR link, since the UCS is not presented. A weakly established original CR may extinguish before the new bond can be formed. For example, a new driver from the U.S. would more easily adapt to driving on the left side of the road in England than would a driver with 20 years experience of driving on the right side in the U.S.

Special Examples of Classical Conditioning

The principles of classical conditioning can provide interesting perspectives on other psychological principles. Three of these are the concept of blocking, the development of secondary (conditioned) reinforcers and the establishment of phobias.

Kamin's Blocking Effect

Leon Kamin has shown that pairing a neutral stimulus with a response-producing stimulus does not always lead to the same degree of linkage for all subjects. This suggests that previous conditioned experiences intervene to affect the strength of a response acquired through conditioning.

In experiments, Kamin conditioned two groups with a multiple conditioned stimulus (such as a tone and light). One of these groups had previously been conditioned with one part of this compound stimulus (light alone). Although both groups received the same UCS (such as food), when they were tested after the pairings the group with the previous conditioning showed poor acquisition of the tone-response linkage when compared with the group for whom both stimuli were new. This indicates that the information provided by each event is important in the total conditioning experience.

Secondary Reinforcement

Secondary (conditioned) reinforcers are developed when a previously neutral stimulus (CS) is paired with a reinforcement (UCS) and the CS takes on reinforcing properties. Quite frequently, secondary reinforcers are verbal stimuli that become meaningful as reinforcers only after pairings of this sort.

Being told by a teacher that your work is "excellent" may serve as a reinforcer. Yet if you had never learned the word excellent or had learned it in a context where it was paired with poor performance and punishment, the meaning would be lacking or different, and the word would not be reinforcing.

Money is an example of a secondary reinforcer. Humans learn to accept money as a reinforcer because they know that money can in turn be used to purchase other secondary reinforcers, or primary reinforcers such as food or heat.

Phobias

Phobias are intense, compelling fears thought to be established in the same manner as other classically conditioned responses. A previously neutral stimulus (CS) is paired with a fear-producing stimulus (UCS), and the CS comes to take on fear-producing (motivating or emotional) attributes.

Imagine stepping into an elevator that then plunges 20 floors before the emergency brake saves you from crashing at the bottom of the shaft. It is probably easy for you to understand that your next confrontation with an elevator might be highly fear-producing. The previously neutral stimulus (the elevator) would have taken on fear-producing qualities because of the single CS–UCS pairing.

Operant (Instrumental) Conditioning

Operant conditioning is a learning process that involves changing the probability of eliciting a particular response by manipulating the consequences of that response. An operant response is defined most simply as a response that leads to an effect or a goal.

Operant conditioning is also called instrumental conditioning or Skinnerian conditioning. The term *operant* is used because responses are frequently operations upon the environment. They are instrumental in that they often produce on effect or lead to a goal. The term *Skinnerian* gives credit to the work of B. F. Skinner, a leading investigator of the many principles of operant or instrumental conditioning.

Characteristics of Operant Conditioning

Operant conditioning is concerned with the acquisition and retention of operant responses as well as the elimination of undesired responses.

The Operant Response

An operant response is a voluntary response made by an organism. Voluntary does not mean necessarily that the person has complete choice in the matter, or that the action is purposive, but rather that it involves voluntary muscle actions and some degree of mediated responses. These responses may be learned in an ordered sequence (or chain of behavior), making the end result the attainment of the intended goal.

Contingency of Reinforcement

Generally, operant conditioning occurs in situations where the actual delivery of a reinforcement depends upon the appropriate responses being made. This is called the contingency of the reinforcement upon the response.

Suppose, for example, a salesman is told that he must make a certain number of sales before he will receive a bonus payment. This is a contingency situation. The completed sales are the operant responses, the money is the reinforcement, and delivery of the bonus money is contingent upon the successful completion of the sales.

Noncontingent Reinforcement

An organism may link a particular response and reinforcement when such an association is inappropriate. The result may be the development of a superstitious behavior, in which the organism performs as if the response will produce the reinforcement. In fact, no contingency actually exists. This is called noncontingent reinforcement.

People involved in sports often show superstitious behaviors. For example, a coach wears a particular plaid coat on a night when his team wins a very convincing victory. Although the coat in no way influenced the result of the game, the coach continues to wear it at games as long as a victory streak continues.

Law of Effect

E. L. Thorndike proposed the law of effect, which states that a response that is followed by a satisfying stimulus or by the termination of an annoying stimulus will become conditioned. Subsequent research has generally supported this proposal. (These contingency situations have come to be called, respectively, positive reinforcement and negative reinforcement, both of which will be discussed later in this chapter.)

Comparison of Operant and Classical Conditioning

There are two major differences between operant and classical conditioning: how voluntary the response is and how identifiable the stimuli are in each situation.

Voluntary Response

In general, operant conditioning involves responses that are voluntary or emitted by an organism, while classical conditioning involves responses that are involuntary or elicited from the organism. Operant conditioning does not involve forcing the response being studied, while the response of interest in classical conditioning is elicited by the unconditioned stimulus.

Stimulus Identification

In classical conditioning, both the conditioned stimulus and the unconditioned stimulus are readily identified, and the association of the CR to the CS can be easily studied. By contrast, in operant conditioning there is no identifiable UCS that elicits a response nor is there a CS to which the response becomes attached. The key relationship in operant conditioning is not between stimuli, but rather between the response and the reinforcement.

Acquisition of Operant Responses

Several factors are important in the acquisition of operant responses, including how this acquisition is measured, initiated, and extinguished.

The Cumulative Record

The most common means of determining whether or not an operant response has been conditioned is to use a cumulative record of that response. A cumulative record simply indicates the number of responses made in a given time period.

A type of apparatus used frequently in operant conditioning is called an *operant conditioning chamber* (known popularly as a *Skinner box*). A basic form of this is represented in Figure 9.4.

An untrained and hungry laboratory rat that is placed in equipment such as this may eventually learn to press the lever, which in turn will activate the feeder mechanism and cause

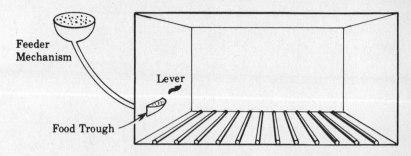

Fig. 9.4

pellets of food to be delivered to the food trough. A cumulative record of the lever-pressing responses might be illustrated as in Figure 9.5.

Shaping

Shaping is the reinforcing of closer and closer approximations of a desired response. In some cases, it may be necessary to encourage the first response so that it may be reinforced and begin the progression of shaping.

For example, when a naive rat is placed in an operant conditioning apparatus, it often is possible to speed the acquisition of the lever-pressing response by using a shaping procedure. With a remote-control apparatus, the experimenter can reinforce the rat's approaches to the lever, any indications of interest in the lever, placing a paw on the lever, and finally pressing the lever—in essence, a sequence of responses that leads to the appropriate response.

Language learning frequently involves shaping. At first a child's approximations of a desired word are reinforced, as are the better and better attempts produced later. At first, a child may say "baaaaa," followed by "brrrrr," "bud- da," and finally "butter."

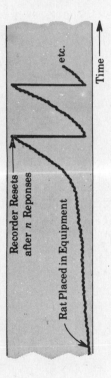

Fig. 9.5

Fig. 9.6

Extinction (in Operant Conditioning)

Extinction in operant conditioning is accomplished by terminating the delivery of reinforcement following the response. The result of this procedure should be a decrease in the rate of responding until it reaches the preconditioning level.

Suppose, for example, a rat has been conditioned to make the lever-pressing response in order to receive food pellets. Extinction is accomplished by simply turning off the feeder mechanism so that additional responses will not lead to the delivery of food pellets. Although the rat may continue to respond for some time, the expected change in response rate should be observed eventually. A cumulative record of extinction might be illustrated as in Figure 9.6.

Partial Reinforcement Effect

Generally, the effect of partial reinforcement in operant conditioning is the same as in classical conditioning; that is, conditioning achieved through partial reinforcement is more resistant to response extinction than that achieved through continuous reinforcement. In addition, certain special effects of the PRE in operant conditioning have been studied extensively. Some of them are described below.

Schedules of Reinforcement

Partial reinforcement has been investigated by arranging the contingency conditions according to several different principles. These various arrangements have been termed schedules of reinforcement.

Schedule Characteristics

Four types of schedules of reinforcement are common. These are as follows:

Fixed Arrangement: The schedule never changes.

Variable Arrangement: The schedule may change, although usually around some average value.

Ratio Scheduling: Based upon the number of responses made.

Interval Scheduling: Based on time.

Basic Schedule Formats

The four basic schedule formats are described as follows:

Fixed Ratio (FR): The reinforcement is contingent upon the subject's making a certain number of responses (or *n* responses). This number remains constant throughout the procedure. For example, in the operant conditioning chamber the rat must make ten lever presses before a food pellet will be delivered to the trough. The speed or pattern of responding does not matter, as long as ten responses are made.

Fixed Interval (FI): The reinforcement is contingent upon a response being made at the end of a specified time interval. This time interval never varies. Here, the rat must make one correct response at the end of a 30-second interval. Responding is not required at any other time during the interval, and the interval never changes.

Variable Ratio (VR): The reinforcement is contingent upon the subject's responding. However, the number of responses required varies from trial to trial, usually in a random pattern. (There may be an average number of responses required, but this will not be readily apparent to the subject.) Here the rat is reinforced after 3, 13, 7, 10, 7, 15, 17, 10, and 5 responses. While this pattern averages ten required responses per reinforcement, sometimes fewer are needed, while at other times many more must be made before the reinforcement will be given.

Variable Interval (VI): The reinforcement is contingent upon the subject's giving a correct response at the end of a period of time, but this time period changes, usually in a random fashion. (There may be an average amount of time, but this will not be readily apparent to the subject.) Here the rat is reinforced when a correct response is made at the end of 15-, 27-, 45-, 30-, 33-, 10-, 30- and 50-second intervals. Although the average time is 30 seconds, the interval may be either shorter or much longer.

Expected Performance

Each of the basic schedules of reinforcement will usually produce a particular or distinctive pattern of responding, as follows:

Fixed Ratio: Bursts of responses closely matching the required number of responses will be followed by brief pauses just after the reinforcement is delivered.

Fixed Interval: No responding or very slow responding during the early part of the interval will give way to a high rate of responding just as the interval nears completion.

Variable Ratio: A constant, high rate of responding can be expected as the subject learns that more responses mean more reinforcements; however, the subject is unable to determine how many responses must be made for each reinforcement.

Variable Interval: A slow, steady rate of responding occurs. (The rate of responding is not important, but responding at the end of each interval is required.) The subject "protects" against missing an interval by continuing with the steady performance.

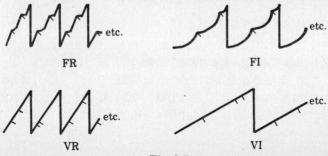

Fig. 9.7

The cumulative record of responses under each of the four basic formats would tend to look like the results shown in Figure 9.7. (Note: Each "hash mark" denotes delivery of a reinforcement.)

More Advanced Schedules

Combinations or variations of the basic schedules lead to more complex schedules of reinforcement, including multiple schedules, compound schedules, and concurrent schedules.

Multiple Schedule: Requires the subject to satisfy two or more independent schedules that are presented successively, each in the presence of some cue stimulus.

Compound Schedule: Reinforces a single response according to the requirements of two or more schedules operating at the same time.

Concurrent Schedule: Reinforces the subject when two or more responses are made to satisfy two or more schedules at the same time.

Generalization and Discrimination

In some operant conditioning situations, discriminative cue stimuli indicate to the subject when responding is appropriate or inappropriate. These are not considered conditioned stimuli because they do not elicit specific responses, but they do serve as signals for the general class of operant responses.

Stimulus Generalization

Just as in classical conditioning, stimulus generalization in operant conditioning is shown when the subject responds not only to the original (discriminative) stimulus, but to other, similar stimuli as well. In other words, the same operant response is made in several similar situations.

Differentiation (Discrimination)

Differentiation (or discrimination) occurs when the organism distinguishes between the original discriminative stimulus and other similar stimuli, making the operant response in the presence of the original stimulus, but not to other, similar stimuli.

Reinforcement Characteristics

A major factor in operant conditioning is the delivery of reinforcement following responding. Several characteristics of reinforcement have been studied, including positive reinforcers, the effects of aversive stimuli, various conditions of learning or feedback serving as reinforcers, and delay of reinforcement.

Positive Reinforcement

Positive reinforcement means that the presence of a particular stimulus serves to strengthen or maintain a response.

Aversive Stimuli and Negative Reinforcement

An *aversive stimulus* is one the subject finds noxious or unpleasant. *Negative reinforcement* means that the removal or absence of a particular stimulus (usually an aversive stimulus) serves to strengthen or maintain a response.

For example, with a grid-type floor in the operant conditioning chamber, it is possible to deliver an electric shock to the rat. The electric shock can be terminated by the rat by pressing a lever. The electric shock is the aversive stimulus, while the termination of the shock is a negative reinforcement that strengthens or maintains the lever-pressing response. (Note: Almost everyone would find electric shock aversive, but many other stimuli may be judged aversive by some and not by others. Previous experience may be important in determining the properties of a stimulus situation.)

Escape, Avoidance, and Punishment

In the example above, the lever-pressing response terminated the aversive shock. Such a response represents *escape behavior*—that is, responding that removes an already-present aversive stimulus. *Avoidance responding* means that an organism responds in a way that keeps an aversive stimulus from being delivered. *Punishment* occurs when a response leads to or is followed by an aversive stimulus.

It should be recognized that punishment situations usually involve a contingency relationship; that is, the aversive stimulus occurs *because* the response was made. However, occasionally, an aversive stimulus may occur contiguously with some response although no contingency exists. In such cases, a superstitious relationship may develop.

Behavior as simple as running may fit all three categories: escape, avoidance or punishment. If the aversive stimulus of a rain shower is present, one may run to escape from it. If one fears heart trouble, one may run for conditioning with the hope of avoiding later physical difficulties. An athlete who misbehaves may have to "run laps," a punishment situation.

Feedback and Using a Response as Reinforcement

Earlier in the chapter, the development of a conditioned reinforcer was described. In this type of learning, a previously neutral stimulus takes on reinforcing properties. Two other special cases of reinforcement are feedback and using a response as reinforcement.

Feedback occurs when a subject is informed of the results of a response. The feedback may serve as either reinforcement, lack of reinforcement, or punishment for the response, increasing or decreasing the likelihood that the response will be made again.

Using a response as reinforcement may be accomplished by

making performance of that response contingent upon performance of some less probable response.

This is sometimes referred to as "Grandma's Rule." A child may be informed that an "if-then" contingency situation exists: only when a particular low-probability response (such as shoveling snow from the driveway) has been completed will a high-probability response (such as going sledding) be allowed. Sledding thus serves as a reinforcement for snow shoveling.

Delay of Reinforcement

Delay of reinforcement means that, although a contingency relationship between a response and reinforcement does exist, some time elapses between the completion of the response and the delivery of the reinforcement. In general, the effect of delay of reinforcement is to reduce learning efficiency.

Uses of Operant Conditioning

There are many possible uses for operant conditioning in family life, education, business, clinical psychology, animal training, and other areas. Two examples of the practical applications of such principles are in programmed learning and behavior therapy.

Programmed Learning

Programmed learning is an instruction or review technique in which material to be learned is presented in successive, well-planned steps. The material may be presented in a textbook format, by a teaching machine or possibly with a computer. Subjects are expected to respond to a certain problem and then to check to determine if the answer they have given is correct or incorrect. The answer provides feedback or reinforcement, generally immediately (a no-delay situation).

Two varieties of programs are *linear programs* (in which each person follows the same program in the same sequence) and *branching programs* (in which the sequence may vary, depending upon the answers given). Linear programs make certain that all subjects study the same material, but may prove boring to some or too difficult for others. Branching programs allow each person to investigate the most important areas according to the responses made, but not all people study the same materials and follow-up may be more difficult.

Behavior Therapy

The basic premise of behavior therapy is that acceptable responses will be reinforced and unacceptable responses will be extinguished or suppressed, sometimes by using both negative reinforcement and punishment. Such a technique does not place high value on understanding the causes of behavioral symptoms, but it has been beneficial in creating responses that are socially acceptable and thus in helping patients return to a relatively "normal" life. (See Chapter 16.)

Learning by Modeling

Learning by modeling has also been called observational learning, learning by imitation, no-trial learning, vicarious learning, identification learning, and social learning. No matter which label is used and which particular emphasis is stressed, the basic premise of learning by modeling is that one person or animal observes the behavior of another and is then able to perform some or all of that observed behavior.

Comparison with Other Learning Forms

Learning by modeling differs from classical conditioning and operant conditioning in several important ways, including species limitations, the significance of reinforcement, and the importance of the type of response made.

Limitations by Species

Imitative behavior is limited to some extent by species membership. Animals as well as humans are able to demonstrate learning by modeling, but in most cases can only imitate activities that are within the skill range of their species and that are appropriate to their species' pattern of behavior. There are limitations on the types of learning an organism can accomplish through classical conditioning or operant conditioning, but the limitations of species membership on learning by modeling seem more rigid. Fewer animals appear to learn by modeling than by classical or operant conditioning.

Effect of Reinforcement

Reinforcement appears to facilitate learning by modeling; it does not simply elicit a response, as in classical conditioning, or develop a contingency relationship, as in operant conditioning. An imitated response is more likely to *remain* in the behavioral pattern if it is followed by reinforcement: however, the imitated response *gets into* the behavioral pattern because it has been observed, not because of the reinforcement. In other words, reinforcement serves only as a motivating condition for learning by modeling.

Importance of Modeled Responses

For the safety of the learner or others, some responses are best learned through modeling. In some cases, eliciting a specific response is impossible, and learning by shaping an operant response might place the learner, teacher or others in jeopardy.

Learning to shoot a pistol or rifle could be accomplished by classical or operant conditioning techniques. However, such techniques might turn out to be very dangerous. In classical conditioning, for example, a learner's orienting responses might result in an unintentional firing of a weapon; and in operant conditioning, the trial-and-error shaping of an appropriate response might very well be time-consuming and unsafe. By contrast, the correct, safe use of a weapon could be modeled with relative safety and speed.

Types of Modeling

Modeling may take place in several different ways, although the basic premise is the same in all cases.

Live Modeling through Observation

Perhaps the most common form of learning by modeling is the direct observation of a live model by the learner. This usually occurs in social situations, involving individuals with whom the observer has frequent contact, such as parents, teachers or peers.

One theory of learning and personality development is called social-learning theory, or SLT. This theory suggests that much of our learning, especially in such areas as aggression, courtship behavior, and social roles, is brought about by our direct observations of and participation with people in our environment. One very important consideration in SLT is what persons are available to be modeled.

Vicarious Learning

Vicarious learning occurs when an observer is able not only to note the response the model makes, but also to observe the consequences of that response. The actual response and the resultant reinforcement or punishment are observed together with the vocal, postural or facial gestures that may reveal the model's emotional reactions. The observer does not actually make the response at this point, nor does the observer receive directly any reinforcement or punishment. However, the vicarious experience can serve to arouse the observer and may influence later responding.

You may easily recall vicarious learning if you have ever

observed someone else suffer a very painful burn. For example, suppose you have watched a friend lean against an electric range where one of the surface units has just been turned off. You no doubt saw the nasty burn that your friend received. This was sufficient to arouse your anxiety and understanding, and you did not have to lean on the hot unit and also get burned in order to know that it could hurt you. This is a case of vicarious suppression of a response; situations involving positive reinforcement for the model may lead to vicarious facilitation of a response.

Symbolic Learning and Verbal Modeling

Some modeling depends on verbal representation of a behavior rather than an observation of an actual behavior. This is called verbal modeling. More than any other single characteristic, this ability distinguishes humans from other species and is what makes a human's behavioral range so broad. Activities represented in verbal codes can be retained (or stored) for later use. As guides for the imitation of appropriate responses, they may considerably reduce the time and effort involved in learning a certain behavior.

Suppose, for example, you discovered a time-saving shortcut from your home to a local theater. You could use a verbal description to represent this path to a neighbor. In effect, that neighbor will be modeling your behavior, but no direct observation of the short-cut is necessary. The neighbor relies instead on a sequence of verbal guides, such as, "Left on McKenzie until you reach Riverside, then right to High Street...."

Pure Imitation

Some modeling involves exact imitation of another's response. In some cases, this may mean there has been imitation without understanding. That is, the response is copied, but the meaning of the response is not recognized by the imitator.

Sometimes pure imitation leads to humorous situations. Many stories have been told about children singing Christmas carols without learning the correct words. However, when one listens carefully, the children may be singing about "Round John Virgin" or "Hark the hairless angels sing." These are good attempts at imitative modeling, but are obviously done without understanding.

Factors Influencing Modeling

The fact that someone is exposed to a particular behavior does not guarantee that the behavior will be modeled. A number of factors influence whether or not learning by modeling will occur.

Attention

The single most important factor in learning by modeling is attention. It is necessary that the observer attend to the behavior being shown by the model. Lack of attention may result in partial or incorrect modeling, or no learning by modeling at all. Attention may be affected in turn by many factors, such as those that influence perception (see Chapter 5).

Proximity

Attention must be directed toward a model if observational learning is to take place. In general, the observer is most likely to select as a model someone who is close by rather than someone remote. This means that parents, other close relatives, and good friends, for example, are more apt to be chosen as models than are strangers.

Model Status

Research has shown that observers are selective in their choice of models. This selectivity seems to be based upon the status of the potential model, including such characteristics as the position the model holds, the role the model plays, the power or influence the model has, and the ability of the model to communicate.

Most evidence supports the findings that high-status models are more likely to be imitated than are low-status models. While the determination of status may vary according to the observer, position (such as parent, teacher or minister), role (such as leader of a peer group), and power (such as having the right to administer or withhold reinforcements) are important factors in the direction of attention. Combined with the model's ability to communicate, these factors incline the observer toward or away from the model.

Junior high school students are often very favorably impressed by teachers who are able to talk in the idiom and at the level of the students and still manage to teach. Such teachers are recognized as "special" and are usually held in high esteem by the students. If such a teacher suggested that certain kinds of behavior such as smoking were inappropriate, the students might stand a good chance of adopting the suggestion. If such a suggestion were put forth by a low-status teacher, the students might not follow it.

It is the observer who grants status to a model. Each observer may choose differently, depending upon the qualities he or she judges most important.

Retention (in Modeling)

For learning by modeling to be successful, the observer must be attentive to the model and retain a memory of the model's behavior to be used at a later time. (Retention is fully discussed in the following chapter.) The observer may retain a particular visual image or a verbal representation of the model's behavior. As mentioned previously, verbal modeling allows a model to present an almost unlimited range of behaviors to an observer, even when actual demonstration of those activities is not possible. Visual images may be very strong, and in some cases almost impossible to keep from conscious memory, but the extent of retention and later transmission of a model's behavior may depend on the observer's language development.

Architects, for instance, often have a "feel" about a particular building, yet may be unable to express this to the client. In such a case, the visual image is stronger than the architect's ability to express it. Quite frequently, the architect will construct a model of the structure, putting the images into a three-dimensional form that can then be discussed, revised, and eventually shown to the client. This process may be repeated several times during the development of plans for the building, and it is sometimes possible for the client to learn to imitate the behavior of the architect: the client, after a while, may be able to visualize changes in the plan without actually seeing them in a revised model.

Reinforcement and Punishment (in Modeling)

As mentioned earlier, reinforcement facilitates learning by modeling, but is not necessary for modeling to occur. The same holds true for punishment: it may be used to encourage learning by modeling, but it does not guarantee that such learning will take place.

Reinforcement or punishment may affect an observer through vicarious learning as previously mentioned. The observed effects of the behaviors of others can be very important, and observers may develop attitudes of self-arousal or self-reinforcement based upon the behaviors and reaction they have seen in models.

Self-Arousal

A person who observes others succeed, fail or perhaps be punished for a particular activity may retain an image or verbal representation that can be recalled at some later time and serve as a motivating stimulus. One need never have spoken to a large group of people, for example, in order to feel fearful of public speaking. Most people, in fact, feel somewhat anxious just thinking about such a situation. Simply observing the public-speaking experiences of others is often enough to create the anxiety.

Self-Reinforcement

Observers may establish independent standards for their own performance on the basis of what the model appears to accept. There may also be some sort of interaction, however. If the model is judged as a low-status person, for example, the observer may try to set higher standards for himself or herself; if the model is seen as a high-status person, the observer may accept lower standards.

Relationship of Vicarious Reinforcement to Actual Reinforcement

Vicarious reinforcement (through learning by modeling) seems to be quite helpful in many situations for learning a new, previously untrained response. However, vicarious reinforcement is unlikely to maintain that response because over time the learner will come to expect actual reinforcement.

For example, having observed a salesperson use a particular technique and be highly rewarded, you might attempt to imitate the same behavior. If your efforts were not rewarded, however, you would probably not continue to use this technique, particularly if you continued to see the other person being rewarded.

Special Concerns of Learning by Modeling

The discussion of modeling in this chapter has so far been very much confined to cases in which one observer attends to the behavior of one model. It should be recognized, however, that over a period of time a person will tend to blend the actions of several different models. Thus, a personal style of behavior, which differs from the behavior of any one model, will emerge.

It is very difficult to determine just how much influence any one model has had on a person's behavior. However, even if percentages of influence cannot be decided, the fact that multiple influences play a role in any one person's behavior is hard to dispute.

Socialization and Conflict

Learning by modeling is the source of many social behaviors. The attitudes and behaviors modeled in and reinforced by certain cultures or subcultures are adopted at an early age, and are often maintained throughout life.

A person who grew up in one culture or subculture may, of course, observe behaviors from another, and may even take these other behaviors as models. This could create a conflict for the person. The resolution of such conflict will in part be determined by the strength of the two behaviors: the stronger or more valued of the two would most likely be adopted.

Teenagers, for example, often find themselves in serious conflict situations of this sort. Their peer group may claim and demonstrate that smoking marijuana is an acceptable and desirable activity. A conflicting set of standards would be shown by adults. In such a situation, the teenager will have to decide which model to imitate. Such choices are not easy, particularly because anxiety over possible rejection (by the peer group) or punishment (by the parents) will occur.

Inhibition and Disinhibition

Learning by modeling has been used to make response patterns more or less probable by using the model's activities as a guide for the observer. If the observer is performing some response that is judged inappropriate, a model experiencing very negative or aversive consequences for such behavior or a model experiencing positive consequences for a contradictory behavior may be used. If the observer is unwilling to act in a given situation, a model who does act and experiences positive consequences may be used. The basic purpose of these conditions is to try to inhibit those responses judged inappropriate or to "release" the observer from inhibitions regarding behaviors that would be appropriate.

These principles have been adopted, in part, into a therapeutic technique known as desensitization. Modeling often play a very important part in a patient's approach toward more normal behavior. (See Chapter 16 for a discussion of this therapeutic technique.)

CHAPTER 10

Acquisition and Retention

The learning process can be divided easily into two sub-categories: the acquisition of new materials and the memory of those materials as measured by later retention. This chapter discusses some of the variables that influence the initial learning, or acquisition phase. It then surveys what psychologists have learned about long-term and short-term memory, and considers some of the reasons we forget what we have learned.

Acquisition

The acquisition of learning is affected by a number of factors, among them the attention process, the degree of motivation and preparedness of the learner, the type of practice followed, the kind of material to be learned, and whether or not there is transfer of training.

Selection of Learning Materials: The Attention Process

Attention is one important factor in determining what materials we will learn. If a subject does not attend to the materials, the chances of learning are markedly reduced. Several features of the attention process appear important in determining the extent and success of acquisition.

Sensory Gating

Sensory gating is a process in which the brain sends messages to some of the sensory systems to decrease the amount of information they have to deal with. At the same time, the brain allows other sensory systems to remain fully functioning. This seems to be a physiological analogy to the concept of selective attention, in which the subject pays attention to certain aspects of the environment while ignoring (or giving less attention to) others.

Sensory gating does not imply total blockage. The sensory systems not "featured" at the moment continue to operate, and if an unusual stimulus occurs, the focus of attention may change rapidly. An author, sitting at a desk, may concentrate on the words on a page while "damping" other sensations such as the noise of a fan in the office or an automobile outside. However, if the fan suddenly begins to make strange noises, the author's concentration on the words is apt to be broken, and auditory sensitivity is likely to increase. (As an experiment, try shifting your own sensory attention right now. What sounds can you recognize that you were ignoring moments ago?)

Parallel vs. Sequential Attention

Parallel sensory processing occurs when the brain processes several different stimuli simultaneously. This type of processing is usually incomplete and seems useful only during the elementary stage of the acquisition of new materials.

Sequential attention is a higher level of sensory processing, in which we treat each unit of information separately and in a sequence. The subject gives special attention to each sensation, and the careful processing of each results in the acquisition and retention of information.

Feature Extraction

In effect, the sensory system selects which incoming stimuli to process. The next stage of acquisition appears to be establishing meaning for these stimuli. This is done by what is known as feature extraction, or the identification and "decoding" of the most relevant aspects of the stimuli.

Feature extraction is important, for example, in determining that an r was an r and not a t or F. Careful inspection reveals that there are distinguishing characteristics (features) that can be recognized (extracted) so that the observer will respond, "That's an r," rather than, "That's a t," or "That's an F."

Characteristics of the Learner

The qualities a learner brings to a situation may affect how acquisition progresses.

Individual Differences

Just as there appear to be individual differences in physical development, the influence of motivation, the expression of emotions, and many other behaviors, there are individual differences in acquisition abilities. Indeed, many of these above-mentioned factors may serve to influence the progress of acquisition.

Many interactions of these factors may be observed. A person who is highly motivated to become a professional singer may be tone deaf. Another, who cares little about singing, may have perfect pitch. Such differences will be reflected in their abilities to learn to sing. A person whose capabilities, interests, and opportunities all blend and lead to a successful career, for example, is truly fortunate.

Preparedness

Some psychologists have argued for a concept of preparedness as an influence on acquisition. These psychologists believe that some organisms have evolved so that they are prepared for acquisition of certain types of materials, unprepared for learning others, and possibly predisposed not to learn still others. Such a concept might explain why some types of learning seem to occur easily, while other types proceed with great difficulty at best.

The concept of preparedness might help explain language learning by chimpanzees (see Chapter 11). Research studies have indicated that chimpanzees are almost totally unable to imitate human speech. They are able, however, to acquire and use American Sign Language (ASL). It seems that gestural communication has evolved for chimpanzees, while oral communication has not.

The Learning Curve

Psychologists have attempted to illustrate the progress of acquisition with pictorial or graphic representations of performance plotted as a function of the amount of time spent, or of the number of trials. We call these representations learning curves. One must keep in mind, however, that performance is not always an accurate indicator of learning.

One might, for example, investigate how the number of hours of practice time affects one's accuracy in pitching horseshoes. The performance measure used could be the number of ringers made, which would be plotted against practice time. Different subjects might show quite different patterns of performance, as illustrated in Figure 10.1. Each of these lines repre-

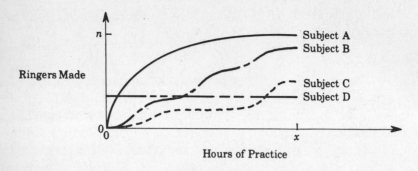

Hours of Practice

Fig. 10.1

sents a learning curve, although subject D doesn't seem to be learning at all.

Plateau

Occasionally, during the course of the trials, the learning curve will "flatten out," and no apparent progress will be made. Following this period, performance once again improves. We call this period of no improvement, preceded and followed by periods of improvement in performance, a plateau in the learning curve.

Asymptote

When a subject achieves maximum or near-maximum performance, the learning curve levels off. This final leveling of the curve is called an asymptote. (Note: The asymptote may be less than the maximum that some subjects could achieve, but is maximum or near-maximum for the subject being tested.)

Incremental vs. One-Trial Analyses

A continuing controversy in the psychology of learning is the debate as to whether learning of any given unit of information takes place in small, cumulative steps (incremental learning) or in a single acquisition experience (one-trial learning). Although research evidence seems to favor the incremental interpretation, some dispute continues because contradictory results do exist.

General Factors Influencing Acquisition

Educators and psychologists have devoted much time and effort in an attempt to determine the factors that help or hinder acquisition of new materials. Some of the most important findings are reported in this section.

Overlearning

Suppose we represent learning by some criterion of performance, such as one perfect recitation of a poem. Once a subject has recited the poem perfectly from memory, we can say that he or she has learned successfully. Any practice that occurs after this criterion has been reached is called overlearning. Overlearning is usually reported as a percentage of the time or a percentage of the number of trials that was needed for the original learning.

Assume a subject took sixteen trials to learn a list of nonsense syllables (consonant-vowel-consonant sequences, such as YOF, which do not make a word). If the subject then continued to practice the correct order of this list for eight more trials, 50 percent overlearning would have occurred.

Research has shown that the law of diminishing returns seems to operate for overlearning. While 50 percent overlearning usually results in a significant improvement in a subject's acquisition and retention of material, 100 percent overlearning helps some more, but not tremendously. Overlearning beyond 100 percent (such as 24 overlearning trials in the example above, which would equal 150 percent) seems to result in little additional improvement. (Note: Overlearning helps increase acquisition and retention of responses, but one must be careful to determine that the responses being practiced are the desired ones.)

Knowledge of Results: Feedback

Any information about the effect of a response is called knowledge of results (KR), or feedback. Two findings indicate the importance of KR in acquisition situations: KR leads to faster acquisition of new materials, and immediate KR is often more beneficial than delayed KR. It appears that in many circumstances, the subject treats KR as if it were reinforcement, and delay of KR is equivalent to delay of reinforcement.

Distribution of Practice

In general, the distribution of practice, where blocks of acquisition trials are interspersed with rest periods, seems to improve acquisition performance. When acquisition trials are massed together, performance suffers. A practical application of this principle occurs in study situations. Acquisition of new materials seems to proceed more easily if we divide studying into study sessions and breaks. Of course, this assumes the study segments are not too short and the breaks are not too long.

Whole-Part Distinction

One can attempt to learn new materials all at once (the whole method) or only segments of the material at one time (the part method). In the part method, a subject may divide the material into several units, studying each separately and trying to bring them all together only after learning each unit individually. The subject may also incorporate an "add-on" technique, in which one unit is mastered, then a second is added to it, and so on. We call this latter method the *progressive-part method*.

Research indicates that the decision to use the whole, part or progressive-part method may best be made by analyzing the materials to be learned. Certain tasks seem to lend themselves more to one type of procedure than to another.

Diving provides a good example of how method selection may depend upon the task to be learned. A simple forward dive from a standing position is usually taught by using the whole method. A running approach may be practiced as a separate skill and then be connected with the dive. It is best to practice more sophisticated dives, such as a somersault with a full twist, with the progressive-part method.

Active vs. Passive Approach

Careful study of the acquisition of new materials has shown that a subject who plays an active role in acquisition generally shows better performance than does a passive subject. Educators have translated this result into a "recitation-reading" comparison, showing that active discussion of new materials is likely to promote acquisition of those materials, while a more passive reading-only approach is less likely to do so.

One aspect of an active approach to learning is warm-up. It appears that for some tasks, an initial period of adjustment and introduction is necessary before acquisition can take place. Figure 10.2 shows a learning curve revealing warm-up effects.

Primacy and Recency Effects

Two fairly common influences on acquisition are the primacy and the recency of the materials being learned. Primacy refers to those materials that are presented first in a series; recency refers to the items presented last. In general, the

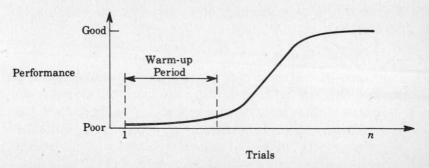

Fig. 10.2

primacy and recency effects tend to encourage acquisition, whereas presenting materials in the middle of a series does not.

Context

A context can influence acquisition in two basic ways. First, we can infer the meaning of the material we are learning from the practical application of that material in a particular setting. And second, associations that promote acquisition may result when certain materials are presented in a particular setting. We sometimes refer to this latter phenomenon as state-dependent learning.

Consider a simple example of context effects. Suppose you did not know the meaning of the "word" *abvoc*. However, in conversations with others you find that abvocs are cute, that some abvocs cry, wet, and have moving parts, and that children love abvocs. Such statements might provide sufficient information to allow you to develop a meaning for *abvoc*.

Verbal Learning

Word usage, the basis for verbal learning, appears to be a species-specific behavior for humans. The extent of human communication appears almost boundless because of this unique capacity. We will discuss language skills in Chapter 11; the focus here is on techniques for studying verbal learning and on approaches to understanding the factors that influence verbal acquisition.

Methods of Study

Three techniques are commonly used in verbal-learning studies. In *serial learning*, the subject is presented the materials in order and must learn them in that order. In *free recall*, the materials may be learned (and later produced) in any order the subject prefers. In *paired-associate learning*, a particular stimulus is linked with a particular response; given the stimulus, a subject must be able to make the correct response. A paired-associate task might use numbers as stimuli and nonsense syllables as responses: 43-YOF, 22-NAH, 68-GIP, 97-TEC, 14-XUH, 50-ZEM. Subjects are required to learn the appropriate pairings and give the correct response when presented with a stimulus.

Suppose subjects are presented with only the list of nonsense syllables: YOF, NAH, GIP, TEC, XUH, ZEM. In serial learning, the subjects must learn the correct letter sequences of each item and to give YOF first, NAH second, and so on. Free recall also requires that the subject learn the correct letter sequences, but any item could be given first, second or in any other position in the sequence.

Factors Influencing Verbal Learning

Psychologists have studied the factors that influence acquisition of verbal materials. Some of the most important influences are similarity, meaningfulness, imagery, and organization.

Similarity. We learn certain verbal materials easily and retain them because they are similar to previously learned materials. In verbal learning, similarity may be based upon physical similarity (primary stimulus generalization) similarity in meaning (secondary stimulus generalization), or similarity that arises from some personal association the subject makes.

Meaningfulness. Research has shown that verbal materials judged meaningful are more likely to be learned and retained than are materials that are judged less meaningful. (We can judge meaningfulness through the number of associations evoked by the material being learned.)

In paired-associate learning, the meaningfulness of the response to be learned seems to be an especially important variable. The pairing of a "high-meaning" stimulus and a "low-meaning" response is more difficult to learn than the pairing of a "low-meaning" stimulus and a "high-meaning" response. In other words, acquisition and retention are easier with "low-high" (or "high-high") pairings of stimulus and response than "high-low" (or "low-low") pairings.

Other features of the materials that appear related to meaningfulness include pronounceability (we more readily learn items that are easily pronounced than items that are difficult to pronounce), discriminability (how distinctive the item is), and frequency (how commonly used the item is). For this last factor, it should be noted that the frequency with which a word is used differs in written and spoken language. Thus, mode of presentation may be important as well.

In the examples used earlier, we would be more likely to learn the nonsense syllable TEC than the nonsense syllable XUH. TEC has a higher meaningfulness value (based on studies of associations), is more easily pronounced, and is relatively easy to discriminate. Furthermore, in English, we encounter the letter sequence TEC much more frequently than the sequence XUH.

Imagery. Imagery refers to the quality of a stimulus that evokes "mental pictures." In general, it is easier to create mental images for concrete stimuli than for abstract stimuli. We can expect better learning, in the form of more rapid acquisition, for high-imagery stimuli than for low-imagery stimuli. This seems especially true in paired-associate situations, where high-imagery stimuli benefit the learning of pairs.

It is easy to illustrate imagery values by simply trying to create mental pictures representing words such as *basis* and *women*. These two words are used frequently in both written and spoken English, but differ considerably in how easily we can translate them into mental pictures.

Organization. Organization is a factor that can influence both acquisition and recall, and may be imposed either by the material itself or by the learner. More organization, if it is sensible and does not contradict other factors of the materials, usually leads to improved acquisition and recall. This appears to be especially true if the learner takes an active part in developing the organization of the material.

Transfer of Training

Transfer of training (also called transfer of learning) occurs when the learning of one set of materials influences the later learning of another set. Some psychologists claim this is the most important learning principle that can be applied to educational situations.

Positive and Negative Transfer

Transfer can either facilitate learning behavior in a new situation, in which case it is called positive transfer, or hinder new learning, in which case it is called negative transfer. Positive transfer is illustrated by a person who has learned to drive a stick shift car and is now learning to drive a stick shift truck. While some new learning may be required, many of the principles mastered in the process of learning to drive the car will facilitate learning the new task. Negative transfer would prevail when a student who has been studying French for three years in high school begins studying German in college. The vocabulary and constructions, accents and syntax with which the student has become so familiar over the past three years can now interfere with the learning of the new language, which is different.

Learning to Learn

A person may learn general principles rather than specific items of information and then use these general principles in later learning situations. In such a case, the subject has learned to learn. Learning to learn takes place when the subject has learned how to go about doing a task and has been able to transfer this knowledge to a later learning situation.

A child might show learning to learn in constructing a series of jig-saw puzzles. Having learned the general principles of how to put the pieces together, the child may apply the principle to each new puzzle confronted, determining the specific technique that works for each.

Retention

The following section is devoted to the second aspect of learning—the retention of materials after they have been acquired.

Definitions

Several different terms are used when discussing retention. *Retention* is thought of as the storage of learning over some period of time, called the *retention interval*. Memory includes both retention (storage) and *retrieval*, which is getting the response out of storage. If for some reason the subject is unable to produce the response at the end of the retention interval, *forgetting*, the loss of retention or the inability to retrieve, has occurred.

Information-Processing Approach

We can study and evaluate retention with what we call the information-processing approach. Psychologists interested in trying to represent human learning functions in terms of computer programming have analyzed the learning process as an input-processing-output sequence. By knowing the stimuli to which the subject is exposed and the response the subject later makes, they hope to program computers to simulate the learning process and thus better understand acquisition, retention, and retrieval.

Computers have been programmed to play games as simple

as tic-tac-toe or as complex as chess. The computer can play quite well and, in fact, will never lose (but may tie) at tic-tac-toe. However, computers cannot yet duplicate an expert chess player's ability. It appears that chess requires both retention and creativity of an order computers cannot yet attain.

Types of Storage

While debate has not completely resolved the question of what types of storage humans may have, a fairly widely accepted theory proposes three: sensory storage, short-term storage, and long-term storage.

Sensory Storage

The basic notion of sensory storage is that items are held in an unprocessed sensory form before being "read out," categorized or interpreted. This kind of storage is thought to last for only a short period of time, although the length of the retention interval may vary (from hundredths of a second to several seconds) depending on the sensory process involved. This theory proposes that materials are either processed from sensory storage into short- or long-term storage or they are lost or discarded.

An ingenious investigation of sensory storage makes use of a tachistoscope, a device that can control in fractions of a second the length of time a visual stimulus is presented. Subjects are given a very short exposure (perhaps one-tenth of a second) to a stimulus item. This is followed by a very brief delay interval, and then a marker (such as an arrow) indicates what part of the stimulus item is to be recalled. The subject does not actually see the image projected by the tachistoscope at this point. Instead, the subject "sees" a visual trace of that image. Research of this type has shown that visual trace persists for less than two seconds.

Short-Term Storage

Short-term storage extends from 1 to 30 seconds after exposure to a stimulus item. Initial processing of the material, in which information is taken from sensory storage, takes place during this period. We view short-term storage as a temporary or interim period. It is one step past the unprocessed sensory storage, but if further processing does not take place, the material will be lost or discarded.

Suppose a newspaper has neglected to print the starting times for a movie you particularly wish to see. You might call the theater to get that information. Looking in the telephone book, you would find the correct number, dial it, and wait for your call to be completed. The processing necessary to make the call requires only short-term storage; the number is quickly used and discarded. If one hour later you were asked for the theater's number, you would probably not remember it.

Long-Term Storage

Long-term storage occurs when materials in sensory storage or short-term storage are processed, rehearsed, encoded or otherwise treated for retention over a period of more than 30 seconds (and maybe for 30 years). As long as initial acquisition does take place and the person maintains the ability to make the appropriate response, items in long-term storage may have unlimited retention intervals.

You probably can recall an event from your childhood. Perhaps you remember a happy moment, such as receiving a special present from your parents; or maybe you remember a sad incident, like the death of a favorite pet. All such memories are retrieved from long-term storage.

Just what processes are involved in long-term storage (or, for that matter, in sensory or short-term storage) remains a matter of conjecture. Obviously, activity in the central nervous system is required, and memories are somehow stored in the brain. Just what changes take place, however, has not yet been determined.

Measures of Retention

Psychologists have devised a number of different ways to evaluate retention. Each method attempts in its own way to measure the amount of information held in storage.

Recognition

In recognition measures of retention, we present the subject with the correct answer as one of a number of available answers. The subject then responds by selecting the answer he or she thinks is correct. The objective scoring of such tests is possible because a result, such as the number of correct answers, can be determined without the possibility of scorer bias.

Matching or multiple-choice questions are usually recognition tests of retention. Suppose you are asked, "Name the city represented by a baseball team named the Red Sox: *(a)* Boston, *(b)* Cincinnati, *(c)* Kansas or (d) Chicago." You should select answer *(a)*, recognizing that it is the correct answer, and eliminate all the others.

Recall

In recall measures of retention, a minimum cue statement or question is presented and the subject is required to supply additional information. Correct or incorrect answers are not presented before the subject responds.

Essay questions and "completion" questions are often recall tests of retention. For example, suppose you are asked, "What are the names of the major-league teams in Cincinnati, Kansas City, Chicago, and Boston?" No selection of names is furnished; we expect the respondent to generate the answers without any additional prompting.

Relearning

In some situations, a subject may have to relearn materials he or she has learned before. We can then compare the amount of time or the number of trials required for relearning to the amount of time or number of trials required for the original learning. Measurement of retention can then be computed in terms of what is called the *savings score* shown in relearning:

$$\text{Savings score} = \frac{\text{original learning} - \text{relearning}}{\text{original learning}}$$

By multiplying this value by 100, one arrives at a percentage to report as retention. We can see how this works through the following example:

On Wednesday, it takes Fred 20 minutes to memorize a vocabulary list for one perfect recitation. On Friday, when he is tested for retention, Fred relearns the list perfectly in 5 minutes. Thus, his savings score (retention) is 75 percent:

$$\text{Savings score} = \frac{20 - 5}{20} \times 100 \text{ percent}$$

$$= \frac{15}{20} \times 100 \text{ percent}$$

$$= 75 \text{ percent}$$

Comparison of Retention Measures

It is important to recognize that an estimate of retention may vary, depending on the measure of retention that has been used. Because of the differences in presentation and scoring, recognition tests would never give a zero value for retention, while recall measures may. Relearning, however, may show a negative score if the time or number of trials necessary for relearning exceeds what was required for the original learning.

A subject, for example, might be taught the names of all the major-league baseball teams. Having accomplished this, the subject might then learn the names of all the major-league hockey teams. Later, when retention for baseball team names was tested, a recognition test using matching might yield a score of 45 percent, recall might be 20 percent, and relearning might be 7 percent. The last result might occur because of the subject's difficulty in getting the New York City teams correct, switching back to the *Mets* and *Yankees* from the *Rangers* and *Islanders*.

The Curve of Forgetting

Early in the history of psychology, a German named Hermann Ebbinghaus devoted much of his career to studies of acquisition and retention processes in verbal learning. One conclusion he reached has remained relatively unchallenged: The general pattern for loss of retention is that the greatest loss will occur soon after acquisition, with the rate of loss diminishing after that. This is represented by what he called the curve of forgetting, shown in Figure 10.3.

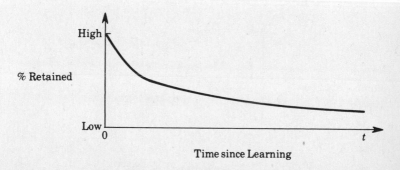

Fig. 10.3

While the general form of the curve seems to hold for many cases, the exact level and shape may vary somewhat, depending upon individual variables such as motivation, materials learned, and amount of rehearsal.

Reminiscence

The acquisition of some tasks often produces accompanying fatigue, which may become pronounced if the acquisition trials are massed together rather than distributed. As a result, tests of retention that are given following practice and a subsequent period of rest may yield better performance than will those given immediately after practice is completed. We call the increase in performance after practice and a rest period *reminiscence*. (Note: This assumes no change in motivation or reinforcement conditions that might produce a similar jump in performance.)

The von Restorff Effect

An especially distinctive stimulus that is inserted into any part of a serial list will be learned and remembered very well. This phenomenon is called the von Restorff effect (or sometimes the isolation effect). It is illustrated in Figure 10.4. The remainder of the items in the list will show a fairly typical position in the curve of retention: the first and last learned will be remembered better than those in the middle of the list.

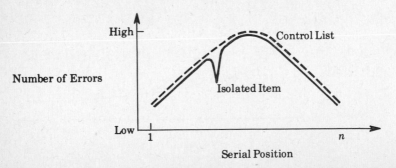

Fig. 10.4

Suppose we ask a group of subjects to memorize the items in the following list: horse, cow, mouse, dog, bicycle, cat, sheep, pig. The von Restorff effect would be shown if the subjects tended to learn and retain the one distinctive item—bicycle— better than they learned and retained the others in this list.

Theories of Forgetting

No one single theory of forgetting has gained predominance in psychological literature. Theories based on retrieval difficulties, loss of memory trace, lack of motivation, and interference have been proposed and supported in part by research results.

Forgetting as Failure to Retrieve

One theory suggests that forgetting is the result of a person's failure to retrieve materials that are already stored. The theory suggests that acquisition has taken place, but that poor organization in storage, poor prompting, inappropriate motivation, or some other variable keeps the person from performance that would reveal the stored materials. Changes in the cue, suggestions for new ways to organize the material or other alterations in attempting retrieval have often shown that the subject's performance can improve considerably.

For example, a young child who is asked to "replicate the design you just saw" may appear to have no recollection of the stimulus. However, if we change the request to "Draw me a copy of the picture you just saw," the child does much better. In this case, a change of cue makes the task much more comprehensible.

Forgetting as Fading of the Memory Trace

Another theory of forgetting proposes that loss of retention occurs because of the disuse of learned materials. Failure to call upon the information in memory means that this information will somehow "fade," and the memory will be eventually lost. To counteract this "fading," a subject must practice. Evidence for this theory comes from research studies in which the typical curve of forgetting appears even though there is no indication that anything except the passage of time has contributed to the loss of retention.

Highway restaurants sometimes entertain their waiting customers by putting puzzles on the tables. One of these is a block of wood with a triangular arrangement of holes drilled into it. All but one hole in the block are filled with golf tees. The task is to try to "jump" one tee over another, always removing the one that has been jumped, until only one tee remains. Customers find this challenging and somewhat difficult, but often discover a pattern that allows them to succeed and then repeatedly practice this successful solution.

On their next visit to the restaurant, many customers reach for the puzzle confidently, only to find that they cannot remember the solution they previously found. Statements such as, "I knew how to do this. Now, just a moment," are fairly common. Because it is doubtful that they have encountered other puzzles of this nature in the interim period, it would appear that the trace of the previous solution must have faded through disuse. However, it would be very difficult to determine that some other contributing factors were not operating in addition.

Forgetting as Distortion

Another theory suggests that forgetting occurs because of distortions of the material stored in memory. This theory suggests that some materials incorporated into memory are only partially accurate representations of what was learned or that inappropriate descriptive labels have been attached to them. In either case, the altered meanings of stored materials will make accurate recollection impossible. Again, some research evidence supports such a conclusion: When inaccurate labels are provided for learned materials, distorted memories may result.

Motivated Forgetting

The psychoanalytic theory of repression suggests that some forgetting comes to pass because a person wishes to forget something. Originally proposed by Freud, this view suggests that forgetting is an ego defense mechanism: a means by which an individual can "protect" his or her personality. See Chapter 13 for a more thorough discussion.

Freud believed that readily accessible memories are found in the preconscious. Memories that might arouse great anxiety are pushed "deeper" into memory, into the unconscious, where they cannot be called forth easily. Repression is likely to put memories into the unconscious, but Freud believed that such memories continue to influence behavior in the form of unconscious motives.

While experimental evidence to support the notion of repression has not been produced, repression is commonly cited in case histories to account for forgetting.

One clinical case history can illustrate how repression occurs and how it affects behavior. Hilda, a young girl, misbehaved badly one day and ran away from her parents. In the process, she fell into a rushing stream and ruined her best clothes. Although she was hurt and in need of attention and comfort, her parents did nothing more than punish her. The memory of that day became very anxiety producing for Hilda. She eventually managed to repress her conscious memory of these events, but unconscious aftereffects persisted. The key stimulus appeared to be the rushing water, and as Hilda grew older she found comparable stimuli (such as a running shower) very anxiety producing. Fortunately, she was able to uncover the repressed memory and ultimately overcome her fears.

Forgetting as a Result of Interference

Another explanation of forgetting is that loss of retention results from interference from other materials. This has been studied with what are known as proactive inhibition (PI) and retroactive inhibition (RI) experimental designs. In each case, the question investigated is what effect one learning task will have upon the retention of some other learning task.

Proactive Inhibition. The experimental design for proactive inhibition (PI) is as follows:

	Step 1	Step 2	R	Step 3
Experimental Group:	Learn A.	Learn B.	E	Test B.
Control Group:	Put in time.	Learn B.	S	Test B.
			T	

If, when the material of Task B is tested, the control group does better than the experimental group, it may be concluded (assuming no experimental flaws exist) that PI has taken place. That is, the Task A materials interfered with the later retention of Task B materials.

Retroactive Inhibition. Retroactive inhibition (RI) is studied using the following experimental design.

	Step 1	Step 2	R	Step 3
Experimental Group:	Learn 1.	Learn 2.	E	Test 1.
Control Group:	Learn 1.	Put in time.	S	Test 1.
			T	

Again, if the control group's performance is significantly better in Step 3, Task 2 learning has interfered with the retention of Task 1.

Most research on both PI and RI has studied interfering or inhibiting effects in an attempt to determine reasons for loss of retention. If one learning makes retention of the other appear easier, however, *facilitation* is said to have taken place.

Learning names to go with faces may eventually lead to either PI or RI when similar-looking people are involved. Recalling a first-learned name when a second would be appropriate is an instance of PI. If the second-learned name is called forth when the first is appropriate, RI is shown. This is a difficulty people in public jobs, such as teaching, often encounter.

Special Issues in Retention

Retention is not without its unusual aspects. Two of these are called the tip-of-the-tongue phenomenon and confabulation.

Tip-of-the-Tongue Phenomenon

Retrieval of information from long-term storage is sometimes not readily accomplished. For example, you may sometimes feel ready to give the desired answer—it's right on the tip of your tongue—only to find you cannot. Quite frequently, approximations of the answer are attempted. For example: Was that animal an ascot? Asclot? Osclot? No, it was an ocelot.

Similar sounds, number of syllables or the same initial letter may be used in attempts to determine the correct response. Such a memory search is not at random. Because of similar meaning, words such as *tiger*, *puma*, or *jaguar* might come to mind as you try to think of *ocelot*.

Confabulation

Confabulation is a memory error that occurs under conditions of high motivation. Asked to recall a particular event, people very anxious to do so may manufacture a report that seems appropriate. In such a case, the person may believe that the report is true even when it contains combinations of several recollections or mixtures of fact and fiction. Questioned about such errors, subjects frequently cannot identify the mistakes.

The most obvious cases of confabulation are found in brain damaged patients, but it is probable that everyone confabulates to some extent, retrieving some key features and filling in the rest.

CHAPTER 11

Thinking, Problem Solving, and Language Development

Once psychologists gained some knowledge of the processes of acquisition and retention in learning, a number of them turned their attention to examining some of the uses of learning. Many areas have been investigated, with several emerging as major aspects of study. This chapter concentrates on three of these areas of cognitive psychology: thinking, problem solving, and the development of language.

Thinking

Thinking is symbolic mediation, or the use of symbols to span the time interval between presentation of some external stimuli and the responses made to them. Thinking is an internal, personal process, often attributed to activity of the mind. Thinking cannot be observed directly, but must be presumed from observable behaviors.

One college instructor demonstrated the individuality and "hiddenness" of thinking to classes by asking the entire class to "think of the dirtiest word you can!" The instructor then pointed out that unless one of the students called out the word, there was no way for any member of the class to know what choice another made. However, one of the students could speak, write or gesture in such a way as to indicate his or her thought. The other students could then interpret this as representative of the student's thinking.

Directed vs. Autistic Thinking

Much of our thinking occurs in attempts to solve problems. Such thinking is called directed thinking, implying that the thinking occurs for a purpose. Thinking that uses symbols in a seemingly aimless fashion, as in some forms of daydreaming, is called autistic thinking.

Symbols

A symbol is any stimulus that has become a commonly accepted representation of some object, event, action or idea. A symbol may take any form or any meaning, as long as there is general agreement that the symbol stands for some other particular thing.

Concepts

Concepts are symbols that summarize or generalize attributes typical of several objects, events, actions or ideas that are dissimilar in other important aspects. Concepts may have different levels of generality, while symbols are usually quite specific. For example, the word *horse* would be considered a very general concept, referring to an entire class of animals. The word *thoroughbred,* on the other hand, represents a more limited concept within the general class of horses. The name *Secretariat,* in this context, is a symbol for one particular horse.

Types of Concepts

Concepts are classified as simple or complex. Complex concepts take several forms, as shown below.

Simple: Concepts that represent a single stimulus property, e.g., all things are either blue or not blue

Complex: Concepts that represent more than one stimulus property at the same time

Conjunctive: Concepts in which two or more properties are represented simultaneously

Disjunctive: Concepts based on two or more properties, but in which any one property or combination of properties is adequate to satisfy the concept

Relational: Concepts that establish a relationship between two properties

The various types of complex concepts can be illustrated by considering beverages. The word *highball* represents a conjunctive concept because to satisfy (or fit into) the concept, a cocktail must have at least two properties: the presence of alcohol and some other fluid (such as water or soda). The word *beverage* itself is a disjunctive concept because any one of a number of drinks (such as water or beer or milk) or a combination of drinks (such as coffee with milk) satisfies the concept. Any comparison, such as the statement "Milkshakes are thicker than sodas," expresses a relational concept.

Concept Hierarchies

Almost all concept classifications contain a number of items. When asked to report the items in a conceptual class, most people will start with their strongest associations and then continue to add items until they can think of no others. The resultant list represents a concept hierarchy, in which there is some kind of ranking of the members of the concept category.

For example, if asked to list modes of transportation, most Americans would start with items such as automobile, plane, bus, train or the like. Lower on the list (and therefore lower in the hierarchy) might be modes such as rickshaw, dog sled or sampan. A person from another culture would probably have a very different hierarchy.

Developing Concepts

Concepts do not simply spring, completely developed, into a person's consciousness. Generally, it is necessary for a learning process to occur. Often, this learning process involves hypothesizing about the concept category, testing that hypothesis, revising the understanding of that concept on the basis of the test results, reformulating the concept, and then repeating the process.

People appear to use various kinds of strategies in developing concepts. In some cases, they may consider all stimulus attributes simultaneously (a *holistic* approach). In other circumstances, they may consider only one characteristic at a time (a *partistic* approach).

Representations of Thinking

As mentioned earlier, thinking is a personal and private event unless a person represents the thought processes in some observable way. Research on thinking has shown that there are two very common thinking processes: inner speech and imagery. *Inner speech* occurs when a person makes verbal representations of thought processes. *Imagery* occurs when a person recalls or generates sensory stimuli. Investigations of inner speech or imagery usually depend on verbal reports of the processes made by subjects.

Problem Solving

A major consideration in the study of thinking and learning has been problem solving. Problem solving occurs when an individual or group establishes some goal and seeks ways to reach that goal. As previously indicated, the thought processes involved in trying to solve a problem are called *directed thinking*, while aimless daydreaming or fantasizing is called *autistic thinking*. Directed thinking is consciously motivated and is therefore affected by the motive conditions that influence other kinds of behaviors.

The Problem-Solving Sequence

Careful research of the process of problem solving has disclosed a fairly common sequence of events leading to the goal. Generally, the steps seem to be as follows:

1. *Recognize there is a problem.* Not being able to understand that there is a problem would stop the process at this point.

2. *Define the problem accurately.* This involves recognizing concepts that are pertinent to the problem. If the key concepts are not available, the problem may not be solved.

3. *Produce hypotheses about the problem's solution.* Based on the concepts selected in the previous step, guesses about how to resolve the problem are developed.

4. *Test the hypotheses.* Each hypothesis should be either confirmed or disconfirmed. While several may solve the problem, it is often possible to select the single best hypothesis.

The sequence of events leading to a goal could be easily demonstrated if you wished to drive to a particular city. Suppose you wanted to go to University Park, Pennsylvania, from Pittsburgh. If you did not realize that you didn't know the route, you might drive aimlessly and only arrive by chance. However, once you recognized the problem, you might then seek out the relevant concepts (for example, route numbers or distances), consider alternate possibilities, do some calculating to determine which might be the best route, and finally select one.

While this example is fairly straightforward, it should be recognized that the same sequence might apply to a problem as complex and subtle as a personality difficulty or an emotional disturbance. An individual must first recognize there is a problem, then determine the key concepts necessary for solving the problem, and finally complete the problem-solving process as described.

Reasoning

Reasoning is a type of thinking in which a person tries to solve a problem by incorporating two or more aspects of past experience. Not all reasoning takes the same form. Programmatic reasoning is said to exist when already-existing systems of thought are used. Generative thinking involves the creation of new systems of thought. Both styles of reasoning are difficult to study because many of the processes are internal, or "hidden," and may not be available to the psychological researcher or even to the person being studied.

Programmatic Reasoning

Logical thinking is an example of programmatic reasoning, requiring the use of already-established conventions or rules for the solution of a problem. There are two major types of logical reasoning: inductive reasoning and deductive reasoning. In solving problems, we use either or both types of reasoning.

Inductive Reasoning. This type of reasoning involves arriving at general principles from specific cases or facts. For example, if we notice that every automobile we have ever seen has four wheels and an engine, we may reason inductively that all automobiles have four wheels and an engine.

Deductive Reasoning. Deductive reasoning works in the opposite way from inductive reasoning: it involves working from the general principle to specific cases. If we are told that all automobiles have four wheels and an engine, then every time we see a vehicle with four wheels and an engine, we recognize it as an automobile, no matter what its color, size or body style.

Generative Thinking

Generative thinking requires the creation of new thought processes, or new ways of looking at or solving the problem. Some of the great discoveries in science, philosophy, and the arts came about because one individual was willing to suspend belief in logic and arrive at apparently illogical conclusions. Einstein's theory of the relativity of space and time—totally illogical by the standards of his time—is one such example. So, too, is the art of Jackson Pollock, which looks like a child's scribble to the untrained eye.

Variables Affecting Problem Solving

Problem solving is a kind of performance, and it is subject to some of the same influences that affect other types of behavior. For example, variables such as motivation and past experience will influence problem-solving performance.

Motivation

The inverted-U curve of performance described in Chapter 7 is seen also for problem solving. Very low levels of motivation yield poor problem-solving performance. As motivation levels increase, so too does performance, but only up to some point. Very high levels of motivation will usually yield poor performance. In addition, a particular motivation may influence a subject's attention, directing the subject to certain problems or aspects of the environment and away from others.

Past Experience

Previous experience may predispose a subject to respond in a certain manner when trying to solve a problem. In discussing this phenomenon, psychologists usually distinguish between a *habit,* which implies a long-term tendency to respond in a certain manner, and *set,* which is the temporary tendency to respond in a certain fashion.

Many familiar jokes or tricks derive their humor from an inappropriate set. For example, ask a person how to pronounce a series of words, and start spelling out a group of names beginning with Mac, such as MacDonald, MacBride, MacIntyre, and so on. Then, spell out the word *machine.* Usually the person responding will pronounce this familiar word "Mac-hine." This is caused by the temporary mental set (beginning each word with a hard "Mac") imposed by the previous conditions. The temporary set confuses the person's habitual knowledge of how *machine* should correctly be pronounced.

Using a citizen's band radio in one's automobile illustrates the difference between habit and set. Most of the people who use these radios employ a special language when broadcasting, but they do not talk in this manner when not broadcasting. Rather, they return to a more "normal" or typical form of talking. The use of the special CB dialogue represents a set, a temporary tendency to respond in a certain way in a particular situation. Outside that situation, people return to their habitual form of conversation.

Functional Fixedness

One form of set that has been studied extensively is called functional fixedness. This occurs when a subject is unable to see any other use for an object except its normal or usual one, although some novel response might be both useful and appropriate for solving the problem at hand.

In a famous research investigation of functional fixedness, two strings were suspended from the ceiling of a room. One string was near a corner of the room and the other was near the center, and a pair of pliers was available. The subject's task was simply to tie the two strings together. However, the strings, though long enough to meet, were not long enough to allow the subject to hold one and still reach the other, even when using the pliers to grasp the end of one string.

Those subjects who viewed the pliers only as a grasping tool could not solve the problem. (These subjects were said to show functional fixedness.) On the other hand, some subjects were able to use the pliers in a different manner: they tied the pliers to the end of the central string and started it swinging in a pendulum motion. It was then easy for them to go to the corner, grasp the other string, and catch the swinging string when it came near enough. In other words, by using the pliers as a weight (and not a grasping tool) they were able to solve the problem.

Insight

Insight is said to occur when, after a problem is posed, there is a period of no apparent progress in solving the problem, and then a sudden solution. The key characteristic of insight is the suddenness of the solution: a swift determination of a hypothesis that can be confirmed. Insight seems to be very personal and because of that, is difficult to describe as a psychological process.

Creativity

One special consideration in problem solving is creativity, which is shown when a subject generates an original, productive, and unusual solution to a problem.

Psychologist J. P. Guilford made an important distinction between *convergent thinking,* in which an individual follows established rules to solve a problem, and *divergent thinking,* which involves generating novel or different approaches to solving a problem. Divergent thinking is the more creative of the two.

Guilford pointed out that traditional tests that ask questions for which there is only one correct answer are designed to reveal convergent thinking, whereas tests for divergent thinking ask questions designed to elicit many kinds of answers, allowing a person to display original and creative thinking. One such test presents the plots of two stories and asks the person to list as many titles as possible for each story. The person who gives the most clever titles scores highest on divergent thinking.

In attempting to measure creativity, psychologists have generated many different types of tests. One of these involves presenting the subject with a minimal visual cue and asking the subject to complete the drawing. For example, the subject might be shown drawing *(a)* in Figure 11.1 and be asked to complete it. A response such as drawing *(b)* would be judged much less creative than a response such as drawing *(c).*

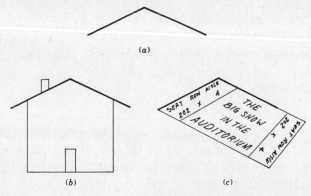

(a)

(b)   *(c)*

Fig. 11.1

Simulation

In an attempt to identify the processes involved in problem solving, some psychologists have turned to the use of the computer. Given a knowledge of the input (stimuli) to which the subject is responding and the output (responses) the subject makes, these psychologists attempt to program the computer to simulate this functioning. They then study the program in an attempt to analyze what processes must be involved. Studies of this nature are generally more successful when the problem is one requiring convergent thinking rather than divergent thinking.

In one experimental procedure, called "Turing's test," after the father of the modern computer, an "expert" compares the output of a human and that of a computer. When the expert cannot reliably tell which is which, the program is said to accurately reflect the cognitive processes of the person.

Language Development

Language development is one of the major areas in the study of learning and cognitive psychology. Psychologists who study this area are called *psycholinguists,* and they are interested in the relationships between an organism and its language. Their work covers the acquisition, structure, and usage of language.

Signs vs. Symbols

Signs and symbols are both signals, or stimuli, that can be used for communication. They differ in that a *sign* has meaning because of its very nature, while a *symbol* has its meaning because a number of people (or other organisms) have chosen to accept that meaning. Any agreed-upon designation (a word, drawing, gesture, and so on) may serve as a symbol.

For example, if you made a noise like the sound of a cow,

you would be using a sign, a stimulus that has meaning because it corresponds (at least somewhat) to the sound naturally made by a cow. Writing or saying the word "moo," however, would be using a symbol. The word does not duplicate the naturally occurring event, but has only come to have a meaning that is generally accepted.

Written vs. Spoken Language

The development of written and spoken language in humans generally progresses differently. Written language depends upon the visual presentation of words, while spoken language depends on the production and reception of sounds.

In general, word usage in written language differs somewhat from word usage in spoken language. Words are used with different frequencies, are arranged differently, are repeated more often in spoken language, and generally take a more casual form in spoken language and a more formal form when written.

Expressive vs. Receptive Language

Expressive language is the words used to convey a message. Receptive language is what is understood from the words used. Expressive and receptive language may not be the same thing; that is, the message-producer may intend to convey one message while the message-receiver may interpret the same words in a quite different manner.

Multiple meanings for words may make it particularly difficult for communication to occur. For example, the word *bread* had at one time at least two meanings: it meant both a food and money. When a person producing a message said, "Wow, I sure would like more bread," the receiver could understand the statement in at least two ways.

Word Development and Usage

Psycholinguists have studied the construction and use of words in great detail. These investigations have resulted in the development of the following terms and findings:

Phonemes

Phonemes are the basic sound components of a spoken language. Young children seem to have the ability to produce phonemic patterns of many languages, but soon learn to limit their patterns to those appropriate to the language being learned. Most analyses suggest that English has about 45 phonemes.

Syllables

While phonemes are the basic units of speech, they are not what are "heard" or concentrated upon by the producer or receiver. Instead, the producer or receiver concentrates on syllables, which are composed of one or more phonemes.

Morphemes

Morphemes are defined as the smallest meaningful unit of a language. Not all syllables are morphemes, because not all syllables have meaning when they stand alone. A morpheme may contain one or more syllables.

The words *male* and *female* can be used to illustrate the difference between a syllable and a morpheme. *Male* is a single-syllable word that is also a morpheme. The word *female* has two syllables, but the *fe-* syllable cannot be considered a morpheme because it does not have a specific meaning by itself.

Words

Phonemes, syllables, and morphemes may be considered the structural components for words. Words are the symbols used in a language.

Phrases, Clauses, and Sentences

A *phrase* is a meaningful combination of gramatically related words that does not contain a subject and a predicate. A *clause* is a construction containing both a subject and a predicate, and forming part of a complex or compound sentence. A *sentence* contains both a subject and predicate, and presents a complete statement.

Word combinations build phrases, which in turn may be developed into clauses or sentences. Sentences may have several clauses, but when they do, the receiver's typical pattern is to treat each separately.

Surface Structure and Deep Structure

Psycholinguists have looked at how the arrangement of words may vary and what effect this has upon the meaning being conveyed. The arrangement of the words has come to be called the surface structure of the language, while the meaning being transmitted is called the deep structure.

Two sentences such as, "Glenn took the test," and "The test was taken by Glenn," have the same meaning or deep structure, although their surface structure is different. One could alter the meaning of the second sentence by substituting the word *purse* for *test*, so that it would read, "The purse was taken by Glenn." This would leave the surface structure almost the same, but alter the deep structure considerably.

Development of Language Rules

In general, children in all cultures develop the rules for language at about the same age and in approximately the same sequence, regardless of the specific language. In addition, children of all cultures tend to make word-usage and grammar errors that require them to learn both rules and exceptions to rules.

Behavioristic vs. Cognitive Interpretations

A controversy in the study of language development has produced different explanations for why a child learns a language. The behavioristic approach suggests that language develops because the child learns it in the same manner as any other learning; that is, because of classical conditioning, operant conditioning, or modeling. In all of these models, emphasis is placed upon reinforcement of language patterns.

While the principles of reinforcement and imitation do seem to be operating in language acquisition, studies have shown that the usual learning models cannot fully account for the rapid growth of the child's vocabulary, the speedy mastery of grammatical rules, the use of new words that the child has never had an opportunity to imitate, the uniformity of language acquisition by other children in different cultures and environments, and the existence of important similarities in acquisition across all languages.

Noam Chomsky (of the Massachusetts Institute of Technology) and others, offering a cognitive explanation, claim that there is an innate ability for language acquisition that is independent, for the most part, of the child's conditioning. These theories view language development as part of our neurological capacities, enabling the child to understand intuitively the rules of grammar. Chomsky points out that there are areas of the human brain concerned primarily with speech control that enable the child, given the proper linguistic experience through interactions with the environment, to form the native language out of the universal language. Thus, according to this view, the child's ability to use language is primarily maturational; given the normal environment, it unfolds naturally during the course of development.

normal environment, it unfolds naturally during the course of development.

Chomsky's view has been criticized by the learning theorists and others for underestimating the importance of learning and environmental factors, which they consider crucial to the acquisition of language. It appears, however, that both innate mechanisms and learning processes are importantly involved in language development. It is now widely believed that the development of grammatical usage follows an orderly sequence, as if it were programmed into the individual. While learning (by observation or conditioning) is very important in language development, there seems to be some mechanism in the brain that is concerned with language and is responsible for this programming.

Language in Animals

Extensive research on language development in primates (especially the chimpanzee) has shown that while these animals have little or no success learning written or spoken language as humans know it, they can be taught to communicate using American Sign Language or other symbolic forms. Rather extensive vocabularies have been developed, along with some grammatical understanding. Communication has occurred between humans and primates trained in the use of these symbols, and it has been observed between one member of a species and another (for example, between one chimpanzee and another).

CHAPTER 12

Intelligence

Intelligence is not a unitary concept but rather is made up of many abilities such as memory, reasoning, and comprehension. There is a difference of opinion among psychologists, however, as to whether intelligence is a collection of these abilities or whether there is one kind of general intelligence that includes all these specific abilities. In this chapter we will look at different theories of intelligence, ways in which it can be measured and expressed numerically, and how it influences or is influenced by other aspects of our lives.

Definition of Intelligence

Since 1916, a number of different tests of intelligence have been created, but no single definition of intelligence has gained dominance in the field. Intelligence has been simply called that which intelligence tests measure. Other definitions suggest that intelligence is composed of lasting personal characteristics that allow problem solving. Another definition explains intelligence as the combination of a person's inherited potential and measured performance.

Theories of Intelligence

The composition (or structure) of intelligence has been described in several different ways. One quite common approach has been statistical analysis. Another is to organize intelligence according to developmental stages. Still other proposals have attempted to separate intelligence into habitual and novel forms. Each of these attempts leads to a theory of what constitutes intelligence and how intelligence incorporates other concepts.

Factor Analysis

The statistical technique most often used to try to determine aspects of intelligence is factor analysis. This technique arose from the work of Charles Spearman and was used by other theorists in constructing their own models.

Spearman's Two-Factor Theory

In the early 1900s, English psychologist Charles Spearman collected scores on various psychological test items and noted the correlations between them. He reasoned that because there were positive correlations between the scores on the different items—which tested mechanical ability, musical ability, and mathematical ability, for example—there must be one common factor of general intelligence responsible for the relationship.

In addition, Spearman felt that each specific task, such as finding a solution for a mathematical problem, required specific abilities such as facility with numbers, memory, and so on. His reasoning led him to describe intelligence as a general factor, which he called the G factor, and a number of specific factors, which he called S factors.

Spearman's research resulted in the development of the statistical procedure known as factor analysis. Using factor analysis techniques, psychologists can identify and interrelate the many factors included under the heading of intelligence. Moreover, the study of many specific problem-solving tasks and their solutions allows psychologists using factor analysis to identify characteristics of intelligence that seem to be correlated.

Thurstone's Factors of Intelligence

L. L. Thurstone also used factor analysis to develop what he saw as the seven basic characteristics that make up intelligence. Thurstone identified these seven aspects of intelligence as follows:

Verbal comprehension: Definition and understanding of words

Word fluency: Being able to think of words rapidly

Number: Being able to do arithmetic problems

Space: Being able to understand spatial relationships

Rote memory: Being able to memorize and recall

Perceptual: Being able to rapidly grasp the similarities, differences, and details of objects or stimuli

Reasoning: Being able to understand the principles or concepts necessary for problem-solving

Thurstone, like Spearman, suggested that there is a general factor (or G factor) that represents some general intelligence linking these separate characteristics.

Guilford's View of Intelligence

J. P. Guilford has developed a model that represents the structure of human intellect as a three-dimensional figure. One dimension is composed of five kinds of mental operations, such as cognition and memory. The second is composed of four kinds of content involved in intellectual operations, such as semantic (verbal) or symbolic (nonverbal). The third dimension represents six different outcomes, or products, which are specific ways of thinking about a subject that result from the various operations as they are applied to different kinds of content. Intelligence, Guilford argues, is the result of the interaction of these three dimensions.

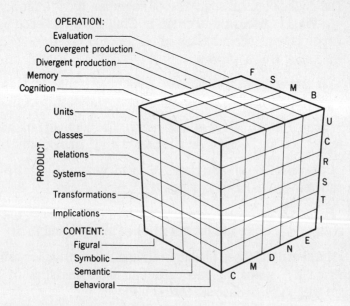

Fig. 12.1 *Guilford's Model of Intelligence* The dimensions of this cube are the contents (kinds of information), the mental operations, and the products involved in intellectual ability. Each of the 120 small cubes in this model represents a unique intellectual ability—a combination of contents, operations, and products. (From J. P. Guilford, *The Nature of Human Intelligence,* McGraw-Hill Publishing Co., New York, 1967)

To give a very simple example: In the task of studying a vocabulary list for a test, the content would be semantic (words), the mental operation would be memory, and the product would be the list of words or units the subject recalls when tested.

Guilford's model allows for 120 separate factors of intelligence (five times four times six) and he has devised tests to measure many of them. His model broadened the concept of intellect beyond that tapped in existing intelligence tests.

Piaget's Stages of Cognitive Growth

The developmental sequence of cognitive growth proposed by Jean Piaget (discussed in detail in Chapter 4) has been used as an approach to understanding intelligence. Piaget's cognitive growth stages are as follows:

Sensorimotor Stage (birth to 2 years): Understanding of sensations and basic cause-and-effect relationships

Preoperational Stage (2 to 7 years): Conceptualization and representation by using language, drawings or symbolic play

Concrete Operational Stage (7 to 11 years): Logic tied to concrete things; series of ideas

Formal Operational Stage (11 years and above): Use of abstract concepts and formal rules of thought and logic

It has been proposed that an individual's intelligence can be estimated by comparing the particular characteristics of the person with the sequence set forth by Piaget.

Crystallized vs. Fluid Intelligence

In an attempt to describe intelligence some psychologists, influenced by the work of Raymond Cattell, have distinguished between crystallized and fluid intelligence. Crystallized intelligence is observed in the application of what has been learned already; this use of intelligence tends to become habitual or unchanging. Fluid intelligence is seen in the ability of a subject to adapt or adjust to new and different situations. Fluid intelligence is thought to be flexible and used when the person is confronted with previously unencountered problems.

The ability to solve word-usage problems, such as fill-in-the-blank definitions, requires reliance on previous learning and thus uses crystallized intelligence. However, solving anagram problems requires both knowledge and flexibility, and thus involves fluid intelligence. Completing the sentence "Wearing apparel for a foot is called a _____ " requires crystallized intelligence, while recognizing that the letters in the word *shoe* can be found in the word *honest* requires more mental flexibility, or fluid intelligence.

Measurement of Intelligence

The first standard measurements of intelligence were developed by Alfred Binet, working in Paris in the early 1900s. Binet was interested in predicting the academic success of school children. Binet's test was later revised by Lewis Terman, of Stanford University, for use with children in the United States, and was released in 1916 as the Stanford-Binet Intelligence Test. A revised form of this test is still in use today.

The Concept of Mental Age

Binet made two major contributions to mental testing. One was the notion that intelligence is not just one ability but a range of abilities, such as language, memory, common sense, and so on. Accordingly, he devised a large variety of subtests of these specific abilities that identified those children who were bright, those who were average, and those who were below average in each of these areas.

In addition, Binet assumed that just as children grow taller as they get older, so do they grow in mental ability. And, just as not every child is at the same stage of physical growth at a particular age, not every child is at the same stage of mental growth at a particular age. In other words, some children of five are taller than others of the same age, and some children of five are brighter than other children of the same age.

Binet set up age norms, or standards, for this test and arranged the subtests according to age level. It thus became possible to report each child's score in terms of his or her mental age, expressed in years and months. A mental age of six years means that the child's mental ability is equal to that of the average child aged six years. If the chronological age of this child were five years, he or she would be considered advanced; but an eight-year-old child with a mental age of six would be considered slow.

Let us look at an example of how this works. Paul passes all six subtests at the seven-year age level, five subtests at age eight, three at age nine, three at age ten, one at age eleven, and none at age twelve. In this testing situation, Paul's basal age (the mental age level at which all items are passed) is seven and his ceiling age (the level at which none is passed) is twelve. His mental age is calculated as follows:

$$MA = (7 \times 12) + (12 \times 2) = 108 \text{ months, or 9 years.}$$

Because each test passed is worth two month's credit (one-sixth of a year), in this equation, the 7 refers to basal age (multiplied by the full 12 months) and the (12 x 2) refers to the total number of tests passed beyond the basal age (5, 3, 3, and 1) multiplied by the two months credit for each test. The final value obtained for mental age represents the performance that would be expected from the average person at that age.

If Tina is tested and obtains a mental age of 108 months (9

years), she and Paul have the same mental age, regardless of their actual age. They both can be expected to perform at a level comparable to the average nine-year-old.

The Concept of Intelligence Quotient

Because not all subjects achieving the same mental age value on a test are the same age, a ratio was developed to try to express the differences implied by the observed performances. This ratio is called the intelligence quotient (IQ) and is equal to the value of the mental age divided by the *chronological* (or actual) *age* (CA) multiplied by 100.

$$IQ = \frac{MA}{CA} \times 100$$

In the previous examples, both Paul and Tina obtained a mental age value of 9 years (108 months). Paul is 9 years old, while Tina is 6 years, 9 months old. Using these chronological age values, Paul's IQ would be 100, while Tina's IQ is approximately 133. Calculations of these values would be as follows:

$$\text{Paul's IQ} = \frac{9}{9} \text{ or } \frac{108}{108} \times 100 = 100$$

$$\text{Tina's IQ} = \frac{9}{6\frac{3}{4}} \text{ or } \frac{108}{81} \times 100 = 133$$

The work of Binet and Terman revolutionized the understanding of intelligence. However, it was later found that the variability in scores is not the same at all ages. As a result, psychologists have created tables of typical performance at each age for the Stanford-Binet (and other tests of intelligence) and use those to estimate intelligence. Although still referred to as IQ, the value no longer is actually determined as a quotient as in the formula above.

Distribution of IQ Scores

When a sufficient number of IQ values have been obtained, the distribution of scores will approximate the normal probability curve (see Chapter 2), usually with a mean of 100 and a standard deviation of 15 or 16 points, depending upon the test used.

Using the standard deviation value of 16, which is used in the Stanford-Binet test, a person scoring 116 would be in the eighty-fourth percentile when compared to the total population, while the percentile value for someone scoring 68 would be two and one-half.

Exceptional Subjects

Arbitrarily, those persons who obtain scores that differ from the mean by two or more standard deviations have been designated as exceptional. Those two or more standard deviations below the mean often are referred to as mentally retarded, while those two or more standard deviations above the mean are called gifted.

Mentally Retarded

Simply designating a person as mentally retarded because he or she obtained an IQ value two or more standard deviations below the mean has not proved to be an adequate description of the individual's capabilities. As a result, subgroups within the category of mental retardation have been developed. These subgroups, along with their IQ cutoff points, are as follows:

70–50: Mildly retarded (educable)

50–35: Moderately retarded (trainable)

35–20: Severely retarded (minimal skills)

20–0: Profoundly retarded (custodial care)

The Gifted

The exceptional subjects classified as gifted are not divided into further subgroupings. Some studies have shown that subjects with very high measured intelligence (IQs of 180 or more) may have adjustment difficulties because they are misunderstood by parents or peers. But most research indicates that the gifted, as a group, are better adjusted and healthier than are people of average intelligence.

Ratio vs. Deviation IQ

The concept of intelligence quotient was developed on the basis of work with the Stanford-Binet test, in which IQ was defined as a ratio of mental age to chronological age. However difficulties with using this ratio arise as subjects approach adult status. There is no way for a ratio test score to measure mental age in a way that would take into account the ever-increasing chronological age of a subject.

As a result, David Wechsler proposed the idea of deviation IQ, basing the reported IQ value on the normal probability curve. The Wechsler Tests of Intelligence have a mean IQ value of 100 and a standard deviation of 15. When the subject has completed the test, the administrator determines the obtained IQ by comparing the subject's performance against that of others at the same age and using the normal probability distribution for that age to establish the percentile and IQ score for the subject.

Group vs. Individual Tests

As with other psychological tests, intelligence tests can be administered either to individuals or to groups. Individual tests are thought to be more sensitive and are used frequently when the subject's motivation may be suspect. However, they are more expensive to administer to subjects, assume more training of the administrator, and require more time for the collection of data from a larger number of subjects.

Infant Intelligence Tests

A number of measures have been developed to assess infants' intelligence. These tests center around the evaluation of perceptual and motor skills such as turning, pointing or visually following a moving object. Tests at later ages focus more on language skills, which cannot be used when testing infants. The result of this is that generally, correlations between scores obtained on infant intelligence tests and later tests of intelligence are quite low. Results on infant intelligence tests seem not to be good predictors of test results later in life.

Relation of Intelligence to Other Factors

Much research regarding measured intelligence has been devoted to trying to establish the relationships between intelligence and social or cultural or physical variables. Some of these variables are discussed in this section.

IQ and Heredity

Research studies have shown that, in general, the closer the genetic relationship of individuals, the greater the similarity of their measured intelligence. This is comparable to the finding for other personal characteristics such as personality. (See Chapter 4 for more on heredity.)

IQ and Age

The stability of measured intelligence over a lifetime has been a major research area. Results of the research have consistently supported the stability of IQ throughout adulthood (at least from age 25 through 60). Yet, there have been suggestions that IQ stability depends in part upon the life experience of the individual being tested. For an adult, IQ may rise or decrease slightly, remain the same, or show a more focused increase or decrease in specific areas only. Changes in IQ seem to be influenced by the person's health, drug use and abuse, continued familiarity with testing situations, type of employment, lifestyle, and other experiences.

IQ and Gender

Comparisons of the measured intelligence of males and females have shown that overall IQ values are approximately the same. This makes sense insofar as intelligence tests are usually geared to avoid an overall bias favoring one sex or the other. While some gender differences have been noted on IQ subtests, on the whole these are so small as to be negligible. Moreover, although there are still gender differences in some standardized tests (such as the SAT), the gap between female and male performance has been on a consistent decline over the past decade.

IQ and School Success

Intelligence tests were originally intended to predict how much students would profit from additional academic instruction, and they have suited this purpose better than any other for which they have been used. Predictions are not perfect because of the influence of variables such as motivation, health, and family circumstances, but IQ scores are found to correlate with academic performance in the range of +0.30 to +0.75.

IQ and Expectations

An interesting facet of the measuring of intelligence, or the use of IQ values as predictors, is that results may be influenced by the expectations of the person administering the test or by the person taking the test. This unintentional bias may lead to inaccurate or incorrect interpretations.

Robert Rosenthal and his colleagues have studied this expectation effect. In one study, at the start of the school year students selected at random were mentioned to the teacher as potential "intellectual bloomers." The teacher thus expected that those students would show increased IQ scores at the end of the school year. When intelligence tests were administered at the end of the year, some of these selected students had indeed shown significant gains in measured intelligence as compared to the other (control) students. Rosenthal suggested that the teacher's expectations may have contributed to this increase.

IQ and Occupation

The general findings regarding the relationship between IQ and occupations indicate that persons with higher measured intelligence tend to be found in what are judged to be the higher status or more prestigious jobs. A second aspect of this relationship is that measured intelligence is a fairly good predictor of how well a person will train for a job, but not as good a predictor of how well the person will actually perform on the job after training.

Research studies in industry have shown that the correlation between measured intelligence and job performance is sometimes very low (below +0.15). Some of the jobs for which this type of finding was obtained include pottery decorators, welders, meat-packing workers, and electronic-parts assemblers. In fact, for jobs involving one simple assembly task, IQ and job performance showed a negative correlation.

IQ and Race

As mentioned previously, the closer the genetic relationship of individuals, the greater the similarity of their measured intelligence. One related finding is that IQ scores obtained for black populations have been slightly lower than those obtained for comparable (at least as far as geographical location is concerned) white populations.

This finding has led to a major controversy. One interpretation suggests that the poorer performance of blacks can be attributed to heredity, while a second interpretation is that blacks have had inferior environmental opportunities that have slowed individual intellectual development. Arguments have been advanced supporting both viewpoints, but the consensus seems to support the environmental explanation of the differences in scores.

Creativity

A creative act is one that is novel or original, purposeful, useful or worthwhile, and represents a unique solution to a problem. Creativity is discussed in more detail in Chapter 11.

Convergent vs. Divergent Thinking

Convergent thinking will lead to problem-solving responses that are correct but considered routine or common. Divergent thinking leads to attempts to use exceptional or novel responses to solve problems. Divergent thinking often leads to responses that are viewed as creative acts.

The Creative Person

While measured intelligence does not seem to be an important aspect of creativity, there are several characteristics that seem to differentiate creative people from noncreative people. In general, the creative person is quite flexible in thinking patterns, is interested in complex ideas, and shows a fairly complex personality pattern. Additionally, the creative person tends to be aesthetically sensitive, is interested in the unusual or novel, and shows a relatively open personality.

Measurement of Creativity

Several attempts have been made to develop measures of creativity. All have in common the aim of evaluating the unique or novel solutions to problems that might reveal the characteristic of creativity. Among such tests are the following:

Unusual uses tests: Present an object and determine how many unusual uses the subject can generate for it.

Remote association tests: Present several stimulus words and determine if the subject can "find" the associate that is common to all.

Anagram tests: Present a stimulus word and determine how many and what smaller words can be created using the letters of the stimulus word.

Drawing completion tests: Present a partial stimulus and ask the subject to finish the drawing.

In a drawing completion test, for example, the administrator might present a stimulus such as Figure 12.2 *(a)* to the subject and ask the subject to "complete" the drawing in any way he or she wanted to. Response *(b)* might indicate a lack of creativity, while response *(c)* would be considered creative.

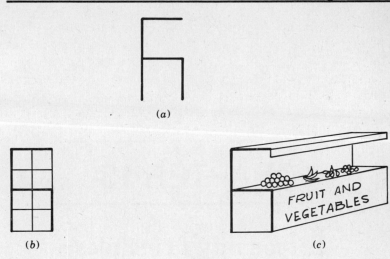

(a)

(b)

(c)

Fig. 12.2

CHAPTER 13

Personality Principles

An individual's personality consists of those enduring attributes that are representative of his or her behavior. These attributes may be acquired because of the person's unique experiences or because of experiences shared with others. The attributes may also result from the influence of heredity, or the interaction of heredity and environment.

This chapter surveys the main theories of personality development. After a brief review of the general factors that influence personality, it looks in detail at the personality theories of Freud, including the psychoanalytic theory of the ego defense mechanisms. Other motivational theories of personality discussed include those of Jung, Adler, and Erikson. Also considered are type theories, trait theories, humanistic and learning theories of personality.

General Factors Influencing Personality

Regardless of the theory proposed to explain personality,

two general factors are seen to influence personality development: a person's experiences within the environment and that person's hereditary background.

Environmental Experience

A person's experiences within the surrounding environment may have major effects upon the development of personality characteristics. These experiences may be unique to that one person or common to many people.

Imagine a man who lives in a fishing village and works on a fishing boat. The experiences of living in the village can be thought of as shared experiences, common to all the people who live there. But suppose the man in question once spent several hours alone in the open sea after falling from a boat. In this respect at least, his experience is unique. The experience of being adrift may influence his personality in ways that would differ from the influences of the village experiences, which he shared with other people.

Hereditary Effects

The particular genetic pattern established at the moment of conception influences the personality characteristics a person will develop. In very obvious forms, inherited brain damage or birth defects may have pronounced influence upon the person's behavior. In addition, somatic (bodily) factors such as height, weight, skin coloration, and the functioning of sense organs may affect personality development.

Interaction of Heredity and Environment

Many personality attributes result from the combined effects of heredity and environment. In most cases, it is difficult or impossible to assign percentages of importance to hereditary and environmental influences, but it is easy to see that the two do interact.

Diet provides a good example of this interaction at the many stages of human development. The mother's diet may affect the uterine environment, and thus influence the expression of the hereditary characteristics in the embryo or fetus. Later, a person's diet may affect his or her weight, and thus personal appearance. This in turn may dispose the person to act in certain ways or lead others to react to the person in a particular manner.

Genetically identical twins reared together are more likely to show similar personality patterns than are genetically identical twins reared apart; but even twins reared apart would more likely be similar than would nontwin siblings who are also reared apart.

Freud's Motivational Theory of Personality

The best-known theory of personality was formulated by Sigmund Freud, a Viennese physician. In his theory, Freud put emphasis on the concept of mental illness and the use of psychotherapy to try to help people with problems. (See Chapters 14 and 15 for a discussion of abnormal personality patterns and therapies.) A theory of personality emerged from Freud's attempts to develop successful therapy techniques.

The Structure of Personality

Freud believed that personality has three basic components: the id, the ego, and the superego. The personality is motivated throughout life by the fundamental drive called *libido*. Libido provides psychic energy that is devoted to the achievement of goals. The essential feature of libido is that it has a sexual quality that, because of social restrictions, cannot be expressed directly. Instead, libido has to find release in substitute or indirect fashion. These expressions begin in the first year of life, but change radically as the child matures and passes through what Freud called the psychosexual stages.

The Id

According to Freud, the id is the most primitive or instinctive part of personality. The id operates according to the *pleasure principle*—that is, seeking pleasure and avoiding pain regardless of societal beliefs or restraints. This means actions generated predominantly by the id are likely to be inappropriate in a social context, especially for adults. The behavior of young children, for example, often shows id control, indifferent to the social rules and regulations that influence adult, ego-oriented behavior.

The Ego

In Freud's approach to personality, the ego is the problem-solving part of personality, which operates according to the *reality principle*. The ego seeks pleasure and avoids pain in rational ways that society approves. The ego thus seems to take the demands of the id and determines how to satisfy them in an acceptable manner.

The Superego

The third component of personality, according to Freud, is the superego. The superego reminds the person of what would be ideal behaviors and what behaviors are totally unacceptable. The superego tries to block the impulses of the id, particularly those of an aggressive or sexual nature, and to substitute moralistic goals for realistic ones. The superego, like the id, is unconscious and must, therefore, depend on the ego to carry out its wishes. The *conscience* is found in the superego.

Let us consider an example of how these work. Shopping in a supermarket, Louise, her teenage son, and her one-year-old daughter stop in the aisle beside the fruit display. Each is occupied, so that no one of them is watching the other. The daughter sees an apple, reaches out, picks it up, and begins happily munching; she simply seeks pleasure and satisfies the motive, having no idea she is doing something that might be called wrong. The son spots some grapes, thinks to himself that everybody else "rips off" the store a little, and takes a small handful and starts eating. Louise sees some peaches she would really like to have, but feels they are too expensive. Momentarily, she considers having a few weighed and priced, then putting some more in the bag after the grocery clerk has gone on to his next customer. However, she realizes this would be dishonest and decides to do without the peaches. Louise's actions reflect superego influence, her son seems to have been under ego control, and her daughter was under the control of motivation from the id.

Psychosexual Stages of Personality Development

Freud proposed that the development of personality advances through several psychosexual stages. In each of these stages, the libidinal energy finds a particular focus, an area of the body known as the primary erogenous zone. If the individual progresses through each stage without serious difficulties, a mature adult expression of libidinal energy would eventually be achieved. However, excessive frustration or excessive gratification during one of these childhood stages could lead to fixation at that stage, meaning that later in life a person responds to situations (or to feelings) in a manner more appropriate for a young child than for a mature adult.

The Oral Stage

The first psychosexual stage is called the oral stage. Libidinal energy centers around oral activities, particularly feeding and weaning. This stage lasts from birth into the second year of life. Fixation at this stage means that a high level of oral activity may be shown by the adult.

Fixation at the oral stage may be represented by activities

such as excessive gum chewing, fingernail biting, talking or eating. These behaviors are thought to occur either because the person has been satisfied too much during the oral stage or because the person has not had enough satisfaction during this stage.

The Anal Stage

In the anal stage, libidinal energy is directed to the anal area, and defecation becomes an expression of one's will. The way the parents (or other significant adults) conduct toilet training will affect adult personality characteristics. Fixation at this stage may result in adult difficulties with the giving or withholding of love or approval, with stubbornness, and with conflicts between neatness and sloppiness.

The Phallic Stage

In the phallic stage, the source of libidinal pleasure is in the genitalia. Characteristic behaviors at this time include exploration of the genitals, infantile masturbation, and interest in the anatomical differences between the sexes. Inability to achieve adult sexuality and responsiveness may result from fixation at this stage.

Freud believed this is the period when what he called the *Oedipus complex* (for boys) and the *Electra complex* (for girls) had to be resolved. Freud proposed that a child has sexual desires for the parent of the opposite sex and feels rivalry with the parent of the same sex. However, fear of punishment causes the child to identify with the parent of the same sex and to adopt similar behaviors. According to Freud, failure to complete this identification process may result in incomplete gender identity and unsuccessful adult relationships with the opposite sex.

The Period of Latency

At the end of the phallic stage (about age 5 or 6), according to Freud, the child enters a latency stage, when preoccupation with sexual concerns no longer exists. During this period, libidinal energies are reduced dramatically. Latency is primarily a period of socialization for children: they begin their formal schooling and develop important attachments with peers.

Adolescence and Adulthood

With the onset of puberty, a person goes into the final stage of development. At this point, the libidinal energies are rearoused, and the individual attempts to achieve adult sexuality. If there have been difficulties at earlier stages, the giving and receiving of adult (mature) love may be difficult or impossible to achieve.

Suppose a person experiences considerable frustrations during the period of toilet training. It is possible that the residual fixations may cause the person to be stingy, stubborn or extremely fussy. All such characteristics might prevail against the mature expression of giving or receiving love.

Defense Mechanisms of the Ego

Freud proposed that actions or events that offend the super-ego and do damage to one's self-image result in anxiety in the ego. To keep this damage and anxiety to a minimum, a person develops and uses ego defense mechanisms as a way of protecting the self. Some examples of ego defense mechanisms follow.

Repression

The most common defense mechanism is repression. In its most basic form, repression simply means forgetting, although it is a motivated form of forgetting—one prompted by unconscious forces. Whatever causes us pain or provokes anxiety becomes a likely candidate for repression and is then no longer accessible to our conscious mind. In general, the superego, our sense of what is right and what is wrong, is instrumental in blocking from consciousness those memories that would cause us conflict.

Projection

Projection is the process of attributing to another person one's own unacceptable thoughts and feelings. A person who feels that no one likes him, for example, may be projecting internal feelings of hostility onto all of the people around him.

Reaction Formation

Reaction formation is a defense mechanism that is often difficult to recognize. Simply stated, this mechanism involves acting in a way that is in total contradiction to the way one unconsciously feels. While the individual is acting in this way, however, he or she is not aware of unconscious feelings and is, therefore, unable to recognize the mechanism at work.

Let us say, for example, that a woman is experiencing some unconscious hostility toward a friend but that her ideas about what friendship should be preclude such feelings from her conscious mind. "If you like your friends, you will never feel angry at them," the unrealistic expectation goes. One way of handling this unconsciously is to react to this anger. She may, for instance, feel compelled to buy her friend an expensive present, one well beyond her means; a present given not for love, but rather for self-protection. The giving of the present is a direct reaction to the unrecognized feelings of hostility.

Intellectualization

Intellectualization is a defense mechanism that makes itself felt when a person understands something intellectually, but not emotionally. Examples of intellectualization include describing a person in technical, nonemotional language and relating to others through planned, impersonal techniques rather than through spontaneity and genuine feelings. Intellectualization is avoiding the reality of another person and seeing him or her as an object instead.

Denial

The defense mechanism of denial is sometimes confused with repression and reaction formation because of the similarities among the three. Denial, in its most general form, occurs when the conscious mind denies feelings from within or situations from without that prove threatening to the ego. A husband, for example, may fail to recognize that his wife is experiencing hostile feelings toward him, thereby blocking out of his perceptual world an important part of their relationship. Parents are sometimes prone to deny their children's angry feelings toward them. Sexual feelings are a class of feelings that are often subject to denial.

Rationalization

When a person uses rationalization as a defense mechanism, he or she develops a false explanation for actions, or attributes false, more favorable motives to explain behavior.

Rationalization is sometimes demonstrated when a person who reads a pornographic magazine claims that he or she is reading it because of its "great literary content." Comparably, one person who crushingly defeats another in a game of tennis may claim to have done so in order to teach the loser to cope with defeat, when in fact the winner may have done so in order to increase his or her own sense of power.

Displacement

Displacement involves the shifting (or replacement) of the object of a feeling or drive. A man employed in a personnel department, for example, may take out some of the aggression he feels toward his supervisor by displacing it onto clients who are safer objects for his wrath. In general, displacement involves displacing to a safe object feelings unconsciously held toward a more dangerous or threatening object. Since there is an imbalance of power in many interpersonal relationships, the use of displacement can make the person in the lesser-power position a victim of the other. Often it is displacement at work when one person says to another, "Why are you always picking on me for things I didn't do?"

Regression

Regression means "returning," particularly returning to an earlier stage of emotional or intellectual development. When a person becomes overpowered by feelings he or she can no longer handle, one way of dealing with the situation is to return to an earlier level of development in which one was able either to avoid confronting such feelings or to feel comfortable with them. Older children often resort to "baby talk" following the birth of another child in their family. Direct attack toward the new baby would be inappropriate, but the regressive behavior may attract the parents' attention and thus help the older children maintain their feelings of self-worth.

Compensation

Someone who feels deficient in some way may defend himself or herself by emphasizing some behavior that "covers up" the deficiency. This is called compensation, and it may take two forms. Using direct compensation, the person will emphasize behaviors that are specifically meant to be reactions to the felt deficiency. Using indirect compensation, the person will stress behaviors that are not associated with the felt deficiency, but rather are substitutes. For example, a person who stutters may exhibit direct compensation by mastering public oratory skills or acting. On the other hand, a person who is physically weak may exhibit indirect compensation by becoming an emotional bully, picking on other people in a way that does not require physical strength.

Introjection and Identification

Introjection and identification are two mechanisms that are often confused with each other. Introjection occurs when an individual's personality incorporates part of another person. For example, the student may introject a part of the teacher; that is, take on some of the teacher's values and beliefs—which can be educationally productive. Freud initially used introjection to explain the learning of values by the child. A child introjects— takes inside—the parents' system of values, and they become a part of the child.

Identification is the process whereby an individual confuses his or her identity with the identity of someone else. With identification, the person may either extend identity into someone else, borrow identity from someone else, or fuse his or her identity with someone else's. A commonly cited example of the mechanism of identification is the phenomenon called *identification with the aggressor,* where an individual exposed to an aggressive and threatening person who makes her or him feel endangered, begins to act and feel as aggressively as the threatening person.

Defense Mechanisms in Everyday Life

While all of us make use at times of these various defense mechanisms, they can present difficulties for us, especially when used to extreme. Defense mechanisms distort perception and block off part of the world. Theoretically, the better adjusted an individual is, the less need he or she will have for defense mechanisms. But even the most well-adjusted person will at times have no choice but to use them.

Other Motivational Theories of Personality

Freud was the first person to popularize what have been described as motivational theories of personality, but several other theories were developed by his associates and by psychologists who came later. The theories of Jung, Adler, Erikson, and Sullivan serve as examples of these other motivational approaches.

Jung's Theory

Carl Jung accepted many of Freud's explanations of personality, but he differed with him on several important aspects. In comparison to Freud, Jung placed emphasis on current events rather than childhood experiences and on social and biological motives rather than sexual drives. Jung also proposed a quite different conception of the unconscious, suggesting that there are actually two: (1) *the personal unconscious,* similar to the unconscious proposed by Freud because it contains an individual's personal memories and repressed desires; and (2) the *collective unconscious,* which contains personality characteristics inherited from ancestors. This latter kind of unconscious carries traits that have developed over many generations to become typical of all people within a culture.

All human beings share the same collective unconscious, since its contents go back to the beginnings of the human race. These contents are organized in the form of archetypes, or primal images. They are universal ideas that contain a good deal of feelings. For example, everyone has a "mother archetype," a preconceived idea of what mother is and how she will be perceived. The reality of one's own mother, and one's personal experiences with her, will also influence a person's perception of her. Thus, Jung asserts that all our behavior is a product of the interaction between our collective inheritance and our actual experiences.

Jung is also credited with developing a system of character types that has become a part of our language of personality description. He speaks of a twofold typology: the introverted person, who is primarily concerned with his or her own inner world, and the extraverted person (Jung's spelling), who is primarily concerned with objects and people in the outside world, and is usually very vocal and outgoing. Jung believed that if one attitude is dominant in one's conscious life, the other is dominant in the unconscious.

Adler's Theory

Alfred Adler also stressed social motivation rather than sexual drives. For Adler, the key to personality was a striving for superiority. Every child is born helpless, dependent on others, and, therefore, overwhelmed by feelings of inferiority that he or she must struggle to overcome for the rest of his or her life. People do this by striving for superiority, which becomes a major motivation in a person's life. In the healthy individual, the striving for superiority is in accord with the needs of the society, and the person acquires such traits as courage, independence, and a healthy sense of ambition. If development is not normal, a person may grow up with feelings of inadequacy, suffering an inferiority complex.

The process by which a person overcomes these feelings of inferiority is called *compensation*, which plays a crucial role in personality development. For example, an individual who is constitutionally weak may compensate by developing the body, perhaps by studying karate. Or, a child who stutters may grow up to become an actor or singer.

According to Adler, each person has a unique life-style that enables him or her to compensate for inferiority feelings and to strive toward superiority. The style of life is formed very early in childhood, by the age of four or five, and is determined largely by one's experiences within the family. Adler pointed out that the position a child occupies in the family—in terms of birth order and chronological distance between siblings—influences his or her personality development and style of life. This factor is known as *ordinal position*.

Erikson's Theory

Erik Erikson tried to combine Freud's emphasis on sexual drives with the emphasis on social motives stressed by other theorists. The result was an eight-stage theory characterized by a crisis that has to be resolved at each stage. The successful or unsuccessful resolution of each conflict affects the developing personality. The stages, along with the crises faced, are as follows:

Oral-Sensory Stage: Trust vs. Mistrust

During this stage, the infant is functionally helpless and dependent on his or her relationship with the parents. How the parents react to the infant's needs and demands determines whether the infant forms a positive feeling of well-being and trustfulness in his or her surroundings, or whether the infant develops basic feelings (not conscious thoughts) of distrust and fearfulness toward the world because of unmet needs.

Muscular-Anal Stage: Autonomy vs. Shame and Doubt

Erikson suggested that this stage involves the child's struggle to make individual willful decisions, partly in the context of the parental demand for toilet training. A successful resolution of the conflict brings feelings of individuality and a willingness to attempt to solve problems, while a negative resolution brings doubt about decision-making powers and shameful feelings about self because of punishments from parents for unintentional mistakes.

Locomotor-Genital Stage: Initiative vs. Guilt

This stage is characterized by the child's efforts at independent, self-motivated behaviors. The crisis arises from the conflicts between the child's expressions and responses from the adult world. These responses may be supportive or discouraging. With a positive resolution of this crisis, the child learns to make things happen and to experience from the "conquest" a sense of pleasure in reaching desired goals. Negatively, as a result of too much parental punishment, criticism or correction the child may acquire feelings of guilt about attempted actions and may become a dependent or irresponsible person.

Latency Stage: Industry vs. Inferiority

Erikson described this struggle as one of industry versus inferiority because at this stage, children must develop a sense of purposefulness about working at tasks and accomplishing something specific. With a negative resolution, the child may acquire feelings of inadequacy or inferiority because of lack of confidence in basic skills.

Puberty and Adolescence: Identity vs. Role Confusion

This stage is a culmination of the preceding stages and results in the integration of feelings about self with perceptions about how others feel about you. In a very real sense, it is a time of "getting it all together," and experimentation with different roles or types of behavior is quite beneficial. People who fail to resolve the identity crisis do not necessarily dislike themselves so much as they fail to be aware of or to act on their own capabilities.

Early Adulthood: Intimacy vs. Isolation

The young adult is caught in a struggle of intimacy versus isolation in an attempt to establish personal relationships with others and to avoid becoming a "loner." During this period, he or she finds a partner with whom to share the basic life values and commitments that developed during the earlier stages.

Young and Middle Adulthood: Generativity vs. Self-Absorption

Here, the adult is engaged in a struggle to provide for future generations, either financially, culturally or in other ways that give one a feeling of meaning by being part of the future. Success in this stage provides feelings of productiveness and contribution, while failure brings feelings of personal impoverishment.

Mature Adulthood: Integrity vs. Despair

In the final stage, as characterized by Erikson, the older person either finds that the experience of living culminates in a sense of satisfaction and fulfillment or, negatively, becomes cynical and fearful of dying.

Sullivan's Theory

Harry Stack Sullivan, an American psychiatrist, stressed the social nature of personality. He viewed personality in terms of definite stages of development, during which social influences play a crucial role, beginning in infancy and continuing through late adolescence. He stated that individuals can be understood only in relation to the significant people in their lives, and he focused his attention on the interpersonal situation and not just the person.

Sullivan suggested that personality manifests itself only when a person is behaving in relation to one or more other people. These people do not actually have to be present, and they can be fictional (existing only in the person's imagination). But, he maintained, all psychological processes (including dreaming, remembering, and thinking) involve a person's relationship with others.

Sullivan spoke of the self, or self-system, which is a product of interpersonal relations. He said that our concept of ourselves is based on our experiences with others, primarily with our parents. In order to avoid anxiety, we engage in what he called security measures, which allow some forms of behavior and forbid others. This self-system can serve as the cohering force, holding together the different elements of our experience in a functioning personality. But it may also become very narrow and isolated from the rest of the personality, especially if it becomes resistant to new information that might change it. Thus, it can also interfere with our ability to deal effectively with others.

Type and Trait Theories of Personality

Type theories of personality attempt to classify a person in a single category defined by one or more characteristics. Type theories began two thousand years ago and persist to the present day despite the realization by many psychologists that a single label cannot adequately describe a person's personality. A relatively modern version of a type theory was developed by Carl Jung. As we saw earlier, Jung proposed that there is a continuum of introversion-extraversion on which every person could be evaluated.

Trait theories try to categorize the personality on the basis of several observed behavioral characteristics. The decision regarding which characteristics to use in trait theories is often made on the basis of statistical analyses.

The statistical technique of *factor analysis* has been extensively used to determine which characteristics best describe personality. Factor analysis reveals the correlations between various test items and allows common factors or traits to be determined. However, the selection of the original items (perhaps questions to be answered or adjectives to be checked if they describe the respondent) is crucial, because the resulting factors identified will depend upon the material used.

Allport's Trait Theory

Gordon W. Allport, an American psychologist, emphasized the importance of traits. He defined a trait as a determining tendency, or a predisposition to respond. A trait implies consistency in behavior, which, in turn, reflects internal consistency. Allport was interested primarily in the individual trait—that which makes a person unique—rather than the common trait, which is the focus of personality testing and is common to a large percentage of the population.

Allport has also been called an ego, or self, psychologist because he believed that ego functions, such as a person's intentions and distant goals, are vital aspects of an individual's personality. These ego functions account for the consistency in a person's behavior over time and through many different situations. Therefore, to understand an individual's personality, we must have knowledge of his or her long-range purposes.

Cattell's Trait Theory

Raymond B. Cattell views personality as a complex structure of traits, which he defines as mental structures inferred from behaviors that account for behavioral consistency. Like Allport, Cattell suggests that there are common traits possessed by all people and unique traits that apply to a particular person and can be found in no other person in just that form.

Cattell makes the distinction between *surface traits,* which are relatively superficial and seem to go together, and *source traits,* which are more basic to the personality. Thriftiness, tidiness, and stubbornness are examples of surface traits that cluster together. Dominance or shyness would be considered source traits. It is the source traits that are assumed to produce consistency across many situations and are most useful in predicting behavior. Source traits are divided into those that are due to heredity—called *constitutional traits*—and those that spring from environmental factors—called *environmental-mold traits.*

Body-Type Theory

One proposal that attempts to describe personality is known as the body-type theory, developed by William H. Sheldon, a psychologist. Individuals are classified in terms of their body types and the personality characteristics that go with them. The three basic body types and their associated personality traits, according to this theory, are as follows:

Endomorphy: A soft, fat body; and *visceratonia:* a cheerful personality desiring peaceful surroundings and acceptance by others

Mesomorphy: A muscular and tough body; and *somatotonia:* a combative, straightforward personality

Ectomorphy: A slim, frail body; and *cerebrotonia:* the restrained personality of an individual interested in academic pursuits

Psychologists have found so much contradictory evidence that body-type theory is not generally accepted today.

Learning Theories of Personality

Many psychologists attribute the acquisition of personality characteristics to learning. These psychologists have shown how classical conditioning, operant conditioning, and modeling (Chapter 9) may all be important in this acquisition.

There is actually no one behavioral theory of personality; rather, there are several different theories that share the common view that learning experiences play the major role in shaping personality. Generally, advocates of these theories study behavior by using the experimental method (discussed in Chapter 2).

Dollard and Miller's Reinforcement Theory

John Dollard and Neal E. Miller believed that personality is acquired through conditioning. People are driven by physiological and learned needs, which, if properly satisfied, will lead them to satisfy other, similar needs in the same way. If a response reduces a drive (bringing pleasure), the person will repeat the response in the future.

For example, if a child's temper tantrum results in obtaining a desired piece of candy, then the child will throw a tantrum every time he or she wants something. Personality traits are simply acquired responses that were previously reinforced. Responses that are not reinforced are extinguished. The individual's social environment plays an important part in personality development. If the parent gives approval to a particular response, the child will tend to repeat it.

Dollard and Miller agreed with psychoanalytic theorists in stressing the importance of early childhood experiences as determinants of adult behavior. They asserted that conflict arises in the child largely as a result of what appears to be inconsistent behaviors, especially from the parents. They called attention to four situations that are particularly likely to arouse neurotic conflicts: feeding in infancy, toilet training, early sex training, and training for control of anger and aggression. Adjustment difficulties in each of these areas can be explained in their theory by inappropriate or inconsistent reinforcement.

Social-Learning Theory

A number of learning-oriented approaches to personality are often classified under the heading social-learning theories. The basic beliefs of such theories are that social behaviors are learned in the same manners as any other kinds of responses, that differentiation of social behaviors is learned according to the environmental circumstances that are present, and that these learned characteristics can be observed in everyday living.

One of the leading proponents of such a theory is Albert Bandura, who has written extensively on social learning through modeling. In investigating a variety of behaviors, and aggression in particular, Bandura has concluded that much important learning and personality development take place when an individual observes the behavior of another and learns to imitate that behavior or in some way model himself or herself after the other person.

The other person or persons need not actually be present. The modeling may be vicarious. Individuals are influenced by presentations, such as those shown in movies, on television or in cartoons, as well as by live models. This may explain why children who are exposed to much violence and aggression in films and on TV tend to act more aggressively, according to some sociologists.

Family and Peer Influence

In studying the effects of social behavior on the development of personality characteristics, psychologists have focused attention on two major areas: the influence of the family and the influence of peers. General findings indicate that both sources are very important in disposing the person toward certain patterns of response. Furthermore, it seems that peer influences become relatively more and more important as a child grows older.

Conflict of Influences

Contradictory patterns of responding may be elicited by a single situation, thus bringing different aspects of the personality into conflict. Resolution of such conflicts follows the same principles as in other conflict situations, with the strongest motive dominating the choice.

For example, while waiting in the checkout line of a discount store, Deborah sees one of her best girlfriends take a book from a boy's briefcase and slip it into her backpack. Deborah realizes her friend is stealing the book, but wonders whether or not to tell the boy about it. Her difficulty in deciding reflects the fact that she has learned that stealing is illegal and immoral, but she also has learned that one doesn't "tell on" good friends. When she chooses to say nothing, her inaction reflects the relative importance of the two values.

Humanistic Theories of Personality

Humanistic theories of psychology put emphasis on studying the whole human being and helping humans try to achieve their fullest potential. Subjective experience is considered as important as objective reports, and the unusual or exceptional is studied as well as the general or usual. Moreover, the humanistic theories offer a positive sense about people, seeing them as essentially good and in the process of growth.

Rogers's Self Theory

Carl Rogers, a leading proponent of humanistic psychology, developed a self theory, which stresses that the basis of personality is the human's wish to realize his or her full potential. Full realization or potential would mean that individuals would be living in perfect accord with themselves and others. But full realization of potential is also dependent upon one's background—the atmosphere in which one grows up, and upon the responses given by others.

Rogers hoped this facilitative background would reflect an attitude of unconditional positive regard, where individuals are valued, respected, and loved simply for what they are. Unfortunately, Rogers found that most people seem to be raised in an atmosphere of conditional positive regard, where approval and respect are given for some, but not all, parts of behavior.

Conditional positive regard is shown when a parent claims on the one hand to love a child, but at the same time complains about that child's performance in school, making unpleasant remarks and perhaps even threats. The parent who is able to love the child and accept the child's abilities regarding school performance is showing unconditional positive regard, at least in this one situation.

According to Rogers, personality maladjustment occurs when a difference develops between a person's self-image and the reality of a situation. When a person is unable to incorporate new experiences into his or her self-image, anxiety may result and lead to the development of defenses against seeing the truth of the situation. Rogers hoped the person would have a more flexible self and be able to adjust to situations as they occur, thus avoiding personality maladjustment.

Maslow's Self-Actualization Theory

Abraham Maslow, an American psychologist, believed that in every individual there is a will toward health, an impulse toward growth or toward the actualization of human potential. Our behavior, then, is goal directed. Human nature is essentially good; whenever we are unhappy or neurotic, it is because the environment has made us so by distorting our thinking. He argued that human beings have different kinds of needs that are ordered in a hierarchy, certain basic needs must be satisfied before other, higher needs can emerge.

At the bottom of the *hierarchy of needs* are the basic physiological drives (hunger, thirst, and so on) that must be gratified in order for the organism to survive. When these needs are met—and they usually are—the need for safety and security emerges. Once we feel safe and secure in our surroundings, we try to satisfy the need for love and belonging; for affectionate relationships with other people; for being with our group, our home, our family. The need for esteem comes next, the need for a stable, firm, positive evaluation of ourselves. Then, at the top of the list, is self-actualization, the highest goal of all. This represents the need to be all that we can be, to be true to our nature, to accept ourselves as we are. When all our lower needs are met, we can begin to satisfy our higher needs. These higher needs include justice, goodness, order, unity. When these needs are met, Maslow believed, we feel a sense of happiness and well-being, or what he called self-actualization.

Self-actualization is the drive to discover ourselves and to fulfill our potential, to be all that we can be. It is an unlearned, uniquely human drive that impels us to action.

Maslow found that self-actualizing people tend to have a high frequency of what he called *peak experiences,* moments of great happiness and fulfillment. He investigated the nature of these experiences and found that people undergoing such experiences, whether in sexual episodes, during creative activities or when viewing a nature scene, feel more integrated, more in harmony with the world, more autonomous, and more perceptive than usual.

Research in Personality

While it is beyond the scope of this book to discuss research studies in detail, it is worth mentioning that study of personality is not all theorizing: it does include research studies as well. Information is gathered from clinical case histories, naturalistic observations, and laboratory experiments involving both humans and animals.

CHAPTER 14

Psychological Testing and Measurement

In our everyday language, we freely use the word personality as if it were one desirable quality that a person either has or does not have. We might say, for instance, "She has lots of personality," or "He has no personality at all." But psychologists view personality somewhat differently. To them, personality is not just one quality; rather, it refers to a complex of traits that help define the total person. But just what traits are prominent and how they should be measured and assessed relative to each other is still a subject of lively debate. This is not surprising, when we consider how complex the human personality is and how many facets it has. All the basic processes (cognitive, emotional, motivational) influenced both by heredity and environment, combine to form the total personality.

A number of different methods of personality assessment have been devised for this purpose. These personality tests are not like the school achievement tests that measure a person's maximum performance—for example, the number of questions you can answer correctly on a math midterm. Instead, they are designed to assess a person's typical performance in certain situations—for example, whether you usually become very anxious before an exam. There are no correct or incorrect answers on personality tests, since you are merely asked what you usually do in a given set of circumstances, in order that your behavioral tendencies may be described.

This chapter concerns itself with the main characteristics of a good psychological test, the uses and abuses of tests, and some of the basic forms of psychological tests that have been developed. Chapter 12 deals specifically with the traits of intelligence and creativity, which many tests measure.

Characteristics of a Good Test

Psychologists have identified four characteristics that seem to be most important for a good test. These characteristics are reliability, validity, standardization, and objectivity.

Reliability

Reliability refers to the consistency with which a result will be obtained when either identical or supposedly equivalent forms of a test are used. A test is said to be reliable when equivalent results are obtained with the same subject taking alternate forms of the test over a period of time or with matched subjects taking alternate forms of the test at the same time. In testing, perfect consistency cannot be expected, but a high degree of reliability is essential. It would be impossible to make accurate or meaningful predictions from the results of an unreliable test.

Validity

Validity means that a test measures what it claims to

measure; that is, a valid test measures what it aims to measure and predicts accurately what it intends to predict. A test may have several different kinds of validities: content validity, construct validity, and predictive validity.

Content Validity

A test's content validity refers to how well or poorly the test's contents pertain to what the test attempts to measure. For example, if we are testing applicants for police officer positions, it probably would not be valid to ask questions about Shakespeare's sonnets, but it would be valid to ask questions about the law.

Construct Validity

Construct validity determines how well or poorly a test measures some trait, such as intelligence or personality, which we cannot actually pinpoint (since it is intangible) but can only infer. On the police officers' test we might want to measure "emotional stability," a construct term, which is relevant to the performance of a police officer.

Predictive Validity

A test's predictive validity is determined by how well or poorly it predicts a person's success in the area it measures. Do individuals who score higher on the test actually do better on the tasks measured by the test? We could determine this by comparing over time the job performance of police officers who did well on the test against those who did poorly.

It is important to identify just what a test does measure, how well or poorly, and with what degree of predictive accuracy. Improper use of tests may lead to inaccurate predictions and, therefore, faulty counseling or guidance.

Comparison of Reliability and Validity

A test may be highly reliable but still invalid. This can occur when a test measures something consistently but does not measure what it claims to measure. However, a test that is valid will also be reliable. (If the test measures what it intends to measure, then it will have to do this with fairly high consistency; otherwise the test would not predict accurately.)

Suppose you were shown "Keiner's Test of Intellectual Skills," which consists of summing up the following three physical measurements: (1) the circumference of the subject's head; (2) the length of the subject's nose from tip to eyebrow; and (3) the distance separating the centers of the subject's two eyes. You would probably realize that this test could have very high reliability, yet very likely be a totally invalid measure of intellectual skills. This example is purposely absurd, but the principle it illustrates is important; namely, it is possible for a number of people to take specified measurements from one subject and obtain the same results, thus demonstrating the test's reliability. However, such measurements may be completely inappropriate for the purposes stated, and thus have no validity. Test developers constantly guard against the possibility that their tests may be either unreliable or invalid.

Standardization

Standardization refers to how the testing is carried out. All aspects of the testing procedure, including the administration of the test and the scoring and evaluation of the results, should follow the same pattern each time the test is given. If the testing procedure is not standardized, differences among the test performances of the subjects may be the result of variations in test procedures, and not an accurate indicator of differences among the subjects.

Norms

One way to standardize test results is to establish norms, which are scores obtained from groups of people who have taken the test. Once norms have been determined, performances by others taking the same test (in the same manner) can be compared to the norms.

Colleges students who expect to go to graduate school often have to take the Graduate Record Examination (GRE) or a comparable test and submit the scores along with their applications. A copy of the scores is sent to each student, along with norms for the test. Thus, the students know what their absolute GRE scores are and how these scores compare to those obtained by others taking the same tests. Often, these are reported as percentile values. A percentile is the point below which a certain percentage of the population falls. For example, a person who scored in the sixty-fifth percentile would have done better than 65 percent of the people who took the test.

Norms vs. Criterion Orientation

Norms are frequently helpful in interpreting the results of psychological tests, but on occasion they may be misleading. In such cases, it may be better to use a criterion, or an absolute standard, to evaluate a subject's performance.

Suppose you were assigned the task of determining how much aptitude for mathematics a particular child has. Depending on the situation, you might use either a normative scale or a criterion scale of measurement. For example, suppose the child attends a special school for children with high aptitudes for mathematics. You might then avoid the norm approach because your subject, in comparison to others in the special school, might not seem to have much aptitude for math. (The norms in this school would be very high, and the child you are studying might score in a deceptively low percentile.) Thus, caution must be exercised in interpreting test results and in choosing standards of measurement.

Norms and Stereotypes

Because norms are established on the basis of test results and are often reported as statistics, they sometimes take on the "ring of truth" for the naive reader. They can, however, be misinterpreted. For example, a person may look at a norm and follow this train of reasoning: "(1) If this is the average or typical score of a group of people, and (2) Jim is a member of that group, then (3) this score must be typical of Jim." The test results may be typical of that person, but the norm does not provide any assurance that it is so.

Objectivity

Objectivity in testing means that the measuring process is standardized according to listed criteria, without any preconceptions or biases. All measurements made in such a neutral or dispassionate fashion would be the same even if different people did the measuring.

In some cases, the person administering, scoring, and evaluating a psychological test is not told why the person is being tested. This is done so that the person will not form preconceptions. It would be inappropriate, for example, for the teacher who has complained about a student's behavior in class to then give a personality test to that student. Instead, the test should be given by someone who is neutral and will proceed in an objective fashion.

Types of Psychological Tests

In theory, any test of a behavioral characteristic could be called a psychological test. Generally, we divide psychological testing between tests of intelligence or intellectual ability and tests of personality. Chapter 12 discusses intelligence testing at great length. Here, we will look briefly at some cognitive tests and then explore personality testing in some detail.

Intelligence Tests

Intelligence tests are probably best described as a series of aptitude tests that predict scholastic abilities. They are the best known and most widely used psychological tests and have been quite thoroughly researched. Chapter 12 includes a discussion of tests of intelligence and creativity.

Achievement and Aptitude Tests

Achievement tests are designed to measure what a person has accomplished or what he or she knows currently. Aptitude tests are designed to predict what a person may accomplish in the future if given appropriate training. Both of these types of testing are based on the concept of ability, which is a person's potential for acquiring a skill. Achievement tests show how well a person has acquired skills so far, while aptitude tests indicate how well a person might acquire skills in the future.

In a sense, all ability tests are achievement tests, showing only how well the person does on a given test at a particular time. However, the purposes of achievement and aptitude tests differ, and psychologists try to design aptitude tests that measure basic skills that do not require any specific knowledge.

There are two major types of aptitude tests: *scholastic aptitude tests,* which are used to predict future successes in academic pursuits, and *vocational aptitude tests,* which are used to estimate future successes in employment situations.

Personality Tests

Personality tests are designed to try to determine what is typical of an individual, or what the person usually does.

Generally, these tests are related to some theory regarding the structure of personality and therefore attempt to measure traits or characteristics specified by that theory. The basic principles of personality are considered in depth in Chapter 13.

There are several different ways of evaluating personality, including paper-and-pencil tests, projective tests, situational tests, and techniques such as interviewing.

Objective Tests

The objective personality tests are so called because they are administered and scored according to a standard procedure, and the results are affected very little by the opinions of the examiner. As a rule, they are paper-and-pencil tests, easy to administer to large groups at one time. Standardized over a representative sample of the population, they provide a score that can be compared with the scores of other individuals.

Paper-and-Pencil Tests

Paper-and-pencil tests usually used for personality evaluation are often questionnaires containing statements to which the individual can respond with answers such as "yes/maybe/no" or "true/false/cannot say." In other cases, a subject is given a list of adjectives and is able to choose those that he or she feels are self-descriptive. These questionnaires, also called *personality inventories*, may measure either general adjustment or a single personality characteristic, such as aggressiveness or friendliness.

Psychologists are aware that test takers do not always tell the truth—either because they want to look better in the eyes of the tester or because their answers may be influenced by their own attitudes. To help the tester deal with this possibility, good tests contain key items that help reveal false answers.

Two of the most widely used personality inventories are the Minnesota Multiphasic Personality Inventory (MMPI) and the Sixteen Personality Factor Questionnaire (16PF).

Minnesota Multiphasic Personality Inventory (MMPI). With the MMPI, the subject is given statements such as "I am easily awakened by noise," or "I never worry about my looks," to which he or she must respond "true," "false," or "cannot say." The tabulation of the responses yields a total personality profile of the person, divided into ten categories, which include masculinity-femininity, social introversion (avoidance of other people), and psychopathic deviation (antisocial conduct). The test has built into it a validating scale to determine, by the pattern of answers, if the subject is faking responses. The faking usually takes the form of trying to give socially acceptable responses instead of honest ones.

The MMPI is useful in diagnosing disturbed behavior and in yielding a profile of personality that accurately indicates areas in which some difficulty of adjustment, such as in relationships with other people, has been experienced.

Sixteen Personality Factor Questionnaire (16PF). This instrument is an objective test that yields a description of personality in terms of sixteen factors such as dominance and emotionality. The individual being tested is given a series of questions, for example, "It's hard for me to admit when I'm wrong," or "When I'm in a group of strangers, I'm usually one of the last to express my opinion publicly." Each question is followed by a choice of "true," "in between," or "false" or some other equivalent set of choices. The score yields a profile of the individual based on a scale of dimensions. Each of these dimensions is called a trait, and Cattel's theory of personality (see Chapter 13) uses this scale to describe an individual's personality.

Projective Tests

In projective personality tests, the subject is usually presented with a series of ambiguous stimuli and asked for a description of, or a story about, each. The theory of these tests is that the person will reveal some personality characteristics by introducing them into (or projecting them onto) the stimulus provided. The expectation is that, because the testing material has no meaning of its own, any meaning the subject gives it comes from his or her own feelings, motives or anxieties.

Underlying this expectation is the psychoanalytic assumption that people are unaware of many of their needs and desires because they are buried in the unconscious mind. If given a chance to use their imagination, individuals bring to light aspects of their unconscious that influence their personality. A major advantage of this type of test is that since the subjects do not know exactly what is expected of them—that is, what they are supposed to say—they are less likely to fake their answers than when they respond to a personality inventory, to which they can try to figure out the socially desirable responses.

The two most widely known projective tests are the Thematic Apperception Test (TAT), which uses a series of twenty monochrome pictures, and the Rorschach Test, which uses ten inkblots (some of which have color). Scoring techniques have been developed to help maintain some objectivity when using these tests.

Thematic Apperception Test. The Thematic Apperception Test presents the person with a sequence of twenty pictures depicting different situations, and he or she is asked to make up a story that relates to what is happening in each picture. The examiner studies the type of story made up by the individual, noting the particular ways in which the subject has defined the situation or identified with a character in the situation. Recurring themes and particularly inappropriate stories are noted; they play an important part in the interpretation.

Rorschach Test. In the Rorschach Test, the subject is presented with a series of ten cards, each of which has an inkblot on it. The inkblot shown in Figure 14.1 is not taken from the Rorschach Test, but it is similar to the type of figures used in the

Fig. 14.1

test. The subject is shown the figure and asked, "What could this be?" or "What does this remind you of?" After responding to the entire set of figures, the subject goes back through the cards and points out what part of each inkblot determined the response.

The scoring of the Rorschach Test has both objective and subjective aspects. The examiner scores the responses in three categories: (1) how much of the inkblot appears in the response—the whole blot or just a minute part of it; (2) whether form, color, shading or movement was primarily responsible for the subject's seeing the blot the way he or she did; and (3) the actual content of the response. In addition, the examiner must interpret the pattern of the responses and any spontaneous remarks or signs of emotional upset that occur during the test, all of which call on the subjective judgment of the person administering the test.

Interviews

Interviews are face-to-face encounters between people. They may be conducted in order to gather the same information as might be obtained by using a paper-and-pencil test. However, interviews give the interviewer a chance to expand on questions asked or to probe answers the interviewee gives.

When conducted by a skilled psychologist with a specialization in diagnostic interviewing, the interview has some very real advantages. In addition to eliciting direct responses from the subject, the interviewer also notes the appearance, demeanor, and body language of the person during the interview. Does the subject fidget nervously? Does he or she sit up as if wanting to be seen, or slump as if he or she wants to disappear?

The interview method provides a good deal of information about an individual and is, therefore, widely used. However, it has its limitations. As we just noted, in order to obtain the necessary information, the interviewer must be skilled; also, unfortunately, not all interviewers are equally sensitive. Furthermore, when used to make inferences about personality and to predict behavior from these inferences, the validity of the interview is not considered particularly impressive. Psychologists frequently use interviews in combination with objective tests to round out their picture of a subject's personality.

Situational Tests

In situational tests, a person is placed in a previously planned situation and is expected to react. The responses made by the person are evaluated as a means of determining his or her personality characteristics. Several years ago, a favorite situational test in employment interviewing consisted of offering the candidate a cigarette and a light, but not providing an ashtray. The reactions of the candidate to the growing length of ash and the lack of a place to dispose of it were observed in an attempt to determine something about that candidate's personality. As might be imagined, there are serious doubts about the reliability and validity of such "one-shot" tests of a personality.

Rating Scales

The rating scale is a device that permits a test administrator to assess the degree to which an individual possesses particular characteristics. There are several different types of rating scales. The most frequently used form is the graphic rating scale, on which each trait is represented by a line. One end represents an extreme of that characteristic, and the other represents its opposite. The rater makes a mark at the place on the line that represents his or her judgment of the other person with regard to that particular trait.

An important consideration in using rating scales is that for the judgment to be useful, the person doing the rating must know the person taking the test well enough to evaluate him or her on each trait. Also, the rater must be careful of the halo effect—the tendency to be too generous with one's ratings if one likes the person being rated, or to rate the subject too low on all traits because he or she possesses one undesirable trait. For example, a rater who knows that the other person is very intelligent might evaluate that person very highly on other traits, such as dependability or honesty.

Test Batteries

Psychologists may combine several different psychological tests into a series and present them to a person. Such a combination of tests is referred to as a test battery. The results from the various tests often are plotted as a profile of scores, which provides information used in counseling and guidance.

Testing Concerns

Several variables must be taken into account when using psychological tests. Some of the most important are discussed in this section.

Individual vs. Group Tests

One concern is whether or not each individual needs to be tested separately. Sometimes data can be collected from a number of people simultaneously. Individual tests have the advantage of giving the psychologist a chance to closely observe the subject taking the test, and they are sometimes more sensitive than group tests as a means of evaluating special characteristics. On the other hand, individual tests are generally more expensive than group tests, and they often require a more highly trained administrator.

Group tests have the advantage of allowing large amounts of data to be collected quickly. They are also relatively inexpensive and usually do not require skilled administration. As a means of surveying a number of individuals quickly, they work fairly well, although it is difficult to keep accurate track of each subject's effort or motivation.

Speed vs. Power Tests

Speed tests are tests that have a time limit as a significant variable. Subjects are expected to do the best they can within a limited amount of time. For all practical purposes, power tests have no time limits. Subjects are asked to give their best possible performances and not worry about the time involved.

Cross-Sectional vs. Longitudinal Investigations

Psychologists often need to compare the performances of subjects in various age groups. There are basically two ways of making such comparisons. Cross-sectional investigations are tests of different individuals in each of the age groups being studied. For example, a group of four-year-olds and a group of ten-year-olds may be tested and the test results compared. Longitudinal investigations test the same subjects throughout the study. A group of four-year-olds may be retested at age ten and in addition at points in between.

Cross-sectional studies have the advantage of allowing the investigators to collect data very quickly. Cross-sectional studies also have limitations, however. It may be difficult to accurately match samples at the different age levels being tested. For example, the educational opportunities might have been significantly better for those of the younger age group, and as a result the scores obtained might be incorrectly interpreted as a decline in intelligence with increased age.

Longitudinal studies have the advantage of testing the same subjects throughout the study, avoiding the need to accurately match the samples. The differing educational opportunities that might have influenced the results in the cross-sectional investigation would not be an important factor. However, data collection in the longitudinal test is a very slow process, and there is a chance that many subjects might drop out over the course of the investigation.

Suppose a psychologist wanted to test the motor skills of children at ages two, four, six, eight, and ten. In a cross-sectional study, matched groups of children in each age group could be tested in a matter of days. A longitudinal study, on the other hand, would require a testing period stretched out over eight years.

Culture-Free and Culture-Fair Tests

It has long been known that an individual's cultural background can affect his or her performance on some tests of cognitive ability and of personality. Attempts have been made to create psychological tests that do not contain biases against or in favor of certain cultures or subcultures. Culture-free tests attempt to eliminate such biases totally, for example, with performance tests free of any cultural background influence. Culture-fair tests try to choose items that should be equally well known by all cultural groups being investigated. But, most attempts at creating such tests have proved relatively unsuccessful.

Uses of Psychological Tests

Psychological tests are used for many different purposes. It must be remembered, however, that test results should be considered only advisory and that any other information available should be used in making either predictions or decisions. Several typical uses of tests are discussed below.

Selection

Probably the most common use for psychological test results is in the selection of individuals for academic or vocational positions. If there is more than one qualified applicant for a position, the person doing the hiring may administer tests to help in the selection process.

Counseling and Therapy

Ability tests and personality tests may be used by the psychologist who is attempting to aid an individual with guidance or therapy. The results obtained may help the psychologist to formulate a plan for treatment of the individual or to advise an individual about his or her abilities.

Legal Proceedings

Results from psychological tests are sometimes used in courts of law and other legal proceedings. For example, a court may have to make a judgment about the sanity of a defendant in a criminal case.

Statistical vs. Intuitive Judgment

A psychologist may make predictions or decisions based solely on comparing some norm or criterion with the results of a test. In such a case, the psychologist has made what is called a statistical judgment based on the test. In other situations, the psychologist may use the test results together with other pieces of information, including feelings or intuitions about the subject. In such a case, the psychologist has made what is called an intuitive judgment based on the total information.

Abuses of Psychological Testing

Psychological testing has been questioned for a number of reasons, including the extent to which the tests are actually able to predict, the fairness of tests for all groups, the possibility that psychological tests invade a person's privacy, and the ways in which the results of tests are publicized or revealed.

Limited Prediction

Many of the predictions and decisions mentioned earlier can be based on or aided by the results of psychological tests. However, psychologists and others with access to test results must realize the limitations of such scores and not attempt to rely upon them exclusively.

Intelligence tests are sometimes thought to provide results that may predict success in almost any aspect of behavior. Yet, research has shown that other variables—such as creativity, level of motivation, and psychomotor skills—may be as important or more important as indicators of future success. Basing predictions of success solely on intelligence scores might be considered narrow-minded and inappropriate.

Culture Unfairness

As previously mentioned, attempts have been made to try to develop culture-free or culture-fair tests, but success has been limited. Thus, psychological tests may be misused if they are administered to a subcultural group for which they are inappropriate. In an attempt to dramatize the lack of test fairness, a "ghetto" test was developed several years ago. Based upon the slang language of a particular subcultural group, the test showed how results could vary widely, depending on the specific language used in the test.

Invasion of Privacy

Merely administering a psychological test is not necessarily an invasion of privacy; such a test frequently serves the beneficial purpose of assisting an individual in making behavioral choices. However, privacy is invaded if the results of an individual's test are revealed without that person's knowledge or consent.

Anyone with access to the results of psychological tests should respect the privacy of those individuals who were tested, and should consider seriously the consequences of revealing test results. Government regulations that attempt to preserve privacy and limit access to test results have been enacted.

CHAPTER 15

Abnormal Personality

In psychology, one of the most difficult areas to define accurately has been that of abnormal personality patterns. When someone shows behavior noticeably different from the average, it is coloquially called abnormal (away from the norm). Such behavior concerns us when it creates either personal discomfort or difficulties for others in the person's society. Generally, both the quantity and quality of the person's behavior must be evaluated before a decision is made regarding whether or not some attempt should be undertaken to modify or correct the abnormal pattern. Moreover, while it is recognized that the word abnormal means "away from the norm," controversies have arisen because it is difficult to determine what norm or norms to use.

This chapter looks at a wide range of abnormal personality patterns. After examining the incidence of abnormal behavior and some of the predisposing factors, it considers the major psychological models that attempt to explain how abnormal patterns develop. The main categories of abnormal conditions based on the diagnostic system of the American Psychiatric Association, the DSM-III-R, will then be outlined and discussed. Finally, factors that influence abnormal patterns will be identified.

Abnormal Personality Patterns

Definition

An abnormal personality pattern, as the term is used in the psychological sense, refers to maladaptive behavior. This is evidenced by behaviors that produce significant and often persistent discomfort or upset for a person or for others in that person's society. Thus, the expectations and demands of the interpersonal and social settings will, to a great extent, determine whether or not a pattern of behavior is considered abnormal.

For example, a famous television star has a reputation for being insulting. His remarks are often rude and outrageous. However, he makes these remarks in the context of his act, and as a result no significant societal upset occurs. If the same kinds of remarks were made in a different social context, such as in a business meeting or a classroom, a totally different interpretation might be made, and the pattern could easily be judged as abnormal.

Other terms used to describe abnormal personality patterns have included mental illness and emotional disturbance. Some psychologists prefer to avoid such terms because they may imply characteristics that are not present in an abnormal response.

Properties of Abnormal Personality Patterns

Some actions that are temporarily upsetting for either a person or the person's society may not be interpreted as abnormal. Because such interpretations are relatively subjective, both the quantity and quality of the behavior should be considered in judging whether or not the behavior is abnormal. In other words, both the frequency and intensity of the behavior in question should be considered.

For example, practically everyone experiences anxiety at one time or another. Anxiety can be considered a normal part of one's experience from time to time. However, if the frequency and intensity of the anxiety seriously affect a person's actions, it will be considered abnormal. Temporary anxiety about making a public speech would be considered normal, while constant anxiety about life in general would be considered abnormal.

Percentage of the Population Showing Abnormal Personality Patterns

While varying estimates have been made regarding the percentage of the American population showing abnormal personality patterns at some time in their lives, a fairly well agreed upon minimum ratio is one in ten. (This is based on hospitalization rates and clinical records.) Further subdivisions by category of abnormal personality patterns have resulted in the following estimates: About half of these people show relatively-mildly disturbed patterns of behavior. Of the others, 30 percent show some kind of addiction, 15 percent are categorized as having other personality disorders, and 5 percent are labeled as having severe disturbance. If these estimates are accurate, it means that at any given time, 5 percent of the overall population is mildly disturbed (maladjusted), 3 percent is addicted, 1 percent shows other personality disorders, and 0.5 percent is severely abnormal.

Predisposing and Precipitating Factors in Abnormality

The onset of abnormal personality patterns seems to be the result of an interaction between a person's background and the person's current environment. The background factors, which include hereditary patterns and childhood experiences (with parents, peers, and others), are called predisposing factors. The stimuli that finally initiate the abnormal pattern are called precipitating factors. In a few instances, as in the case of brain damage, it may be impossible to distinguish between predisposing and precipitating factors.

A person's childhood experiences could predispose him or her to show an abnormal personality pattern in later life. Parents who show an inordinate amount of concern for cleanliness in their children, for example, could predispose their children to abnormal anxieties about dirt and disorder. Such a predisposition, once it is well established as part of the child's personality, could create great anxieties later in life.

Other Factors for Judging Abnormality

Psychologists have tried to identify characteristics that help distinguish normal from abnormal behaviors. Some of those characteristics include whether or not the person shows voluntary control of the behavior; the productivity of the behavior; the judgment, attention, and planning that go into the behavior; and the frequency of the behavior. Any or all of these factors may be considered in characterizing a behavior as normal or abnormal.

Many people, by virtue of the nature of their jobs, must formulate rather rigid plans of behavior and operate according to them. For example, an airline pilot must go through an exhaustive routine of instrument checks before taking off. Such a routine is time-consuming and must be very exacting, but no one would question its importance or interpret it as a sign of an abnormal personality pattern. If, however, the pilot went through an equally detailed series of checks each time he drove his car, his behavior might very well be considered abnormal. The extremely careful routine appropriate to the former situation would not be appropriate to the latter.

Difficulty in Determining Abnormality

Several difficulties arise in deciding whether or not a pattern of behavior should be called abnormal. One of these has been mentioned earlier in this chapter, that of determining how the behavior compares to the personal or societal norms. The word *abnormal* literally means "away from the normal," but this raises the question of what is meant by the term *normal*. When we speak of normal behavior, we usually mean behavior that society accepts as proper—that is, actions that fall within the guidelines established by society. *Normal*, therefore, is sometimes used to mean "socially acceptable" or "proper."

Another difficulty is that behavior considered abnormal in one culture or period of time may be considered normal in another. In the Puritan society of the seventeenth century, it was considered normal to burn suspected witches. Today, of course, this kind of behavior would be considered severely abnormal.

Clinical psychologists generally use the concept of adjustment— the person's ability to cope with the problems of life—as a standard for judging whether the individual's behavior is normal or abnormal. Thus, normal is equated with adjusted and abnormal with maladjusted. Whenever individuals cannot make the adjustments in behavior necessary to respond to changing environmental stimuli, including interpersonal relationships and social roles, their behavior is considered maladjusted.

Explanations of Abnormal Behavior

Attempts to understand why people behave abnormally have led to several different models of abnormality. Each of these models is derived from a theory of personality development (see Chapter 13). Each supports a different form of psychotherapy (these are discussed the next chapter). While none is sufficient to account for all abnormal conditions, each has made a contribution to our total understanding of abnormal behavior.

The Psychodynamic Model

Originating with the work of Freud, the psychodynamic model places emphasis on internal, or intrapsychic, sources of abnormal behavior. Conflicts residing in the unconscious, or between the unconscious and conscious mind, are thought to cause abnormal patterns of responding.

Freud, for example, believed that a phobia is really an expression of repressed sexual fantasies, usually of an Oedipal nature. These fantasies, or unconscious wishes, may conflict with defense mechanisms mustered to help contain these feelings. Typically, the phobic object, like a symbol in a dream, represents a compromise between an unconscious fear and its defenses which, when psychoanalyzed, reveal the primitive nature of the conflict.

Freud's famous case of Little Hans ("Analysis of a Phobia in a Five-Year-Old Boy," 1910) offers his most detailed discussion of phobia. Hans had developed a fear of large animals, especially horses, soon after witnessing a large horse falling (the "precipitating trauma"). This developed into an agoraphobic response, rendering Hans unable to leave his house. Analysis of the child's unconscious by Freud and the boy's father revealed the causes of the phobia, which, expressed in the terminology of psychoanalysis, involved castration anxiety, murderous Oedipal wishes against his father, and aggressive-erotic fantasies about his parents. These fears were countered by the defenses of repression, displacement, and projection—whereby Hans forgot his primitive traumatic memories (repression), saw the horse as his father (displacement), and imagined the horse wanted to hurt him (projection). Thus, Freud concluded, the unconscious conflict, the repressed rage against the father, emerged in the guise of a phobia.

The Biomedical Model

Biomedical models emphasize the influence of bodily functions upon personality. Disease, genetic inheritance or the condition of the person's nervous system may be seen as the source of abnormal behavior. Therapies based on a biomedical model of personality may make use of drugs or surgery. One of the problems with biomedical models is that a great demand is placed upon psychiatrists, who are expected to give medical treatment for problems that may not really have medical solutions. Another problem is that patients who consider themselves sick may not accept responsibility for their actions, thus making treatment more difficult.

The Social-Learning Model

The behavioral, or social-learning, explanations of abnormal behavior focus on how an individual learns an inappropriate anxiety-evoking response. There are three main paradigms used: classical conditioning, operant conditioning, and modeling.

The origin of a phobia was the subject of investigation in one of the most widely cited demonstrations in behavioral psychology, still an important example decades after publication. John B. Watson and Rosalie Rayner induced a phobia in Albert, an eleven-month-old boy, by using the classical-conditioning model associated with Pavlov and his dogs.

First they observed Albert's natural reaction to small furry animals (rodents were used). Clearly he was not phobic. Then, they instituted the experiment. Whenever Albert reached out to touch the rodent, the experimenters produced a loud, frightening noise. During several trials, they paired this neutral, conditioned stimulus (CS), the rat, with the fear-evoking, unconditioned stimulus (UCS), the noise. In time, the boy came to experience fear whenever he saw the rat, even when the noise was no longer emitted. This had become his conditioned phobic response (CR), the result of pairing the previously neutral stimulus (rat) with the unconditioned stimulus (loud noise). Soon thereafter, he developed a phobia for many furry objects, apparently generalizing the fear of the rat to these other objects as well.

According to the operant-conditioning model of B. F. Skinner, abnormal conditions develop not only from the accidental pairing of stimuli, but also from a person's intentional, voluntary operations on the environment, and from the consequences of these operations. If certain voluntary behaviors become associated with highly unpleasant and anxiety-evoking consequences, they are capable of developing into an abnormal condition.

The modeling (observational-learning) paradigm, developed extensively by Albert Bandura, suggests that most abnormal personality patterns are learned, at least in part, by direct exposure to the anxieties and irrational fears of another, especially one to whom we feel connected, or feel a certain emotional attachment. With this model, neither pairing of stimuli nor reinforcement is required; mere exposure is enough. A two-year-old who sees his mother screaming at the sight of a dog running through the backyard may develop a fear of dogs as he perceives, learns, experiences, and feels along with her at that terrified moment.

Most behavioral psychologists today are not so naive or dogmatic as to believe that a single explanation can account for all abnormal conditions. Instead, they recognize that many forces may interact to cause an abnormal condition.

The Cognitive Model

The cognitive model may be behaviorally oriented or psychodynamically oriented. Both orientations emphasize, in explaining the causes of abnormal conditions, the person's cognitions (thoughts) in relation to his or her overt behaviors.

The Cognitive-Behavioral View

The cognitive-behavioral explanation views thinking as a mediating process between stimulus and response. An abnormal personality pattern develops when the individual's thinking results in distortions that cause certain types of inappropriate responses (combining anxiety and fear with avoidance behavior) to what are really nondangerous stimuli.

The Cognitive-Dynamic View

The cognitive-dynamic view of phobia, represented by Albert Ellis's rational-emotive therapy (RET), extends this further by dissecting and clarifying the thinking processes involved in the distortion. In growing up, Ellis suggests, we are taught to think and feel certain connections about ourselves, others, and things in the world. Connections that are associated with the idea of "This is good," argues Ellis, become positive human emotions, such as love or joy, while those associated with the idea that "This is bad" become negative emotions, colored with painful, angry or depressive feelings. An abnormal condition is an illogical and irrational connection, associating "This is bad" or "This is dangerous" with things that really are not. The difference between the rational-emotive point of view and the psychoanalytic is that in RET the patient's thinking is said to be distorted because of early-life cognitive distortions (as opposed to strictly emotional confusions, as a Freudian would argue). It is not suggested that later in life he or she is "traumatized" or "fixated" at this early level of thinking, thus avoiding the determinism of the Freudian position. As with any thinking, Ellis argues, distorted thinking can be corrected by learning effective strategies of logic and reasoning—an important implication for therapeutic practice of RET.

The Existential Model

The major thrust of the existential model is an emphasis upon present experience, rather than past experience or the history of emotional learning. A basic principle of the model is that a person must take responsibility for all behavior, and not attribute it to past experience or illness. The existential model aims at understanding the person in his or her total existential reality—that is, within the context of the person's total existence and with regard to all areas of functioning.

Combining Models

Some abnormal personality patterns may best be explained by reference to more than one of the above models, and psychologists have come to recognize that each model makes an important contribution to the understanding of abnormal personality patterns. As a result, acceptance of the several models has been quite widespread, and the use of combinations of two or more models is not uncommon.

Diagnosis and Classification of Abnormal Conditions

Over the years, psychologists and psychiatrists who treat people with abnormal conditions have made a number of attempts to categorize them symptomatically in the same way a physician does, namely, through diagnosis. The traditional diagnostic categories used by psychoanalysts since Freud include neurosis, psychosis, personality (or character) disorders, organic disorders, and psychosomatic disorders. These categories are still widely used, but modern perspectives on psychopathology as well as years of clinical experience have reorganized, combined, or further subdivided many of these categories.

Specifically, with the publication in 1979 of the *DSM-III* and in 1987 of the *DSM-III-R (Diagnostic and Statistical Manual of Mental Disorders,* third edition, revised), the official diagnostic manual of the American Psychiatric Association, there have been some modifications and expansions of the traditional psychoanalytic categories. Neurosis, for example, was eliminated as a diagnostic category. The main reason it was dropped from the *DSM-III*, despite its common usage as a diagnostic term and as a general description of behavior, is that there is really no consensus in the field about how to define it. Instead, the *DSM-III* considers a *neurotic disorder* one in which the predominant disturbance or symptom—whether it's anxiety, irrational fear, bodily complaints, or antisocial behavior—is fundamentally distressing to the individual and is recognized by him or her as unacceptable. Under the general heading of neurotic disorders are now included anxiety disorders, phobic disorders, and somatoform disorders. The classificatory system then proposes four other criteria to differentiate neurotic problems from other categories or disorders:

1. Reality testing is basically intact.

2. Behavior does not actively violate gross social norms, although the individual's functioning may be impaired.

3. Without treatment, the disturbance is relatively enduring or likely to recur and is not limited to a transitory reaction to stressors, as with a crisis.

4. There is no demonstrable organic cause or basis for the symptoms.

Psychotic disorders are more severe than neurotic disorders. They are characterized by loss of touch with reality, complete dissociation (separation of sense of self from the reality of interacting with others), inappropriate feelings and responses to other people, and other, sometimes gross and dramatic, symptoms of loss of reality orientation, such as hallucinations and delusions. There are not always clear differentiations among different psychotic states, and historically there have been many changes about the ways we view these disorders. Reflecting the broadness of this category, psychotic disorders are grouped in the *DSM–III* as schizophrenia, paranoid disorders, and "other" psychotic disorders.

Most psychologists currently use (or at least recognize) the *DSM-III-R* organization, which has twelve major diagnostic categories. For example, under "Anxiety Disorders" are included generalized anxiety, obsessive-compulsive disorders, and phobias. "Somatoform Disorders" include body dysmorphic disorder, conversion disorder, and hypochondriasis. Under "Dissociative Disorders" come amnesia and multiple personality. "Mood Disorders" are depression, mania, and manic-depressive (bipolar) disorders. "Personality Disorders" include narcissistic, antisocial, schizoid, and others.

Anxiety Disorders

This category includes a number of symptomatic disorders in which there is an extremely high level of anxiety, which may express itself in any of several ways, directly or indirectly.

Generalized Anxiety Disorder

Anxiety may manifest as a general condition of the person's overall functioning. We all know of overly anxious people who are "worry warts," who never feel comfortable unless they are worrying about something. It is a less specifically symptomatic form of neurotic problem than the other two major types of anxiety disorders.

Obsessive-Compulsive Disorder

In this common type of anxiety disorder, the individual develops obsessions and compulsions.

Obsessions are repetitive thoughts that keep intruding into the individual's consciousness without regard for propriety or relevance. For instance, a man may be obsessed by thoughts of pain, always imagining himself being tortured or torturing others in the worst ways. He hates these thoughts but he cannot get them out of his mind.

A *compulsion* is a behavior that serves no purpose other than to discharge anxiety. It is not performed to accomplish a real end, but if it is not performed the person feels anxious. A person who has to return home at lunchtime several days a week to make sure the front door is locked is exhibiting compulsive behavior. So too is a person who, when walking down the street, avoids all the sidewalk cracks.

A girl keeps thinking, "I have to hold my breath to the count of ten and then my parents won't die, but if I breathe before then they will die," and then goes about holding her breath. The thought is an obsession; the action is a compulsion. Or, consider the case of Larry, who, on the surface, is a seemingly normal although somewhat aloof college student. What others cannot see is that Larry stays away from people because he is continually afraid of getting a disease. Everything he touches has to be wiped first, and he always thinks at night about what germs he has been exposed to during the day. Larry is typical of an obsessive-compulsive, worrying about germs and dirt. Compulsive hand washing and bathing (as well as desk cleaning and so on) are common compulsive symptoms among disturbed latency-aged boys. Often this can be accounted for by their burgeoning sexual awareness.

The perfectionist, a person who is never satisfied and who is always striving to be perfect, is also an example of a compulsive personality. Perfectionists demand the impossible, both from themselves and from others. Often their unrelenting criticism of self leads to as much conflict with other people as does their criticism of others. It creates a negative, unpleasant atmosphere in which no one can function effectively.

Within the context of an interpersonal relationship, the highly critical person is almost always in a state of conflict with someone. It comes as no surprise, therefore, that psychological research has shown perfectionists to be prone to difficulties in their interpersonal relationships, to experience many unpredictable shifts of mood, and in general to be unsatisfied with their lives no matter how much they accomplish.

Phobic Disorder

The third type of anxiety disorder—and perhaps the most common—is the phobic disorder (or phobic neurosis). Virtually everyone suffers from some type of phobia, although it may be so slight that the person does not deem it necessary to have the condition treated.

A phobia is an irrational fear that interferes with a person's healthy functioning. We all have fears, some rational and some not so rational, but it is the *degree* of the fear and how much it interferes with our functioning that determine if it is a serious phobia or not. Phobias may involve fear of snakes (ophidiophobia), fear of numbers (such as 13, triskaidekaphobia), fear of lightning (astraphobia), fear of dogs (cynophobia) or of almost anything else.

Somatoform Disorders

Another major category of neurotic disorder is referred to in the *DSM–III* as somatoform disorders. The word *somatoform* (*soma* = body) means "taking the form of a bodily disorder." Here, the anxiety expresses itself as a physical symptom, or at least what appears to be a physical symptom. The symptom may be a specific paralysis or dysfunction, psychogenic pain, hypochondria, or some more general types of manifestations, or what used to be called hysteria. Somatoform disorders are divided into further categories: body dysmorphic disorder, conversion disorder, and hypochondriasis.

Body Dysmorphic Disorder

Body dysmorphic disorder (*dysmorphophobia*) is a preoccupation a normal-appearing person has about a presumed bodily defect, such as facial wrinkles, body shape or the size of the nose. The individual develops almost an obsession with the way he or she looks, and thinks that others are focusing inordinately on that presumed physical abnormality.

Conversion Disorder

Conversion disorder appears as a physical illness, but has no organic causes. This may be as extreme as paralysis, blindness, loss of limb feelings, and inability to swallow or as mild as a case of chills. Symptoms of conversion disorder seem to rise and fall with the degree of stress the individual is experiencing.

Hypochondriasis

Hypochondriasis is characterized by continual complaining about health, or the neurotic belief that one has a serious illness when one really does not. A hypochondriacal person will obsess about his or her health, misinterpreting an ordinary experience or some sign of mild ill health as an indication that he or she is really very ill.

Dissociative Disorders

People exhibiting dissociative disorders seem to lose contact with or "tune out" part of their consciousness or memory. While these disorders are well-known and have become very popular with the public in dramatized versions such as *The Three Faces of Eve*, in reality they are quite rare.

Multiple Personality

Often mistakenly referred to as schizophrenia, the most unusual form of dissociative disorder is multiple personality. This disorder involves the coexistence of more than one personality, each relatively complete and independent, within one person. Typically very different from each other, each personality is usually not aware of the other(s). Differences may extend not only to behavioral characteristics such as attitudes and speech patterns, but also to physical manifestations, including state of health.

Psychogenic Amnesia

Amnesia involves selective forgetting of past events. While some amnesias can be attributed to physical causes, such as a concussion resulting from a blow to the head, psychogenic amnesia is thought to be caused by stress.

A more dramatic form of amnesia is called *fugue*, where the person not only suffers loss of memory, but also leaves his or her home for an extended period of time, in some cases, years.

Mood (Affective) Disorders

Mood disorders are typified by extremes of mood swing: great elation or deep depression. A person consistently showing elated, hyperactive states is called manic, while a person who shows minimal activity and despondency is called depressive. In bipolar disorder, the person alternates between manic and depressive states.

Depression

Most of us feel blue or moody or depressed at times, especially when things do not go well. However, for the most part, as soon as things get better, we snap out of it and enjoy life again. But many people feel melancholy all of the time or for very long periods of time. They suffer from a lingering form of depression—categorized in the *DSM–III* as a mood disorder—that may fall anywhere on a continuum from neurotic to psychotic, depending on the severity and duration of the symptoms.

Among the symptoms experienced by depressives are feelings of self-criticism, apathy, pessimism, and helplessness. Depressives are often unable to sleep or they sleep too much, and they may suffer loss of appetite or have an insatiable appetite; often their sex drive is diminished. They feel that life is not worth living, and they sometimes have suicidal impulses, which in turn may arouse guilt. Some depressives constantly feel weak and exhausted, and are preoccupied with their bodies. They also frequently worry about diseases.

Learned Helplessness. Martin Seligman developed the concept of learned helplessness based on studies conducted with dogs. After the dogs were exposed to several trials of inescapable shock by being restrained in a harness, they would not learn to escape the shock, even when they were finally allowed to do so. Only after they had been dragged to the safe side of the apparatus did they learn the proper escape route. Seligman and his associates suggested that the dogs' escape response had been extinguished by experiencing the inescapable shock, a phenomenon he called learned helplessness.

Seligman claims that depressed behaviors are learned in a similar fashion. The critical element, he believes, is the individual's perception that he or she is unable to control environmental events. This perception could result from a history of failure in dealing with stress-inducing situations, so that when faced with new crises, the person is likely to give up, even when appropriate coping strategies are available. While there has not been much support for this model in recent years, it does offer a compact and logical explanation to account for at least some aspects of depression.

Bipolar Disorders

Formerly known as manic-depressive disorders, bipolar disorders are characterized by swings between manic and depressed states. Occasionally, these swings parallel the seasons of the year in what has been called *seasonal mood disorder*. Bipolar disorders vary considerably in severity and often include periods of normal behavior interspersed with mood swings.

Personality Disorders

Personality disorders, also known as character disorders, usually begin during childhood and persist through adult life. What distinguishes a personality disorder from a neurotic disorder is that the symptoms of a personality disorder are basically consistent with a person's self-image and are indicative of the person's accepted life-style.

The last part of the distinction is particularly important: namely, that the person exhibiting a personality disorder does not experience neurotic anxiety, is not necessarily made uncomfortable by the disorder, and generally does not wish to change. Thus, personality disorders are particularly difficult to treat. Nevertheless, while a personality disorder may not be as troubling to the individual as a neurotic problem would be, it is potentially harmful to others, especially in the case of antisocial personality disorders. Personality disorders are classified in *DSM-III-R* as "Anxious/Fearful," "Odd/Eccentric," and "Dramatic/Impulsive."

Dependent Personality Disorder

An example of the Anxious/Fearful category is that of the dependent personality disorder. A person with these symptoms has little or no self-esteem, possibly allows others to make all decisions, and seldom is concerned with his or her own needs.

Schizoid Personality Disorder

Unable to form social relationships, someone exhibiting a schizoid personality disorder shows almost no ability to hold warm or caring feelings for another. This is an example of the Odd/Eccentric category.

Narcissistic Personality Disorder

One example of the Dramatic/Impulsive category is that of the narcissistic personality disorder. A narcissistic person is preoccupied with success, has grandiose feelings of self-importance, often expects special treatment, and typically lacks interpersonal empathy.

Antisocial Personality Disorder

Another example of the Dramatic/Impulsive category is that of the antisocial personality disorder. The antisocial person (formerly referred to as a psychopath) is a self-centered, often charming person, without care or concern for others, lacking the basic essentials of conscience that restrain us in many of our actions. Also sometimes referred to as a sociopath, this person believes that he or she is socially superior and more intelligent than other people (although this is not necessarily the case). Feeling free of the social and legal restraints that govern the lives of others in society, the sociopath has no compunctions about committing acts that others would not even consider.

Psychosexual Disorder

A person who engages primarily in destructive or antisocial sexuality is termed a sexual deviate. We must take great pains to qualify our definition with the recognition that a wide range of sexual behavior, although nonnormative, may still be acceptable; that some is borderline and that other behavior is clearly pathological. In the *DSM-III*, some behaviors are classified as atypical sexual behaviors while more serious disturbances are generally categorized as sexual dysfunctions or personality disorders.

Atypical Sexual Behaviors. Atypical sexual behaviors include homosexuality, transvestism (wearing the clothes of the opposite sex), and transsexualism (feeling trapped in the body of the wrong sex). While unusual, these are not considered abnormal.

Sexual Dysfunctions. Sexual dysfunctions include problems such as impotence or inhibited orgasm that interfere with pleasurable sexual intercourse.

Behaviors considered as psychosexual disorders, which would be viewed by clinicians as detrimental to the individual and/or other persons and thus socially disapproved, include *pedophilia* (sexual relations with children); *exhibitionism* (exposing the genitals in public or semipublic places such as parks, stores, buses or movie theaters); *voyeurism* (the acting-out version, where sexual gratification is accomplished by masturbating, as in the case of a Peeping Tom); *sadism* (achieving sexual gratification by inflicting pain on a sexual partner); *masochism* (deriving sexual gratification through experiencing pain or psychological humiliation); and *incest* (having sexual relations with one's relative). The rapist would fall somewhere between the deviate and the antisocial person (see above), since *rape* is not so much a sexual act as an act of brutality and rage against women.

Substance Use Disorders

The abuse of or addiction to any psychoactive substance may result in a substance-induced organic disorder, indicating that the substance brings about an abnormal condition by affecting body chemistry and physiological functioning. The effects can be further broken down according to the substance of abuse: alcohol, amphetamines, caffeine, cannabis (marijuana), cocaine, hallucinogens, inhalants, nicotine, opioids, PCP, or tranquilizers. While abuse of any of these substances may lead to maladaptive behavior patterns and abnormal conditions, the specific symptoms and treatment depend on the substance. For example, alcohol addiction requires a different treatment strategy and detoxification program than does addiction to marijuana.

Substance use disorders are subdivided into two categories:

substance abuse and substance dependence. *Substance abuse* results when there is pathological use of the drug, reduced occupational and/or social functioning, and at least one month's duration of the problem. *Substance dependence* is identified by *tolerance*, the need to increase the amount of drug to achieve the same effect, and *withdrawal*, the presence of physical distress when substance use is discontinued.

A more detailed discussion of psychoactive substances is found in Chapter 5.

Schizophrenic Disorders

Schizophrenia (the word literally means "a splitting of the mind") is a psychotic disorder characterized by a breakdown of personality that manifests itself in cognitive, emotional, and social dysfunctioning. Schizophrenia is not, as the public often thinks, characterized by multiple personalities (which is actually a dissociative disorder).

Many schizophrenics are bright and well educated, but they are unable to perceive accurately the stimuli in their environment or competently process information according to the rational guidelines that govern much of our cognitive processing. Thus, the schizophrenic may also distort his or her thoughts to conform with expectations and beliefs that are totally irrational. These false beliefs are called *delusions*. The most common delusion among schizophrenics is that someone or something outside of oneself is in control of one's thoughts. Schizophrenics may also experience hallucinations, hearing their own or other people's silent thoughts spoken aloud, or they may feel interference with their thoughts and actions. Together, the delusion that an outside force is controlling one's thinking, and the imagined voices giving commands, constitute a basic symptom complex of schizophrenia.

No one knows what causes schizophrenia, and like most of the things we don't know about, we propose many theories.

Psychoanalysts have generally taken a back seat to the physiological and genetic researchers during the past decade, as evidence continues to mount that there is at least some organic, or biological, basis to schizophrenia.

Several subcategories of schizophrenia have been distinguished: disorganized, catatonic, paranoid, and undifferentiated.

Disorganized Schizophrenia

Disorganized schizophrenia is typified by a serious thought disturbance—the flight of ideas and looseness of associations. It may also be characterized by steady withdrawal from reality, leading to a pronounced state of apathy. Feelings and emotions are not appropriate for the situation, and there is often a very flat, unpronounced affect, showing a cutting-off from the normal range of feelings. Babbling and incoherence are common, as are delusions.

Catatonic Schizophrenia

Catatonic schizophrenia is often characterized by motor disturbances. The most widely recognized symptoms of catatonic schizophrenia are total muscle rigidity and a single body position that is held for very long periods of time. A catatonic schizophrenic who suffers from a delusion that the food being served is poisoned may hold his jaw tightly shut, clench his hands behind his back, and turn his head to the side so that he cannot be fed. Any attempts to modify this body position will be resisted strenuously. A second variation of catatonia involves random motor activity and hyperactivity.

Paranoid Schizophrenia

The paranoid schizophrenic usually shows pronounced delusions of grandeur and persecution, accompanied by disconnected thought patterns. The delusions are frequently linked with hallucinations.

Undifferentiated Schizophrenia

A person who is clearly schizophrenic but cannot be categorized by one of the previous three designations is said to show undifferentiated schizophrenia. This type is usually marked by a mixture of symptoms specific to each case.

Delusional (Paranoid) Disorders

There are some people who though they appear to be well adjusted most of the time and to function in a normal fashion, have one symptom that, over a period of time, may become more and more a pronounced part of their personality: they hold a persistent delusion. In contrast to the schizophrenic, discussed above, whose delusions are illogical, often incoherent, and fragmented, the person who suffers from a paranoid reaction usually has one well-organized delusion that is backed by what appear, on the surface at least, to be fairly logical arguments. It is typically a delusion of persecution, in which a person believes that someone or some organization (the FBI or CIA) is out to pursue and even kill him or her.

Paranoid reactions are extremely difficult to treat because individuals with this disorder view all efforts as potentially threatening.

Organic Mental Disorders

This category, which includes the *DSM–III* categories of organic brain syndromes and organic mental disorders, refers specifically to conditions that, although paralleling psychotic disorders in various ways, have an organic—that is, a physical—basis, or some organic cause associated with the brain. Because organic disorders are sometimes difficult to diagnose conclusively through clinical interviews and psychological testing procedures, a series of medical tests usually has to be given. Aside from erratic behavior, organic disorders are characterized by a loss of intellectual ability, memory disturbances, and loss of time and relational consciousness.

Organic disorders often affect elderly people (*senility*), alcoholics (*alcohol-reaction psychosis*), and people who have been injured in accidents (*trauma*) that result in some damage to the brain. Many mind-altering drugs, such as amphetamines, cocaine, barbiturates, and hallucinogens, can bring about an organic mental disorder, through either intoxication or withdrawal. It has also been pointed out that reactions to certain medications can precipitate organic brain disorders. Recent evidence has further confirmed that even some of the more commonly used medications in treating inflammations, heart arrhythmia, and hypertension may have as side effects organic symptoms that mimic psychotic behavior in a number of ways.

Infantile Autism

One abnormal personality pattern that is sometimes classified as a separate type of psychosis is infantile autism, which afflicts children under the age of ten. The predominant characteristics of this type of psychosis are extreme withdrawal from reality and from others, poor communication, strenuous attempts to maintain everything just as it is, and no desire for personal contacts and intimacy. The autistic child often appears to be bright, but does not operate well within a normal environment. This pattern of behavior is not at all well understood and, as a result, treatment techniques have been difficult to develop.

Relationship of Abnormal Patterns to Other Factors

Attempts to establish some understanding of the relationships of abnormal patterns to other factors have been quite difficult because of the problems inherent in trying to label the abnormal behavior. Despite this, research results have tended to support the following findings.

Sex

Research relating gender to various types of disorders has shown that, in general, females are more likely to be treated for neurotic or psychotic patterns of behavior, while males are more likely to show addictions, sexual deviations or brain syndromes.

Age

Careful study has shown that the peak for neuroses and personality disorders comes in adolescence. Psychoses and alcoholism peak during middle age, while brain syndromes reach a maximum in old age.

Marital Status

Abnormal personality patterns occur with the greatest frequency for divorced or separated persons. Single persons are found to be next highest, followed by widowed persons, with married people showing the lowest frequency.

Social Class

A summary of a number of studies has shown that the lower the designated social class, the higher the rate of serious abnormal personality patterns. This may be because the stress of being in the lower social classes leads to abnormal behavior or because patterns of abnormal behavior lead the person to become part of a lower social class. Furthermore, behaviors tolerated in an upper class may be considered abnormal in a lower class.

Ethnic Group

Little or no difference has been found when comparing

different ethnic groups for incidence of abnormal personality patterns. There is no established evidence to indicate that membership in a particular ethnic or racial group leads to a higher rate of abnormality than membership in any other group. However, the specific symptoms of abnormal behaviors may vary considerably from one ethnic group to another.

CHAPTER 16

Therapies

Psychologists have been interested not only in the identification or diagnosis of the abnormal personality patterns we looked at in the preceding chapter, but also in trying to develop techniques to treat these problem behaviors. Before the late nineteenth century people with emotional problems were thought to be possessed by the devil, cursed by God, suffering a character defect or in some way diseased.

The major breakthrough in treatment came at the turn of the century, when Freud developed the psychoanalytic method for helping his patients who suffered from hysterical ailments. This laid the foundation for what is now called psychotherapy, the application of psychological principles to the treatment of behavior disorders. This chapter discusses some of the medical therapies and psychotherapies that have been developed.

Types of Therapists

The overall purpose of therapy is to try to help individuals overcome problems such as those described in Chapter 15. The term does not in itself describe the training, licensing, or orientation of the professional being seen for help. There are a number of different types of therapists, each from a different professional background and with different orientation and training. Probably the best known are psychiatrists and clinical psychologists.

Psychiatrists are medical doctors who have usually had advanced training in the use of drugs, diagnosis, and treatment. They can prescribe medication, hospitalize those in their care, and perform shock therapy.

Clinical psychologists usually obtain a Ph.D. along with specialized training in therapy techniques. They are required to undergo an internship, usually in a mental hospital, where they work under close supervision. *Social workers* usually have an M.S.W. or D.S.W. (master's or doctorate in social work) and have completed an internship, often in an agency setting, which qualifies them to work with individual therapy clients.

Other types of therapists include *psychoanalysts* (usually psychiatrists, psychologists or social workers with advanced training in Freudian or modern psychoanalytic techniques), *psychiatric nurses, licensed professional counselors, marriage and family therapists*, and some *paraprofessional personnel*. (Paraprofessionals are often volunteers with limited training who may work for organizations such as crisis intervention centers.)

Therapy Effectiveness

The effectiveness of therapy techniques has been debated vigorously. There are basically three difficulties in establishing estimates of the effectiveness of therapy techniques:

1. *Biases.* The data collection techniques in therapy are

especially subject to biases, including what is recorded in the case history and what criteria are used for interpreting that information.

2. *Spontaneous Remission.* Some people simply recover from abnormal personality patterns without any therapy.

3. *Placebo Effect.* Comparable to the phenomenon in medicine, there is sometimes a placebo effect in therapy situations. This occurs when the client approaches the therapy situation with such energy and determination that virtually any style of therapy would effect a cure.

Medical Therapies

Physical procedures used to treat abnormal personality problems are called medical therapies, or somatic therapies. Two of these, electroconvulsive shock therapy and pharmacological therapy, are used fairly frequently. A third, psychosurgery, was once used much more extensively, but is no longer in favor.

Electroconvulsive Shock Therapy

Electroconvulsive shock therapy (ECT) involves administering a sedative and muscle relaxant, then tightly strapping the patient to a table, placing electrodes on either side of the head, and passing a brief, high-intensity electric current through the brain. This causes immediate unconsciousness, followed by repetitive controlled convulsions.

ECT seems to overstimulate the brain, but there is no subsequent memory either of the events leading up to the treatment or of the actual administration of the shock. Upon regaining consciousness, the patient will remain in a docile or passive state for several days. Because of this, ECT has sometimes been used simply as a way of making patients more manageable, although a more appropriate and quite successful application has been its use in helping depressive patients obtain relief from their symptoms.

While ECT is not used with great frequency, certain types of behavioral symptoms may prompt psychiatrists to choose this technique. Probably the most common case is the psychotic depressive who is contemplating suicide; in such a case, there is an immediate need for a behavioral change if the person's death is to be prevented. It should be emphasized, however, that ECT is typically employed *only* when other types of therapy have been tried unsuccessfully.

Pharmacological Therapy

The most prevalent of medical therapies today is pharmacological therapy (sometimes called drug therapy); the use of drugs to change brain chemistry and, as a result, to modify abnormal or maladaptive behavior patterns, such as depression. Two advantages of pharmacological therapy are set forth by its proponents: (1) there is no hospitalization and recovery required (as in ECT or psychosurgery); and (2) the person allegedly can be made more open to therapeutic influence.

Today, a large number of drugs designed specifically for psychological problems are available. They are known collectively as *psychotropic drugs*. The three major classes of these drugs are antipsychotics (major tranquilizers), antidepressants, and antianxiety compounds (minor tranquilizers).

Antipsychotic Drugs

A tranquilizer is a drug that makes a person feel calm, or tranquil. A distinction is made between the major and minor tranquilizers according to the power of the drug to reduce anxiety or stress. The major tranquilizers are called antipsychotic drugs, since they do more than calm a patient; they actually alleviate many of the psychotic symptoms.

Most of these antipsychotic drugs are from the phenothiazine family of drugs. The trade names of the most commonly prescribed phenothiazines are Thorazine (chlorpromazine), Mellaril (thioridazine), Stelazine (trifluoperazine), and Prolixin (fluphenazine). Haldol (haloperidol), a nonphenothiazine, is also widely used now in the treatment of psychotic disorders. All these medications have been particularly helpful in permitting the early release of patients from mental hospitals. But they have a number of side effects, such as twitches, tremors, irritability, and sleepiness—and therefore require constant patient-monitoring by a physician.

Antidepressant Drugs

Antidepressant drugs are used in the long-term treatment of severely depressed individuals. There are two main groups of antidepressants: monoamine oxidase inhibitors and the tricyclics.

Monoamine Oxidase Inhibitors (MAOI). These drugs inhibit the actions of certain enzymes in the brain that are believed to be related to depression. Medications of this class include Marplan (isocarboxazid), Nardil (phenelzine), and Parnate (tranylcypromine). But since these drugs can produce serious side effects and require constant dietary regulation, they are less frequently used than the second group of antidepressants.

The Tricyclics. The second group of antidepressant drugs comprises the tricyclics: Elavil (amitriptyline), Tofranil (imipramine), Desyrel (trazodone), Asendin (amoxapine), and Ludiomil (maprotiline). These drugs are considerably safer and more generally effective than the MAOIs. But they take several weeks to begin working and are erratic in their rate of effectiveness. They are typically prescribed for people whose lingering depression leads to sleep loss, nervousness, weight loss or inability to function in some area of living.

Lithium Carbonate. In addition to these antidepressants,

lithium carbonate has come into use in the treatment of manic-depressive (bipolar affective) disorder. While lithium is not effective in treating unipolar depressions, it has been proven effective in the treatment of specific manic-depressive disorders.

Antianxiety Drugs

Antianxiety drugs are less powerful than the antipsychotics. There are two classes of these: the *meprobamate drugs* (Miltown and Equanil) and the *benzodiazepines,* which include Valium (diazepam), Librium (chlordiazepoxide), Tranxene (chlorazepate), and Dalmane (flurazepam). Valium is the most widely prescribed psychotropic drug in the United States, and the problem of Valium abuse, and abuse of benzodiazepines in general, has been growing rapidly.

Cautions in Drug Therapy

Several cautions are appropriate at this point: While pharmacological therapy may relieve symptoms of abnormal personality patterns, this relief may last only as long as the medication continues. Once the medication is stopped, the symptoms may return. Additionally, the individual may become psychologically dependent upon the drugs. In many cases, it may be important to see to it that other forms of therapy accompany pharmacological therapy if an eventual cure is to be expected.

Psychosurgery

Psychosurgery refers to any technique that involves surgical destruction of brain tissue. Such surgery is performed with the hope of modifying severely abnormal behavior patterns. Probably the best known of these techniques is the *lobotomy*, where the neural tissues connecting the prefrontal lobes to the rest of the brain are severed. This technique has proved only partially successful in reducing abnormal behavioral patterns and sometimes caused the patient to become confused and unresponsive. In some cases, it has even resulted in seizures or death, and has thus fallen from favor as a therapeutic technique.

Psychotherapies

Psychotherapies are nonmedical techniques used to try to help a client or patient overcome a problem or problems. There are several different types of psychotherapy, but the concept of psychotherapy can probably be viewed as originating from the work of Sigmund Freud. His view that people can solve their problems by talking about them originally caused him to refer to psychoanalysis as "the talking cure." While many of the early principles of psychoanalytic therapy are not widely ascribed to today because they are considered clinically ineffective, there is no question that its method and theory have influenced the development of many other, more modern, therapies, which are considered more effective treatments.

The aims of psychotherapy vary with each and every case. It is probably safe to say that all psychotherapy has as its overall aim helping the client overcome a particular problem or problems. But the types of problems vary considerably. For example, abnormal personal frustrations, motivational conflicts, maladaptive personality patterns or current living situations may all be dealt with in the course of psychotherapy. Clearly one does not need to have a seriously abnormal personality pattern to encounter these problems.

Psychoanalysis

The foundation principles of psychoanalysis were developed by Sigmund Freud, who believed it is the therapist's responsibility to listen to the patient with "evenly divided attention," that is, with a neutral and calm interest. The psychoanalyst is looking for unconscious conflicts, below the surface level of the patient's awareness. The analyst then interprets to the patient his or her unconscious conflicts and defenses.

Free Association

A major aspect of psychoanalysis is the process of free association. Free association is a technique in which the client lets each thought lead to the next without restriction. The purpose of free association is to get the client to consider all the different factors that might be creating problems. Speaking what comes to mind, without forethought, is supposed to facilitate the release of information from the unconscious. It is hoped that the person will express to the psychoanalyst even those things that seem objectionable or irrelevant, and thus reveal fears or conflicts that cannot be reached through ordinary rational discourse.

Transference

As the therapy progresses, the client often demonstrates what Freud called transference, the development of an emotional relationship with the therapist. Freud believed this relationship represents a reenactment of the association the person had with a parent while a child. He also argued that ultimately the patient would be cured by working out his or her underlying infantile problems through the transference relationship. As the client develops trust in the therapist, it becomes possible to explore more and more of the conflicts that have created the problem. The therapist directs the sessions to try to encourage the person to recognize and evaluate these conflicts.

Resistance

Resistances interfere with the smooth progress of the therapy at every juncture. Freud defined resistance as anything that prevents the patient from gaining access to his or her unconscious. Resistance can take a variety of forms, including failure to appear for sessions, refusing to speak, or forgetting. One of the main tasks of the analyst is to analyze and resolve resistances so that they no longer impede the course of treatment.

Dream Analysis

Freud felt that one way of generating ideas and exploring desires within the therapy setting is dream analysis. He maintained that dreams represent thoughts and wishes the patient holds but is unable to express consciously. Often, even the content of the dream does not express the message directly, but rather through symbolic representation. The patient must recount the dreams to the therapist for analysis and interpretation. The material reported by the dreamer is called the *manifest dream content*; the underlying meaning of the dream is the *latent dream content*.

Wish Fulfillment

To understand the latent meaning of the dream, Freud held, the analyst must be familiar with the symbolic language of the unconscious, as well as with the patient's past experiences and ways of perceiving and reacting. If the dream symbols can be correctly interpreted, they reveal particular urges that the person would hope, at least on the unconscious level, to fulfill. Accomplishing symbolically in dreams what cannot be accomplished in actual behavior is referred to as wish fulfillment. These wishes are often in direct conflict with conscious thoughts and wishes (for example, the unconscious wish to murder a loved one would not be acceptable to the conscious mind).

Freudian Slips

Another source of clues to the unconscious was referred to by Freud collectively as the psychopathology of everyday life. By this, he meant the slips of the tongue and other lapses in normal behavior, such as coming early or late for appointments, forgetting possessions or carrying items away from the doctor's office. These small variations, for which the observant analyst is always on the lookout, give important clues about the client's unconscious needs, wishes, and conflicts. We sometimes refer to these daily errors, especially slips of the tongue, as "Freudian slips."

Adlerian Therapy

Alfred Adler, a colleague of Freud's, broke away from the psychoanalytic circle to develop and popularize his own form of treatment, known as Adlerian psychology, or individual psychology.

Style of Life

Central to understanding Adler's psychotherapeutic orientation is the concept of life-style or, style of life. The term refers to an individual's organized patterns, themes, behaviors, and orientations that are organically expressed (as a total pattern) through his or her life activities.

Each person, according to Adler, has a unique life-style that enables him or her to compensate for inferiority feelings and to strive toward superiority. For one individual, the style of life may be centered around aggressive, manipulative, and exploitative experiences, through which he or she takes advantage of others. This is that person's characteristic style of striving for superiority. For another person, the style of life may be centered around intellectual and social achievement: working toward attaining superiority through the application of intellectual and social skills. Still another person's style of life may be centered around the acquisition of large sums of money or other possessions.

Social Interest

Adler's view of the client, in contrast to Freud's, emphasizes the individual's social nature and the influence of the social environment on development. Adler viewed human behavior as being motivated not primarily by unconscious sexual drives, but rather by a mix of inborn social strivings, which he called social interest. Throughout his writings, Adler suggested that the healthy individual is able to act in a way that is both socially productive and, at the same time, personally fulfilling.

Ordinal Position

A child's position within the family is also central in understanding the forces that shape us into what we ultimately become. Birth order, or ordinal position, means more than simply the numerical order of birth; it refers, rather, to the psychological position of the child in the family constellation. For example, two siblings whose births are separated by many years may both be raised as oldest children. To the Adlerian therapist, the client's ordinal position offers an insight into the forces that helped shape him or her.

Private Logic

Adler's concept of private logic includes a person's logical assumptions and his or her logical processes of reasoning. If either is wildly distorted or out of synch with the rest of the world, some therapeutic intervention is required to correct it. The therapist, by using the client's private logic, helps establish rapport between them because the client feels understood and accepted by the therapist.

Jung's Analytical Psychotherapy

Carl Gustav Jung, the Swiss psychiatrist who was an early supporter and close friend of Freud's, also broke ranks with him to begin his own movement, which is called Analytical Psychology. Jung, like Adler, believed that Freud placed too much emphasis on sexuality. While he was in agreement with many of Adler's points, he differed from Adler on crucial issues, and in place of the Adlerian concepts discussed above, focussed on man's immediate conflicts and his "will to live." Jung opposed much of the rigid Freudian world view, and in its place offered a more flexible view of the individual.

Introversion and Extraversion

Jung contributed a number of original concepts for which he earned fame. He established the personality categories of introversion and extraversion (Jung's spelling), distinguishing between a person who is primarily concerned with his or her own inner world (an introvert) and one who is concerned with outside objects and people (an extravert). He also originated the widely used phrase "a complex" to describe emotionally charged thoughts and belief systems.

Archetypes and the Collective Unconscious

Jung rejected Freud's assumption of a single unconscious, arguing instead that we have two: a personal unconscious and a transpersonal (also called collective) unconscious. The personal unconscious closely resembles Freud's version, consisting of everything that has been repressed during one's development. The collective unconscious, Jung's unique contribution to the theory of psychoanalysis, consists of archetypes—inborn categories derived from the cumulative experiences of the human race.

These categories, which influence and help shape our behavior, perceptions, thoughts, and feelings, are not directly accessible to our consciousness, but appear indirectly and symbolically through the recurring symbols of mythology, folklore, and art. For example, the ideas of a God, of a Hero, of Unity, of the Wise Old Man, are recurrent symbols throughout human history. Although they assume different forms during different cultural ages and take on different manifestations in each person's life, they have consistently appeared in the literature and mythologies of all people throughout the world in all ages.

All of us, Jung suggested, have both masculine and feminine characteristics. Thus, two other important archetypes are the *anima*, the feminine aspect of a man, and the *animus*, the masculine aspect of a woman. Both exist in the collective unconscious and motivate individuals to understand and respond to individuals of the opposite sex. Another important archetype is the *shadow*, the animal instinct that human beings inherit from lower forms of life. It is responsible for our baser thoughts as well as for many of our creative impulses. Finally, the *persona* (from the Greek word for "mask"), the role that a person plays in society, stems from the human social role that has evolved throughout the ages. It consists of those aspects of personality that we show to the world, in contrast to our real, private personality.

There is no formal theory of Jungian therapy. Rather, the process consists of a dynamic and vital interchange between therapist and patient, in which sharing of ideas holds equal importance with the sharing of feelings. This interchange may involve interpreting dreams or looking at the past, but the content is rarely as important as the process of exploration. The goal of this interchange is to bring forth the unconscious mind, in all of its historical, social, intellectual, and emotional dimensions.

Client-Centered Therapy

Another approach to psychotherapy is called client-centered therapy (sometimes referred to as nondirective or Rogerian therapy or counseling) developed by an American psychologist, Carl R. Rogers. The basic principles of this therapeutic approach are that (1) people are basically good inside and are capable of healing themselves and directing their own lives; (2) therapy should be nondirective and nonjudgmental, with the therapist creating an atmosphere that allows the client to grow; (3) emphasis should be on the client, who alone determines the direction of change and the course of the treatment; and (4) in the process of helping the client grow, the client-centered therapist relies primarily on the personal quality of the therapeutic relationship rather than on any specific techniques.

In all his writings, Rogers emphasized the quality of the therapy relationship as the core of therapy. He rejected the notion that the client is sick; for this reason, he preferred the term "client" to "patient." Rogers carefully enumerated the characteristics of the therapist, whom he referred to as the "facilitator." Most important are empathy, unconditional positive regard, and genuineness. *Empathy* is the ability to get into the client's skin, to experience reality as the client is experiencing it. *Unconditional positive regard* is the quality of accepting one's clients as they are and for what they are. *Genuineness,* or authenticity, is the honesty, the willingness of the therapist to give of himself, the stripping away of pretense. It is through the communication of these important qualities to the client, not through any specific techniques, that the client is encouraged and helped to grow.

The client-centered therapist deals with what the client is experiencing here and now. The therapist does not try to get the client to look back into the past or to bring up childhood memories. The focus is on the present. Nor does the therapist attempt to interpret what the client says; instead, the therapist follows the lead of the client and provides love, understanding, acceptance, warmth, and respect.

Gestalt Therapy

Gestalt therapy is based on the idea that the personality must be treated as an organized whole. The emphasis in Gestalt therapy is on the way in which we divide and organize our perceptual field—that is, the many perceptions that confront us at any given moment. From the Gestalt point of view, we organize all these perceptions into figure and ground; in other words, into experiences that are in the focus of awareness and those that are kept in the background.

In practice, Gestalt therapists are extremely flexible in the techniques they use. Fritz Perls, the founder of the Gestalt therapy movement, saw techniques as "gimmicks"—contrivances to help the client better organize his perceptions and live more comfortably in the world.

The Gestalt therapy client is made to experience everything rather than just speak about it. For example, if a person is discussing feelings about his parents, the Gestalt therapist may ask him to imagine that his mother or father is seated in a chair across the room and encourage him to direct his statement to the imaginary figure. Gestalt techniques are designed to direct clients to their current problems and focus their attention on the here and now.

Cognitive Therapy

The basic assumption in cognitive therapy is that each client's primary problem has to do with his or her construction of reality. Individuals, in growing up, develop distorted views of the connections between themselves and the environment. These distortions extend to the way they feel about themselves and the way they take in and process information from the outside world. In order to function appropriately, one should perceive the world and one's relationship with it in a manner that is consistent with the responses one is likely to get to one's actions.

The cognitive therapist integrates a variety of techniques designed to help the client develop better cognitive (thinking) skills, leading to thinking that is realistic and that constructively supports healthy emotional states. Cognitive therapists are primarily concerned with how clients think about their problems. Techniques are aimed at changing thoughts and ways of processing information, often to promote more effective problem solving. These may include homework assignments, readings, role playing, and measuring and reinforcing the client's healthy thoughts and behaviors.

Cognitive-Behavioral Therapy

One popular form of cognitive therapy is cognitive-behavioral therapy, which, as the name implies, combines cognitive techniques with principles from behavior modification (described below). This may involve *cognitive restructuring,* in which old thoughts are examined, changed, and/or discarded; *stress inoculation,* which a person conditions him- or herself not to react physiologically or psychologically to stressors; or *rational-emotive therapy,* in which illogical thoughts are challenged and the irrational "propaganda" from one's past is scrutinized critically by one's present intellectual capacities. In all these cases, false beliefs are challenged by rational evidence, and maladaptive behaviors are changed by reinforcement.

Effectiveness of Cognitive Therapies

There is considerable evidence supporting the effectiveness of the cognitive and cognitive-behavioral approaches, especially for the treatment of depression and phobias. There have also been a number of serious efforts at working with schizophrenics, but at this time there has not been enough research to conclude if these are effective.

Play Therapy

Play therapy, which is used with children, involves creating a permissive and accepting atmosphere in which the child can play with toys, dolls, puppets, art supplies or other kinds of equipment. Such therapy gives the therapist an opportunity to observe behaviors that might not be expressed by the child under ordinary circumstances. The permissiveness of the therapy setting is thus supposed to encourage the child to express, both verbally and nonverbally, attitudes that might otherwise remain unexpressed.

Play therapy may be oriented toward the psychoanalytic, behavioral, Gestalt, or client-centered approach. In any case, the course of play therapy generally includes three states: play, play and talk, and talk. During the first stage, the child is usually shown the toys in the treatment room and is then left on his or her own. The child's behavior in playing with these toys is observed by the therapist, but little or no attempt is made to make the child speak. In this stage, the therapist learns about the child, and the child begins to feel comfortable in the treatment setting.

During the second stage, the therapist encourages talk to accompany the play. This helps the child learn to express himself or herself verbally at his or her own pace. During the final stage, the child will mainly talk about his or her problems, expressing them only in part through symbolic play activities. Thus, the child goes from indirect symbolic expression to direct expression of feelings through talking.

Group Therapy

In group therapy, more than one client is involved in the therapy setting at the same time. The belief supporting such a therapy technique is that the group provides a social setting where resolution of problems first developed in a social setting may be achieved.

A traditional therapy group is one that applies the methods of individual psychotherapy, with appropriate modifications, in the group setting. Its purpose is to help individuals resolve their emotional problems not in isolation with a therapist, but among other people who may have similar problems, or who may at least be able to share some of their problem-solving experiences.

Groups may be made up of several individuals from different backgrounds, or they may, in some cases, be members of one family. Some groups, called *encounter groups,* consist of people who do not necessarily show abnormal personality patterns but who have chosen to meet together to attempt to increase awareness and achieve self-actualization or personal growth.

Behavior Modification Therapies

Based upon the principles developed in the study of learning, behavior modification techniques try to deal directly with the symptoms of abnormal personality patterns. If personality disturbances are learned forms of behavior, this theory states, it stands to reason that they can be modified or eliminated through new learning.

Behavior therapy, then, is based on the application of the principles of learning to neurotic problems. Several different approaches have been developed, all with the common theme of changing an individual's behavior (or response pattern) without delving into the deep, underlying causes. Behavior modification therapies employ a variety of ways to strengthen positive (that is, desired) behaviors while weakening or eliminating undesirable behaviors.

Operant Conditioning Techniques

One way to change a person's behavior patterns is to concentrate on reinforcing responses that are appropriate and that lead to desirable goals, while at the same time attempting to extinguish maladaptive responses (a procedure called extinction). To do this, it is necessary to have a very consistent reinforcement pattern, because even an occasional reinforcement for the maladaptive response may make the response very resistant to extinction. (This is because of the partial reinforcement effect; see Chapter 9.)

One application of operant conditioning in behavior modification is called a *token economy*. In this technique, used mostly in school classrooms, hospitals, prisons, and other institutional settings, participants are able to earn tokens (poker chips, tickets, and so on) that, when accumulated, can be traded in for privileges or rewards. The tokens are awarded for adaptive responses and withheld when maladaptive patterns are shown.

The sophistication of a token economy may advance with the increasing abilities shown by the individual. At first, tokens (and eventually rewards) may be given for behaviors as simple as maintaining personal cleanliness, caring for one's possessions or showing good manners toward others in the setting. As these are achieved, they will continue to be reinforced, but additional responses may be added to the behavior repertoire. For example, rewards may be given for the acquisition of job skills. Eventually, it is hoped, the person will be able to return to normal functioning.

Classical Conditioning Techniques

The classical conditioning model of learning is also used in behavior modification therapy. A correcting experience (serving as an unconditioned stimulus) may be paired with a conditioned stimulus that appears to provoke maladaptive responses. The UCS experiences may be pleasant or unpleasant (positive or aversive), depending upon the type of behavior modification being attempted.

Systematic Desensitization

At the heart of systematic desensitization is the principle of *reciprocal inhibition*, which means that a person cannot make two incompatible responses at the same time; for example, a person who is relaxed cannot also be anxious at the same time.

Systematic desensitization relies upon the pairing of relaxation (a positive experience) with various forms of the anxiety-producing situation. This step-by-step procedure, or hierarchy of stimuli, is designed so that each CS used comes closer to the one that is most anxiety-provoking. The therapist's task is to monitor each experience, providing effective relaxation cues and maintaining a moderate pace through the hierarchy.

If, for example, a client has an intense, compelling fear of the dark, systematic desensitization may be used to help overcome this irrational fear. At first, the person may be asked to read stories about or descriptions of dark places. While this occurs, he or she is reassured and helped to experience relaxation. Successive steps following this might include observing a movie about people going into caves, then actually seeing someone else in a dark room, and finally entering a dark room. Each step would pair relaxation (the new UCS) with images or experiences of the dark (the CS), until the person is able to confront the dark without experiencing intense anxiety.

A different version of confronting the anxiety-provoking stimulus occurs in *implosion therapy*. The client is asked to imagine the very worst possible version of the anxiety-provoking stimulus and to experience all the attendant anxiety. However, this is done in a totally reassuring environment, and the client is made to see that the imagined anxiety cannot hurt.

Aversion Therapy

Aversion therapy is a behavior modification technique used on clients showing self-destructive behaviors. Like systematic desensitization, aversion therapy uses the principle of reciprocal inhibition. Here, however, the therapist pairs painful or unpleasant stimuli as unconditioned stimuli in the situations that induce the maladaptive behavior. The person learns that responding in a self-destructive manner will lead to aversive stimuli, and so the frequency of such responses decreases.

Modeling Techniques

The basic principles of learning by modeling can also be used in behavior modification therapy. By observing someone who is coping successfully with the anxiety-producing situation, the client can discover and perhaps imitate responses that will be adaptive in that situation. It may not be necessary for the client to perform in any particular way in order to learn from modeling; merely observing the model's behavior is often sufficient.

In its most obvious form, modeling is learning by example. If the example is a positive one, then positive behavior will be the likely outcome. For example, a young boy who is afraid of cats can be given the opportunity to observe a model (the therapist) handling a cat and petting and playing with it with no fear. The belief is that the boy will learn simply by watching this behavior. He should be more able to cope with cats by having seen what kinds of successful responses toward cats can be made.

Biofeedback Techniques

Biofeedback uses monitoring devices to provide information to a person about physiological events within his or her own body (such as skin temperature, galvanic skin resistance, pulse rate) that would otherwise be difficult or impossible to recognize. Biofeedback therapy uses that information to help the person learn to control bodily processes, and thus overcome or avoid some problem. Biofeedback therapy may be very helpful in situations involving conversion reactions or psychosomatic disorders.

Therapists using biofeedback procedures have claimed that appropriate monitoring and learned physiological control can help alleviate many physiological problems. One example of this is the treatment of "tension headaches." Chronic sufferers are able to observe feedback from neck and shoulder muscles, learn how to relax these muscles, and thus reduce the tension that appears to contribute to headaches.

Assertiveness Training

Some persons come to a therapist because they recognize they are timid or withdrawn and they wish to change that pattern of responding. While such behavior often would not be called abnormal, the people see it as a problem to be overcome. Assertiveness training, which frequently uses operant conditioning, classical conditioning, and modeling in combination, helps the clients learn how to express emotions and beliefs in a more forthright and confident manner.

Ethical Issues

Although ethical issues pose challenges to professionals in all areas today, they are even more challenging in the psychotherapy field for two reasons. First, because therapists not only advise and guide, but also become intimately involved in their clients' lives, at least in an emotional sense, there are far more opportunities for abuse and exploitation than would be found, for example, in an accountant-client or attorney-client relationship. Whether we call it transference, countertransference, or empathy, there is little question that many clients form powerful attachments to their therapists, and sometimes vice versa.

Second, people's expectations, attitudes, and beliefs about psychotherapy have changed drastically over the past two decades. Now, clients are raising ethical issues that were rarely raised before. These include questions about how well the process works in relation to its expense, the qualifications of the practitioner, safety, alternative treatment plans, and other consumer issues.

Two issues of special concern are confidentiality and sexual contact.

Confidentiality

Most people who enter a therapy relationship, where they know they will be speaking freely about themselves and others in their lives, expect confidentiality. While there are certain instances where this may be broken, the central ethical question is under what circumstances and how. If a client, for example, tells the therapist his plan to kill his ex-wife, to whom does the therapist have a responsibility—the client or the ex-wife? What are the therapist's legal and ethical obligations? Is it only talk or is it a prelude to action? Professional organizations, such as the American Psychiatric Association, American Association for Counseling and Development, and the American Psychological Association, have rules regarding specific cases and how the therapist should (or should not) act.

Sexual Contact

There is now universal agreement (at least by all professional associations) that sexual contact between therapist and client is detrimental to treatment. How should therapists who break this rule be disciplined? If one therapist learns of another who has broken this rule, what are the obligations to report? To whom? These questions are debated forcefully as malpractice insurance rates rise, reflecting the increase in accusations against therapists, especially by their clients and former clients.

CHAPTER 17

Attitude Formation

A major aspect of social psychology is the study of attitudes, which are learned evaluative reactions to objects, events, and other stimuli. An attitude may be defined as a relatively enduring tendency to respond consistently to an object, person or event in either a favorable or unfavorable way.

Attitudes are often categorized according to their level of complexity. A set opinion that can be identified in something like "yes/no" or "good/bad" terms is called a simple attitude. Attitudes that involve several reactions are called multiple or complex attitudes.

This chapter examines the ways in which attitudes are formed, how they are measured, what influences their development, and how they can be changed. It also looks at interpersonal attraction and prejudice as two areas of concern in which the psychology of attitudes has shed light on many complex situations.

Components of Attitudes

To say that an attitude is a learned, evaluative reaction to a stimulus only partially explains the concept. Attitudes have different components that combine to create the overall reaction a person may have to the stimulus. Three components that have been identified and studied are the affective component, cognitive component, and conative component.

Affective Component

The affective component of an attitude is the feeling or emotional reaction the individual has toward the stimulus. Affective reactions may be positive or negative. Moreover, although two people may have favorable attitudes toward an issue, they may have different intensity of feelings. Debbie may be emotionally involved with the question of promoting a healthful environment, feeling very positively toward all those who favor pollution control legislation and feeling deep anger at those who oppose it. Jane, on the other hand, may also favor clean air and healthful living conditions but without becoming angry every time a law fails to achieve passage. Both Jane and Debbie demonstrate the same attitude, but with substantially different affective components.

Cognitive Component

The cognitive component of an attitude refers to the beliefs the individual holds about the stimulus object. These beliefs are essentially the acceptance of some conclusion about the stimulus.

Our beliefs about a particular issue may be based on a great many facts or we may have only minimal knowledge about it. Say we are in favor of environmental protection. The cognitive aspect of this attitude includes our belief that air pollution is harmful to our health and that clean-air laws can reduce air pollution. It may also include a host of other facts and a wealth of detail on cigarette smoke, automobile exhaust, and industrial pollutants. But a person may hold this attitude without knowing these facts. For example, Bruce may be strongly in favor of clean-air legislation because his girlfriend Betty is active in the movement and has encouraged his beliefs. But Bruce's attitudes may not include much knowledge about the issues and facts.

Conative Component

The behavioral tendencies toward the stimulus are called the conative component of an attitude. This aspect describes the actions, either favorable or unfavorable, that the person may take toward the stimulus.

The stimulus in question need not be a tangible or visible one, such as a person, group of people or institution. It may be an abstract stimulus such as the idea of education. It is very possible a person could develop a positive feeling toward education (affective component) based on the belief that everyone can benefit from education (cognitive component). Such a person might very well make a contribution to a local educational institution (conative component).

This example pictures a favorable reaction to or attitude about education. It should be recognized, however, that others may hold exactly opposite attitudes, involving a negative feeling, no belief in the benefits of education, and actions that would work against an educational institution. Both types of attitudes would be learned, evaluative reactions to the stimulus.

Relationship of the Three Components

How closely are these three attitudinal components related to each other? The bulk of research indicates that there is a high degree of consistency among the three elements of a person's attitude toward a single object. It has also been found that consistency is greatest when the person's attitude is extreme. The person who is extremely prejudiced, who feels hatred toward a minority group, is very likely to have negative beliefs and feelings about members of the group and to take aggressive measures against them.

Theories of Attitude Formation

Many aspects of attitudes have been studied extensively. Two that seem to apply quite generally to many different attitude situations are exposure to the stimulus and cognitive dissonance theory.

Exposure to the Stimulus

A number of studies of attitudes have shown that repeated exposure of the person to a given stimulus will usually lead to a more favorable reaction to that stimulus. However, researchers recognize that people select, to a large extent, the stimuli to which they are exposed. This phenomenon is referred to as *selective exposure*. In other words, we can usually choose what we want to see and hear.

Cognitive Dissonance Theory

It is possible to feel two different ways about one stimulus. Cognitive dissonance is the feeling of discomfort that an individual has when he or she holds two cognitions that are psychologically inconsistent with one another. For instance, if you smoke a pack of cigarettes a day and have read the reports that smoking causes lung cancer, you may experience dissonance because of the two cognitions "I enjoy smoking cigarettes" and "Smoking causes cancer and I don't want to get cancer." This dissonance is a very uncomfortable feeling, which should motivate a person to reduce or eliminate it. One can reduce the dissonance in more than one way: by giving up smoking, by belittling the medical evidence, by switching to a low-tar cigarette or by arguing that you could get hit by a car and die tomorrow even if you didn't smoke, to suggest just a few.

Suppose Valerie has had a great desire to attend a rock concert in a city about 90 miles from her home. She has worked extra hours to save enough money to be able to afford the ticket, transportation, and time off from her job. Finally, the night of the show arrives. However, the featured group is late, plays poorly, and uses a bad sound system. Furthermore, the weather is rotten. Valerie is now quite disappointed.

The next day, when she is asked if the show was worth all the effort she put in to go see it, Valerie answers by saying that the show really wasn't great but it really wasn't that bad either; and besides, she really hadn't made such a special effort to be able to see it. Her playing up of the show's merits coupled with her playing down of her extra labors may be viewed as an attempt to reduce cognitive dissonance. To admit that the show was poor would mean that it wasn't worth much effort. Therefore, Valerie reinterprets her previous behaviors to fit better with the result.

Forced Compliance

One interesting effect of cognitive dissonance is accounted for in a theory known as forced compliance. This theory states that conflict between one's public and private beliefs creates dissonance and leads to attitude change. In other words, if a conservative person is forced to assume a liberal position over a period of time (let us say to get elected from a liberal district), there will be a shift in the person's attitudes in the liberal direction. The theory makes another prediction, however, which on its face seems illogical. It states that the greater the reward used to induce people to advocate a public position that is discrepant from their true beliefs, the less dissonance is aroused and, therefore, the less likely they will be to shift their private attitudes.

Experiments designed to test this theory involved paying students either a small amount of money or a large amount of money to give a speech arguing a position contrary to their own personal beliefs and opinions. It was found that the greater the reward for speaking out publicly against one's own beliefs, the less influence the public speaking had on changing one's beliefs. This is explained in the following way: The person receiving a small award cannot personally justify the public behavior, so to resolve the dissonance he or she begins to reassess and change the beliefs. The person receiving a large reward, on the other hand, can justify the hypocrisy more easily because of the magnitude of the reward, and therefore experiences less dissonance and, hence, less need to change his or her beliefs.

Measurement of Attitudes

Two means of measuring attitudes are used more often than other techniques: public opinion polls and attitude scales.

Public Opinion Polls

Public opinion polls usually ask one or only a few questions on any given topic. They are given to a sample of people taken from the general population. The questions are worded to try to avoid eliciting a biased response, and answers are usually of the simple "yes/no" or "agree/disagree/no opinion" type.

Polls are usually used to measure attitudes of whole populations rather than of small groups. By a population, we mean all people in a particular category, such as college students, all farmers, or people over 65. Of course, the polls do not contact every member of the population; instead, they test a sample, which is a small, representative selection of the total group. If the sample is carefully chosen, the responses from a relatively small number of people can be generalized from the sample to the whole population. Techniques of sampling are discussed in Chapter 2. However, two methods that are particularly applicable to attitude measurement are quota sampling and area sampling. (Quota sampling is a form of stratified sampling discussed in Chapter 2.)

Quota Sampling

With quota sampling, different attributes of the population are represented in the sample in proportion to their numbers in the population at large. Some of the bases for such a sampling are age, sex, social class, income, religious affiliation or educational attainment. For example, if education were used as the criterion, the sample would include a proportionately large number of elementary and high school graduates, a smaller number of college graduates, and an even smaller percentage of people with postgraduate degrees. Within each category, the individuals in the sample would be selected on a random basis.

Area Sampling

Area sampling is random sampling of a specific geographic area. Here, candidates for the sample are chosen on the basis of place of residence. If a person is not at home, the interviewer must go back until he or she is contacted. No substitutes may be interviewed.

Accuracy

Because many precautions are now being taken in sampling, public opinion surveys are becoming more accurate. A margin of error is always allowed for, because people do change their minds at the last minute. Widespread use of this tool not only by political candidates and the press but also by large corporations and public interest groups, as well as branches of the government, is making available more and more information about the beliefs and attitudes of our citizens.

Attitude Scales

The other frequently used measurement technique is the attitude scale. Subjects are presented with a group of statements that have been standardized on a large sample (see Chapter 2) and asked to indicate agreement or disagreement (or sometimes the degree of agreement) to each of the stimuli.

A person's attitudes toward various professions, for example, may be determined by using an attitude scale, which often makes use of comparison statements like the following: "A doctor has more prestige than a lawyer," or "A nurse has less prestige than a secretary." A tally of the agreements and disagreements with these statements would allow the investigator to create a hierarchy of prestige for the professions compared.

Development of Attitudes

Our attitudes are learned in two ways: directly, through contact with the attitudinal object, on the basis of one experience or many, or indirectly, through contact with others who hold these attitudes and who influence our thinking. These social influences include our parents, our peers, the educational system, and the mass media of communication. Some of the most important aspects of these social influences will be discussed here.

Parental Influence

For young children, parents are by far the most important source of attitudes. The parents' own attitudes and the reinforcements they give to the child for reacting in certain ways are extremely influential on the child. In general, as the child grows older, this influence becomes less and less important as other influences (as well as the child's increased reasoning abilities) take over.

What happens if a person is a member of a family or group with which he or she does not identify, whose values he or she does not share? This individual may appear to comply with the group's norms in order to avoid disapproval or punishment, but secretly, he or she does not really hold the same attitudes. For example, Andrew, an adolescent, no longer accepts the religious beliefs of his family. Because he lives at home and is being financially supported by his parents, he superficially conforms to the family norm of going to church every Sunday, but basically he is not religious. He actually identifies with the family of his best friend, Henry. Andrew admires Henry's family because they are well educated, liberal, and modern in their outlook. He visits them often and has adopted not only their freethinking religious attitudes but their political views and aesthetic tastes (in art, music, film, books, and so on) as well. This family has become what is called Andrew's reference group, a group with whom he identifies and in which he tries to gain acceptance.

Peer Influence

The single greatest replacement of parental influence (as the child grows older) comes from the child's peers. This begins at a fairly early age (perhaps four to six years) and becomes even more important as the child grows older.

Influence of Education

Another important source of information and reinforcement is education. In general, the more years of formal education a person has, the more liberal the person's attitudes seem to become.

Influence of Mass Media

The mass media may help form attitudes. For example, a number of television shows present factual information regarding political concerns. It is not likely, however, that the information presented by mass media, in and of itself, creates attitudes. Rather, it provides support for attitudes that have already been stimulated by one of the other major sources of influence.

Critical Periods for Attitude Development

At least one proposal has suggested that the decisive time for establishing most attitudes occurs between the ages of 12 and 30. After age 30, the attitudes are said to be crystallized, and are unlikely to change.

In the 1960s, the Beatles introduced not only a somewhat different style of popular music, but also a different fashion for men's hairstyles. Perhaps no one aspect of behavior demonstrated the difference in attitudes between children and parents than the acceptance of these new, longer hairstyles. The adults (at first) were simply unable to accept what they considered to be a radical change; their attitudes were crystallized. Young people and children, on the other hand, had a greater flexibility of attitudes. They changed styles quite quickly.

Interpersonal Attraction

It is possible to consider interpersonal attraction from either a "like" or a "dislike" position. This section will concentrate on why one person is attracted to (or likes) another. "Dislike" will be considered in the section on prejudice.

Primacy and Recency Effects

When we first meet someone our reactions are often determined by what we have already heard about that person. Or, if we have heard nothing, our attitudes may depend entirely on first impressions. In other cases, it may take time before we get any clear impression about a person. These reactions are indicative of the primacy effect and the recency effect.

The Primacy Effect

A person who is forming an impression about someone or something shows evidence of the primacy effect if information presented first is more likely to be influential than information presented later. This effect may not be observed if the person is specifically instructed to pay attention to the later materials or to ignore the earlier information.

The primacy effect explains the importance of first impressions. A shy child who finds it difficult to respond in class during the first few days of the school year may be labeled by the teacher as "dull." Although there may be later evidence that contradicts this evaluation, the teacher is likely to retain the initial attitude. Moreover, the child may realize that the teacher's expectation is that he or she will be dull, and may begin to respond according to that expectation. In this way the teacher's expectation becomes what is called a *self-fulfilling prophecy*.

The Recency Effect

The recency effect is shown when later-presented materials are more influential than those presented earlier. This can be demonstrated experimentally by telling subjects that their first impressions may be inaccurate, or by giving them conflicting information about a person before they meet that person. Information presented over a long period of time is also more dependent on the recency effect, since people tend to remember the later material (or information) better.

Proximity

Proximity, the real or perceived physical distance between one person and another, has been found to be a very important determinant of interpersonal attraction. In general, the greater the real or perceived distance between two people (or groups), the less likely it is that interpersonal attraction will develop.

Similarity

Repeated research studies investigating the correlation of characteristics shared by friends, married partners, and other people with positive interpersonal attractions have shown these correlations to be fairly high. That is, people with similar characteristics are often attracted to each other. This holds for sociological characteristics (such as socioeconomic status, education or the like) and for physical characteristics (such as height, hair color or skin color).

Complementarity

Complementarity occurs when two people have dissimilar characteristics that blend nicely and form the basis for interpersonal attraction. For example, a dominant person and a submissive person might get along well together because they fulfill each other's needs. It should be recognized that both must agree that the dissimilarity is a good foundation for a relationship.

Attractiveness

Another factor that helps determine interpersonal attraction is attractiveness. People who are judged to be physically attractive may often be better liked than those who are rated as unattractive. Such a judgment of attractiveness may influence other people to perceive additional positive qualities in the attractive person. This is called the *halo effect*.

The attractiveness of a person may lead others to expect a certain kind of behavior from that person. Thus, if a man is very handsome, people may expect him to be charming also, and they may perceive such charm regardless of whether or not it actually is one of the man's characteristics.

Anxiety and Attraction

Investigations into the effect of anxiety on interpersonal attraction have shown that as anxiety levels increase, the need for affiliation with others also increases. The explanation of this phenomenon has been summarized by the concept of social comparison: A person who is anxious about something will tend to seek out others in order to compare reactions and possibly find some resolution for the anxiety.

The Principle of Least Interest

The behavior of a pair of people is sometimes the result of the level of attraction each holds for the other. One of the effects of such attraction has been labeled the principle of least interest; that is, the person who has the lesser involvement in the relationship is able to establish the conditions of the relationship, while the person having the greater interest agrees to the other person's conditions in order to maintain the relationship.

Effects of Frustration

The theory that emotional arousal can intensify feelings of love may help to explain why parental opposition to a romance often succeeds in fanning the flames of love. The term *psychological reactance,* or the *Romeo and Juliet effect,* after Shakespeare's play, is used to describe this phenomenon. In the play, a family feud forces the lovers to choose between family loyalty and love, a dilemma that serves to intensify the lovers' feelings for one another.

Prejudice

A prejudice is a learned reaction that is overgeneralized and unjustified. Although a prejudice may be a favorable reaction, most research has centered around unfavorable, or negative, attitudes. Thus, this section will treat prejudices as unfavorable biases.

Developing and Maintaining a Prejudice

Prejudices are developed and maintained in the same way as other learned responses. It is interesting to note that modeling (see Chapter 9) appears to be the most important source of learning a prejudice. In other words, a prejudice is likely to be learned from someone who is prejudiced rather than from actual contact with the people against whom the prejudice is held.

Once developed, prejudices are supported by occasional reinforcements, thus demonstrating the partial reinforcement effect discussed in Chapter 9. Occasional or infrequent support for the prejudice will thus be enough to make it very resistant to extinction.

Stereotypes

The term *stereotype* is frequently used to describe the prejudiced reactions shown by an individual. A stereotype can be defined as an oversimplified and relatively rigid conception of a person or group of people.

Purposes of Prejudices

Holding a prejudice may serve several different purposes. Expressing a prejudice may help a person achieve some goal, satisfy some need, protect his or her self-image (comparable to a defense mechanism) or simply serve as a kind of knowledge, providing an explanation for a particular event. It also is possible that some combination of the above may be operating.

Scapegoating

One term that often appears in connection with the concept of prejudice as a defense mechanism is *scapegoating,* which is the displacement of aggression toward an "available" person or minority group.

Changing Attitudes

Trying to change attitude has been called *persuasion.* The important variables that either facilitate or hinder attitude changes have been studied extensively.

Source of the Message

One of the most important factors in trying to change a person's attitudes is the source of the message or persuasion. Three factors have been found to be most significant: (1) how believable the source appears to be, (2) how attractive the source is judged, and (3) how much power or prestige the source seems to have. Maximizing these three factors should lead to a high probability of accomplishing attitude change.

In the early 1960s, President John F. Kennedy combined very well the three factors of being believable, attractive, and in a position of power. He did this so well, in fact, that many of his followers accepted his statements without criticism. Later historical evaluations have shown that some of his judgments may not have been as good as they seemed at the time.

The Message

Various aspects of the message itself influence attitude change:

1. The phrasing of the message itself may be crucial in determining whether or not it will be accepted and bring about a change in attitude. Because the message must provide the suggestion to be accepted, hopefully without criticism, it must avoid creating a feeling of doubt. For example, the use of biased or domineering terms in a message will make it especially liable to criticism.

2. The order of presentation of information (the primacy and recency effects influence messages, too).

3. Whether one or both sides of an argument are presented.

4. How closely the message corresponds to the receiver's current attitudes (cognitive dissonance).

5. Whether a message is one-sided or two-sided. *One-sided messages*—those that present only one side of an argument—appear to work best when the receiver is either neutral or already somewhat in favor of the message being presented. *Two-sided messages*—those that present both sides of an argument—are more effective when the receiver currently holds the opposite point of view.

The Receiver

The characteristics of the receiver also influence the possibilities of attitude change. Among these characteristics are (1) how open to suggestion the receiver is, (2) how the message affects the needs of the receiver, (3) how selective the receiver is about perceiving information in the message, and (4) how much resistance to the message the receiver may have developed.

Inoculation Effect

One reason resistance may develop is because of what has been called the inoculation effect. Suppose the receiver is first exposed to mild arguments against his or her position. In such a case, the receiver not only is able to learn to cope with such arguments, but also builds up a resistance to stronger arguments that may follow. Thus the term *inoculation;* the person seems to become "immunized" against the stronger arguments that may follow.

Anchorage Effect

A second possible explanation for resistance to an attitude-changing message is called the anchorage effect. Generally, this refers to the development of strong beliefs that are supported by or anchored to, the rules or principles of some organization.

Religious affiliation may provide strong anchorage against attitude change. For example, some religious groups hold beliefs that do not allow the drinking of coffee or cola drinks, while other groups will not eat pork products. People who believe in and practice one of these religions would be very resistant to persuasion that suggested they consume one of the restricted products.

Intergroup Contact

It might appear that increasing amounts of intergroup contact should increase the similarity of the attitudes held by the two groups. This is not always the case, however. Several factors appear to affect the outcome of intergroup contact.

In general, greater similarity of attitudes will develop if the members of the two groups have similar status, characteristics that support change (such as a lack of prejudice), or possibly some sort of dependency upon each other. However, if the intergroup contact supports already-held beliefs, the differing attitudes of the groups will become even more solidified.

Social Movements

Social movements are attempts to cause social change, or a significant alteration in the existing social structure and accompanying changes in attitudes and behaviors. Attempts to resist social change are called *countermovements*.

Examples of social movements in the United States are the civil rights movement, the feminist movement, and the antiwar movement prompted by the Vietnamese war. All of these showed similar patterns of development, including an unevenness of progress, strong recruiting efforts, and the development of formal organizations that carried out public appeals designed to influence behavior and change attitudes.

CHAPTER 18

Social Psychology: Behavior in Groups

Psychology primarily concerns itself with the study of individual behavior, but the influence of group membership on an individual cannot be ignored. One major area of social psychology is the study of the individual's behavior as it is influenced by membership in a group.

The subject matter of social psychology encompasses a broad range of topics, and the list grows from year to year as psychologists develop new techniques for studying individuals interacting with each other and with their social and physical environment. In the preceding chapter we examined how attitudes are formed and how they affect behavior. In this chapter we will see how individuals are influenced by groups in terms of social roles, conformity, obedience to authority, stereotyping, competition and cooperation, and helping behavior.

Relationship of the Individual to the Group

It should be recognized that almost every person's behavior is influenced by membership in groups almost all of the time. Some of these groups are *formal*, with designated titles and rules. Other groups are *informal*; they are organized casually and have unwritten (and perhaps very flexible) rules. The groups may also be *present* (that is, the other members are actually physically in the person's environment) or *absent* (meaning the other people are not physically present, but association with them remains an important influence on the person's behavior).

Socialization

As an individual grows up within a given culture, the family, school, peers, and the community at large furnish many influences that help establish the values and norms by which the individual lives. This rather general process, called socialization, seems to result both from modeling and from the reinforcement of what are considered appropriate behaviors.

Cultural Relativity

The process of socialization establishes values and norms that affect daily life. However, it must be recognized that the values and norms may be appropriate only for the particular culture or subculture involved. The principle of cultural relativity proposes that behavior must be judged according to the cultural setting in which it occurs.

For example, one difference between American and certain European cultural values can be seen in the ways in which men greet one another. American men most often greet each other with a handshake (which may be of several different varieties). In some European countries, men kiss each other on both cheeks when they meet after a long separation. What is considered appropriate and ordinary in one culture might be considered out of the ordinary in another.

Social Facilitation and Social Interference

The presence of others may influence an individual's performance on a task. If the presence of others seems to improve performance, social facilitation has taken place. Social interference occurs when the presence of others seems to impair performance. Quite frequently, social facilitation will occur when the person is performing a task that has been well learned, while social interference may be more likely when the person is performing a task that has not been learned well.

The amount of experience that a person has had in teaching is often reflected in the style with which a lecture is delivered. The "rookie" teacher may have difficulties with pronunciation, remembering the sequence of topics or answering questions asked by the class. The "veteran" teacher, on the other hand, may actually relax in front of the class and in fact be more personable and confident there than in nonteaching situations. The new teacher's difficulties illustrate social interference, while the experienced teacher's abilities illustrate social facilitation.

Competition and Cooperation

One topic in social psychology that has received a great deal of attention is the comparison of competitive and cooperative behaviors. Whether a person is competitive or cooperative may be a function of the expectations of the group to which the person belongs.

The basic intent of competition is to get the best of a situation—that is, to do better than someone else. Cooperation means working with or assisting someone else in the hope of achieving a mutual goal.

Some researchers have claimed that competitiveness is a characteristic of all people. Other researchers have found that a cooperative group is generally more successful than a competitive group in achieving good performance on a task. Within a group, however, there must be successful communication if cooperation is to result in benefits.

Social Roles

It is necessary to understand status to be able to understand social roles. *Status* refers to the position held or the function served by a person at some given time. *Role* is the expected range of behaviors of a person holding a particular status. (Note: The word *status* has a second meaning, implying prestige or standing. The two meanings of status are not necessarily the same, although an individual's position may give him or her prestige.)

Expectancy

Because a role is defined by a certain range of behaviors, the person holding a role can be expected to act in a certain way. In some cases, this is exactly what happens; the person acts in accordance with the role he or she has accepted. Research on social roles has shown that they may influence behavior significantly. A person in a given role may have expectations based on that role, and these expectations may cause certain kinds of behaviors. When a behavior is the result of such an expectation, it is called a *self-fulfilling prophecy*.

Imagine two groups of high school students who are given a lengthy word problem in algebra. One group is told that the solution to the problem will be time-consuming but easy because it involves only a rudimentary knowledge of mathematics. (This description of the problem is accurate.) The other group is told the problem is a real "brainteaser," and is often given to graduate students in mathematics. Such descriptions could create a self-fulfilling prophecy: the students in the second group might be expected to perform less well on the problem because of the expectations created by the false description.

Role Conflict

Interrole Conflicts

No person holds only a single role. The multiple roles one has may not always call for compatible behaviors. When two or more roles are in conflict, so that fulfilling the expectations of one role means being unable to satisfy the expectations of the other, an interrole conflict exists.

For example, Jerry and Marcia have been living together for almost six months when Marcia takes a job with Jerry's firm. Although she is not Jerry's direct supervisor, her position requires broad corporate decision making that affects Jerry's immediate occupational role. On several occasions, her decisions cause Jerry to have to do extra paper work, which requires him to stay late in the office. He is upset about the extra work dictated by Marcia's policy (in her role of executive) and even angrier when he gets home and Marcia (in the role of companion) complains about his staying late at the office. He wants to respond, but finds himself in a conflict between his role as employee/subordinate and his simultaneous role as equal partner in the relationship.

Intrarole Conflicts

On some occasions, a single role may call for more than one possible behavior, and these behaviors may be in conflict. This situation is called an intrarole conflict. Supervisors in factories often experience intrarole conflicts. One aspect of a supervisor's job is to guide the workers and try to help them experience some job satisfaction. Another aspect, however, is to keep production at a level that satisfies management. These two purposes are not always in agreement, so the supervisor must choose which goal to pursue in any given situation, and in the long run find the proper balance between satisfying management and satisfying the workers.

Conformity

What is considered appropriate behavior in a given situation is often established by group opinion. A person who behaves according to the expectations of a group shows *conformity*. A person who recognizes the expectations of a group but acts in an opposite fashion shows *nonconformity*. A person whose behavior is not influenced one way or the other by social expectations shows *independence*.

Group opinion, for example, exerts a powerful effect upon styles of dress. Some of the fashions offered by designers will catch on if many people conform to the style of the moment; other designs will be rejected by the public and become financial disasters for the designers and clothing manufacturers. In the fashion industry, financial success thus depends to a large degree on how many people will conform to a new style or "look."

The Asch Experiment

A classic series of studies on conformity was conducted by Solomon Asch. These studies had naive subjects sit in a group with confederates of the experimenter and make some public judgments. They were asked to judge the relative lengths of some lines, which would seem on the surface to be an objective judgment. The confederates, however, were instructed to give the same wrong answer out loud. Since they all answered in the same way, they were in effect creating a group norm that was incorrect, thus putting the experimental subject under pressure to conform.

Asch found that there was a marked movement toward the majority—about one-third of all the judgments made by the subjects were errors in the direction of the distorted estimates of the majority—but that most of the estimates were correct despite the majority pressure.

When, in subsequent experiments, Asch varied the number of confederates who were present, he found that the conformity rate was greatest when there were three in the opposing majority. Increasing the number beyond three did not substantially increase the amount of conformity.

In other experiments, Asch had one confederate agree with the opinion of an experimental subject—that is, give the correct judgment when all the other confederates disagreed. He found that a naive subject was less likely to conform if at least one person agreed with him and he was not alone in his dissent.

When those who conformed were asked after the experiment why they had yielded, some subjects said they did not want to appear different or inferior to the others. A few said they actually believed that the two lines were equal and were not aware of yielding at all. However, most of the conforming subjects believed that their own perceptions were inaccurate and those of the majority were correct.

Obedience to Authority

One aspect of conformity that has been investigated experimentally is obedience to authority. It seems that if subjects can attribute responsibility for their actions to some other person who is judged superior or in authority, they will do as they are told, even if their actions may be potentially harmful to someone else. This was demonstrated in a famous series of studies conducted by psychologist Stanley Milgram.

Milgram's investigations involved a group of naive subjects

who were asked to act as teachers in a series of so-called learning experiments. They were told to give an electric shock to a learner whenever he made a mistake in a paired associate learning task. The naive subject did not know that the learner was actually a confederate of the experimenter who had been trained for this role.

The subject-teacher was to read a series of word pairs to the learner and then read the first word of each pair, to which the learner was to give the correctly paired term. Every time the learner made a mistake, the subject was to press a switch on an instrument panel connected to a simulated shock generator: an instrument panel indicated how strong a shock was presumably being given. But since this was a fake generator, it did not actually produce any shock.

In these studies, it was determined that under certain conditions a subject will obey an authority figure, even to the point of administering what appear to be fatal shocks to the confederate-learner. In other words, obedience to authority can be a more powerful force than learned ethics, or even common sense.

Milgram pointed out that there were a number of features of the studies that tended to promote obedience, some of which he investigated in later research. For one thing, the investigation was sponsored by and took place on the grounds of Yale University, a very prestigious institution. In a later version, Milgram carried out the experiment in a downtown office building rather than at Yale. The sponsor was said to be a private firm conducting research for the university. Under these circumstances, there was a decrease in obedience from 62 percent originally to 48 percent.

A second factor that was varied in later studies was the immediacy of the authority figure. In the first experiment, the researcher was present the entire time. In the second, he left the laboratory after giving initial instructions but kept in touch by telephone. In a third variation, all instructions were provided by means of a tape recording. It was found that obedience dropped by approximately two-thirds when the authority figure had only telephone contact; and when he was not present at all, the subjects administered only very low levels of shock.

A third factor that Milgram later manipulated was the immediacy of the victim. In the first experiment (the *remote* condition), the learner was in another room and only responses were heard by the subject-teacher until the learner pounded on the wall at 300 volts and then gave no further answers. In a second condition (*voice-feedback*), his distress signals were more elaborate: he began moaning, grunting and groaning at 75 volts; shouted at 120 volts; and cried to be let out at 150 volts. At 180 volts, he said that the pain was unbearable; at 270, he gave an agonized scream; at 300 and 315 volts, he shouted that he would give no further answers; and after that, he did not give any responses other than an occasional shriek of pain. In this condition, approximately 62 percent of the subjects were fully obedient.

In a third condition (*proximity*), the victim was seated in the same room as the subject and could be seen as well as heard. In the final condition (*touch-proximity*), the victim received a shock only when his hand rested on a shock plate. At a predetermined time, he removed his hand from the shock plate, and the experimenter ordered the subject to replace it and to hold it there while he administered the shock. It was found consistently that obedience decreased significantly the more immediate the victim was to the subject. But even in the final condition, 30 percent of the subjects obeyed the experimenter and gave the highest shock.

Stereotypes

Stereotyping is another aspect of conformity that has been widely investigated. Stereotypes are overgeneralizations that suggest that all members of a particular group can be expected to behave in an identical fashion. Thus, a person who thinks in stereotypes may expect all members of a particular group to conform in certain behaviors. (Stereotypes are discussed more fully in Chapter 17.)

Payoffs and Costs of Roles

The role a person fulfills may lead to either payoffs or costs. A payoff means the role has led to a positive event or a reinforcement, while the cost of a role means the result has been aversive, or negative in nature. A commonly observed result of nonconformity is discrimination; that is, a person who fails to conform to the standards of group opinion may suffer rejection and unfair treatment (the cost).

Equity Theory

People generally feel a need to maintain equitable relationships with others. They measure the costs and payoffs of their relationships, determining if the relationship is worthwhile—that is, are they getting as much out of it as they are putting in. In terms of equity theory, people become distressed if they find themselves participating in inequitable relationships and will be motivated to restore equity (justice). If they have behaved inequitably themselves, they can restore psychological equity by distorting their perceptions of the situation.

Group Dynamics

The social interactions that occur within groups have been summarized under the heading of group dynamics. Research on group dynamics has focused on aspects such as the effect of the size of a group on behavior and decision-making processes.

Group Size

A gathering of two or more people is called a group. The size of a group appears to affect the type of social interactions that will develop within it.

Dyads

A group consisting of only two people is called a dyad. Social interactions within a dyad are generally cooperative and positive. A spontaneously created dyad promotes social exchange, a reciprocity of give-and-take. Each person seems to experience superiority in some ways and inferiority in others.

The relationship between an editor and a writer illustrates the principles of social exchange. The writer generates ideas, creating a manuscript. The editor reads and comments on the manuscript, suggesting additions, deletions, and perhaps changes in wording. Each is dependent upon the other: The writer requires the guidance and assistance of the editor, while the editor, of necessity, must have the raw materials produced by the writer. Each must recognize the superiority of the other in certain aspects of the publishing process.

Triads

A group of three people is called a triad. Research has shown that triads are frequently unstable and promote internal competition. A frequent occurrence is that the triad disintegrates into a dyad and one outsider, and the outsider is usually dissatisfied with this outcome.

Perhaps the most famous example of triad relationships is the "eternal triangle," consisting of either two women and one man or two men and one woman. There is an inherent instability in such a situation and the potential for a great deal of competition. Such a triad often dissolves into a stable dyad and an outsider, who will most likely be dissatisfied.

Groups of More Than Three

Study of groups of more than three members has shown that as group size increases, there is an increase in competition within the group. Groups of four or five are thus often found to yield greater satisfaction than larger groups.

Leadership

Attempts to identify the common characteristics that are most important for leadership within a group have generally proved fruitless. Both the purpose of the group and its composition seem to affect the choice of leader. One interesting point is that if a person who is designated by title as a leader refuses to lead, the group may rebel against that person and choose a new leader.

Group Decisions—The Risky Shift

The social interaction produced by a group's discussion of a problem sometimes leads to a phenomenon known as the risky shift: The group, acting as a whole, may take risks greater than those that any single member, acting alone, would dare to take.

The term risky shift developed only because most researchers have studied movement toward taking greater risks. It is also interesting to note that individual decisions may to some extent conform to group decisions, even if the individual was not present when the group made its decision.

The shift need not always be toward greater risk, however. Research into this phenomenon indicates that the shift is made in the direction of the strongest arguments. This role of arguments means that a group's decisions could be more conservative than the decisions of some of its members, depending on the number and strength of the arguments in favor of various courses of action.

Group Decisions—"Groupthink"

Research studies of group decision-making processes have revealed an interesting phenomenon described as "groupthink."

The members of a group may create an atmosphere in their meetings that takes hold and dominates the thoughts or opinions of all the members. Characteristically, the members of such a group believe the group's opinions are invulnerable to outside criticism, and the apparent unanimity of the members' opinions may be enough to convince them of their inherent rightness, in spite of evidence to the contrary. Evidence opposing their viewpoint may be ignored, and dissenters may be urged to change viewpoints to conform with that of the group.

During the early part of World War II, the "groupthink" phenomenon could be observed in the behaviors of some Americans of German descent. People who were otherwise firm in their admiration for democracy and justice would meet to extol the virtues of the changes taking place in Germany. They would also try to encourage other German-Americans to accept these beliefs, and became upset with those who did not. As more information regarding the conduct of the war became available, these people simply could not believe the reports. It was not until later in the war, when the evidence was overwhelming, that they were persuaded to change their thinking about the Nazi regime.

Environmental Psychology

The ways in which the environment shapes and is shaped by our behavior is the primary concern of environmental psychology. An environmental psychologist examines the physical setting—both public space and personal space—to better understand the context of an individual's behaviors and experiences. Among the topics included in the field of environmental psychology are crowding, privacy, personal space, and territoriality. The knowledge that is acquired through environmental research can then be applied to the creation of physical settings for better living.

Crowding

One aspect of group behavior that has been studied extensively is the effect of crowding. In laboratory experiments, rats were allowed to breed until their environment became extremely overcrowded. Such conditions led to many pathological behaviors, including unusual sexual behaviors, high levels of hostility, and even cannibalism. An overcrowded environment like the one that the rats were in has been described as a *behavioral sink*, where the unusual responses occur even when normally adequate amounts of food, water, and shelter are provided. There are weaknesses in this study, however; namely, the rats never really had adequate shelter in terms of a defensible place to hide; and cannibalism is not an unacceptable or abnormal behavior in rats, but rather one that has allowed rats to survive under highly adverse conditions.

A research study investigating a similar phenomenon showed that people in high-density population areas (big cities) are not likely to trust a stranger who comes to the door and asks to use the telephone; people in rural areas are much more likely to be trusting in such a situation. It is unclear to what extent population density (rather than other variables such as crime rate) explains this finding.

Privacy

Of particular interest to environmental psychologists is the issue of privacy. Privacy is not one thing but many things. The term may refer to some kind of need, or motivation, of the person, to forms of behavior, to inner experiences, or to some combination of these.

Research has shown that in most social situations, people seek out privacy. It has also been found that when several people are interacting, they create a social space boundary that deflects others away from them, and the extension of the boundary increases with the size of the group. If a pedestrian is walking down a sidewalk alone, he or she would walk farther away from groups of people who are talking together than from an individual who is standing alone. Moreover, the larger the group, the farther away the pedestrian would walk. Research has also shown that a pedestrian will walk farther away from an individual standing alone than from an empty bench. This demonstrates the force of privacy in everyday life.

Personal Space

Another variable in environmental psychology is personal space. This is the physical distance immediately surrounding a person that the person thinks of as his or her "own." Two factors seem to be important in determining what constitutes adequate personal space. One of these is the standard accepted by a particular culture. The other is the intimacy of the given situation; in general, the distance defining personal space decreases as the intimacy of a relationship increases.

Consider the story of two diplomats at a formal reception. One came from a very "proper" country, where personal space was measured in feet. The second came from a much more "intimate" country, where courtesy called for leaning toward your companion and even making physical contact. When these two met at the reception, they began a conversation. Each time the second diplomat came closer to the first, the first would move back slightly. In this way, the two managed to move almost 40 feet across the reception hall before their conversation was ended.

Territoriality

Territoriality is an extension of the principle of personal space: it is the larger space that a person feels is his or her own. It assures the person room to move about, socialize, eat, dispose of bodily waste, and carry on other vital activities. Moreover, territoriality serves an important social function in the organization of human societies.

The idea of "neighborhood," for example, is a translation of territoriality. When a person has lived in a neighborhood and feels that it is home, intrusions on that neighborhood by foreign (unknown) groups of nonmembers is strongly resented. In nature, moreover, each animal species (or group) carves out its niche, or territory, and will repel all invaders, often fighting a life-or-death battle in the process. Only members of the group can enter the territory designated by the group as its own, and admission into the territory indicates the animal's acceptance by the group, at least temporarily.

Prosocial Behavior

Prosocial behavior (also called helping behavior) exists when one person or a group of people come to the aid of another person or group.

The Bystander Effect

Helping behavior seems to be more likely if only a single person is asked for help or recognizes someone else's need for aid. Groups are less likely to offer aid or agree to help someone in need. The significant factor appears to be the "diffusion" of responsibility: One person alone cannot reasonably expect that someone else will come to the aid of the person in need; by contrast, people in groups can always rationalize their lack of involvement by assuming that someone else will give the necessary aid. This has been called the bystander effect.

The incident that provoked the initial research in this area was the killing of a young woman named Kitty Genovese in New York City in 1964. More than 30 people admitted having witnessed some or all of the incident, yet not one went to the woman's aid or even called the police. When interviewed later, they stated they felt "someone else" could or would take the responsibility. Research studies under controlled conditions have confirmed that this type of behavior is common in many groups.

Justification Reaction and Equity Theory

Sometimes a person who witnesses a crime or an accident and does not offer help may put down the victim, blaming the victim for the incident. One may say, "She had no business walking these streets alone at night," or "He was probably speeding and that's why he crashed into the tree." This is called the justification reaction, and it is a type of rationalization that allows a person to account for his or her lack of helping behavior.

The principle of equity theory (discussed earlier in this chapter) comes into play in such situations as well. A bystander who does not help tries to defend (or deny or minimize) this inequitable (unjust) behavior by distorting the situation. Some popular distortions are derogation, or putting down the victim, minimizing the victim's suffering, or denying one's responsibility for the victim's suffering.

Glossary

Ability A person's potential for acquiring a skill.

Abnormal behavior Behavior that creates a problem for the individual or for society.

Abnormal personality patterns Behaviors that produce significant personal discomfort or create problems for others in a person's society.

Abscissa The x-axis, or horizontal axis, of a graph.

Absolute threshold The lowest level of a stimulus at which its presence or absence can be correctly detected 50 percent of the time.

Accidental sampling In psychological research, the use of any subjects that are available rather than the intentional definition of a sample group.

Accommodation According to Piaget, changing one's responses and thought structures to deal with new information provided by the environment.

Achievement test A test that measures what a person has accomplished to that point in time.

Acquisition In learning, the attaining of a response that becomes part of the behavioral repertoire of the organism.

Action potential The signal that passes through a neuron.

Activation theory In the psychology of emotion, the emphasis on the brain's reticular activating system (RAS) as a component of emotion and emotional response.

Activation-arousal theory A theory that proposes that any organism has a normal (appropriate) level of arousal and that behavior will be directed toward trying to maintain that level.

Adaptation The evolutionary adjustment of an organism to its environment; often made as a means to improve a species' chances for survival.

Addiction Dependency on a drug or chemical.

Adlerian psychology Also called individual psychology, the system developed by Alfred Adler which incorporates social striving with individual growth.

Adolescence A period of postnatal development from approximately age twelve (the onset of puberty) to age eighteen.

Adrenal glands Endocrine glands which secrete hormones that help us cope with emergencies and stress.

Adulthood The final period of postnatal development; from approximately age eighteen on.

Affective component The emotional (or feeling) aspect of an attitude.

Affective disorders Abnormal behavior characterized by extremes of mood (manic and depressive).

Affiliation The motive to associate with others or to maintain social contacts.

All-or-none principle The finding that a signal, once started, will always travel the entire length of a neuron at a fixed intensity.

Amnesia Loss of memory for an extended period of time, often caused by some form of trauma.

Anal stage In Freud's theory of personality, the period when libidinal energy is expended to satisfy the conflicts created by being toilet trained.

Analytical psychology A system of psychology and psychotherapy developed by Carl Gustav Jung.

Analytical therapy A psychotherapy developed by Carl Jung which includes historical as well as personal experiences in the analysis of the unconscious.

Anchorage effect Resistance to attitude change because of particularly strong beliefs or group support.

Anger One of the basic emotions; a response of heightened arousal in the class of rage or hostility.

Anima According to Jung, the archetype that represents the masculine aspect.

Animus According to Jung, the archetype that represents the feminine aspect.

Anthropomorphism The attribution of human characteristics to objects or nonhuman organisms.

Antianxiety compounds A class of medications used to treat anxiety; also known as "minor tranquilizers."

Antidepressants A class of medications used to treat depression.

Antipsychotics A class of medications used to treat psychotic conditions; also known as "major tranquilizers."

Antisocial behavior Behavior characterized by a failure to act according to societal standards and the absence of anxiety about such behavior; also called psychopathic or sociopathic behavior.

Anxiety disorder A disorder in which a person continues to experience anxiety at a moderate level, with occasional intense periods, but does not recognize the cause of the anxiety.

Apparent movement Static stimuli presented in such a way as to give the appearance of movement.

Applied psychology Any branch of psychology that applies psychological principles to the solution of practical problems.

Approach-approach conflict A situation in which a subject must choose between two stimulus situations, both of which have positive values.

Approach-avoidance conflict A situation in which a subject must decide whether to go toward or away from a single stimulus situation that has both positive and negative values.

Aptitude test A test designed to predict what a person may accomplish in the future with additional training.

Archetypes According to Jung, inborn categories such as mother, wise old man, that together comprise the collective unconscious.

Area sampling A method in statistics, in which a random sample is taken from a defined geographic area.

Assertiveness training Teaching someone to express emotions and beliefs in an "open" or forthright but nonaggressive way.

Assimilation According to Piaget, the ability to incorporate new information from the environment into already existing thought structures.

Associationism A system of psychology that studied how and why bonds are established between particular stimuli and responses.

Asymptote In a learning curve, the point at which the performance has approached near maximum and begins to "level off."

Attachment The relationship of a child to parents and other significant individuals; usually develops during the first six months of postnatal development.

Attention The key to perception: if a subject is to perceive something, the subject must give some level of attention.

Attitude A learned evaluative response to a social stimulus.

Attitude scale Pretested attitude statements to which the subject indicates his or her degree of agreement.

Attribution The assignment of causes to explain the acts of other people or oneself.

Auditory localization Identifying the direction from which a sound was produced; often a function of the slight discrepancy between the times at which the signal reaches each ear.

Autistic thinking Chronic aimless thinking, such as fantasizing or daydreaming.

Autonomic nervous system (ANS) That part of the peripheral nervous system that controls the functions of many glands and smooth-muscle organs; divided into the sympathetic and parasympathetic systems.

Aversion therapy A technique that pairs unpleasant (aversive) stimuli with inappropriate responding.

Aversive stimulus Any stimulus the organism judges to be noxious or unpleasant.

Avoidance response Any response an organism makes in order to keep from experiencing an anticipated aversive stimulus.

Avoidance-avoidance conflict A situation in which a subject must choose between two stimulus situations, both of which have negative values.

Axon The single long fiber extending from the cell body of a neuron; carries the signal to the synapse.

Backward conditioning In classical conditioning, a trial in which the onset of the UCS occurs before the onset of the CS.

Basal age The highest year level at which a subject passes all the subtests of an intelligence test.

Behavior Any observable or measurable response of a person or animal.

Behavior modification Procedures that change behaviors by using operant conditioning, classical conditioning, and modeling techniques.

Behavior therapy The use of operant-conditioning procedures to help create socially acceptable behavior.

Behavioral genetics The study of the influence of heredity on behavior.

Behavioral sink The description given to overcrowded conditions that lead to pathological responding, despite environmental conditions that are otherwise normal.

Behaviorism A system of psychology that studied observable stimuli and responses only, and that denied the concept of mind.

Benzodiazepines A class of drugs used to treat anxiety.

Binocular depth cues Cues to depth perception based upon the simultaneous functioning of two eyes.

Biofeedback The use of monitoring equipment to inform a person about physiological responses that might otherwise remain unobservable.

Biomedical model An explanation of abnormal personality patterns emphasizing the influence of body functions.

Bipolar disorder Behavior characterized by swings between manic and depressed states; also known as manic-depressive disorder.

Blind spot The area in the retina where the optic nerve exits to the brain; no vision is possible here because there are no receptors.

Body dysmorphic disorder The preoccupation a normal-appearing person has with a presumed bodily defect.

Body-type theory An attempt to predict personality by identifying the shape of the body and the characteristics that supposedly accompany that shape.

Branching program Those programmed learning situations in which progress through the program depends on the subject's responses; the program may vary for each subject using it.

Bystander effect In the psychology of helping, the principle that a single person is more likely to help someone in need than is a member of a group or crowd who can rationalize his or her lack of action by assuming that someone else will give help.

Cannon-Bard theory of emotion A theory proposing that emotion consists of simultaneously occurring physiological and psychological reactions to an emotion-producing stimulus.

Catatonia A pattern of schizophrenic behavior characterized by extremes of cooperation and activity, the best-known example being total withdrawal accompanied by complete muscle rigidity.

Ceiling age The year level at which a subject fails to pass any subtests of an intelligence test.

Cell body The central part of a neuron, from which extend the axon and the dendrites.

Central fissure A deep convolution running from the top middle of the brain toward the central side.

Central nervous system (CNS) Basically, the brain and spinal cord.

Central tendency A number that best represents a group of numbers.

Cephalo-caudal trend The tendency for the head to develop before and more quickly than the lower portions of the body.

Cerebellum The part of the brain primarily responsible for motor functioning.

Cerebrotonia The personality accompanying ectomorphy; a quiet person interested in scholastic pursuits.

Cerebrum The two cerebral hemispheres, controlling the more sophisticated mental processes of an individual; covered by the cortex.

Chemotherapy A medical therapy involving the use of drugs to try to treat abnormal personality patterns.

Chromosomes Small bodies that contain genes; occur in pairs within each body cell; human body cells have 46 chromosomes, while human germ cells have 23.

Chronological age (CA) In IQ testing, the subject's actual age, which is used to compute the intelligence quotient.

Circadian rhythms Cyclical patterns of change in physiological functions such as hunger, sleep, or body temperature.

Clairvoyance The disclosure of knowledge or information that could not have been received through regular sensory processes.

Class interval Arbitrarily selected portions of a measurement scale; usually equal.

Classical conditioning The acquisition procedure in which a previously neutral stimulus is paired with a response-producing stimulus until the neutral stimulus elicits the same type of response; also called respondent conditioning and Pavlovian conditioning.

Classification According to Piaget, the ability to judge as similar things that are alike.

Client-centered therapy Developed by Carl Rogers, a technique that depends on the concept that people are basically good and in the process of growth if exposed to the right nurturing and accepting environment.

Clinical case history Records or data from a therapy situation used to identify behaviors and to suggest problems that need to be studied.

Clinical psychologist A psychologist who specializes in the treatment of emotional and behavioral problems.

Clinical psychology The branch of psychology concerned with the theory and practice of helping people with behavioral or mental disorders.

Closure In perception, the "completing" of an incomplete stimulus or piece of information.

Cochlea The structure within the inner ear that transduces the mechanical energy of sound waves into signals for hearing.

Cognitive component The part of an attitude revealing the beliefs the person has about a stimulus.

Cognitive dissonance The feeling of discomfort that a person has when he or she holds conflicting attitudes toward the same stimulus.

Cognitive restructuring An approach in cognitive therapy in which old thoughts are examined, changed, and/or discarded.

Cognitive therapy A form of therapy in which illogical thinking is changed to produce more adaptive behaviors.

Cognitive-behavioral therapy A combination of cognitive and behavioral therapy techniques.

Collective unconscious In Jung's theory of personality, the part of personality that holds behavioral characteristics inherited from ancestors.

Color The hue of a visual stimulus, determined by the wavelength of the light.

Combination motives Motives that result from the combined effect of unlearned and learned characteristics.

Common fate Perceptual principle stating that objects moving in the same direction and at the same rate are judged to be part of a single form or unit.

Community psychology A branch of psychology based on the premise that better community functioning can help prevent abnormal personality patterns.

Comparative psychology The branch of psychology that compares the behaviors of one species to the behaviors of another.

Compensation Emphasizing a behavior to account for or cover up some perceived deficiency.

Competition Trying to do better than others in a situation.

Complementarity Instances where people with dissimilar characteristics are attracted to each other, and thus fulfill each other's needs.

Complex A term coined by Jung to describe emotionally charged thoughts and belief systems.

Complex attitude An attitude that involves several reactions.

Complex concept A concept that represents more than one stimulus property simultaneously.

Compound schedules Partial reinforcement schedules in which a response is reinforced according to the requirements of two or more schedules that operate at the same time.

Compulsion An unwanted but not preventable pattern of action that recurs often.

Conative component The part of an attitude revealed by the actions a person takes in response to a stimulus.

Concentrative meditation Meditation that limits attention to one specific object or sound.

Concept A symbol that summarizes or generalizes the attributes of some objects, events, actions, or ideas that are otherwise dissimilar.

Concept hierarchy The "rank" of members in a concept category.

Concrete operational stage According to Piaget, the third state of cognitive development; from approximately age seven to age eleven.

Concurrent schedules Partial reinforcement schedules in which two or more responses are made to satisfy two or more schedules at the same time.

Conditioned reinforcer See secondary reinforcer.

Conditioned response (CR) In classical conditioning, the response elicited by the CS; usually similar to the UCR.

Conditioned stimulus (CS) In classical conditioning, the stimulus that was originally neutral and comes to be response-producing.

Cones The visual receptors that function primarily in lighted conditions; they are located toward the center of the eye and operate for color vision.

Confabulation A memory error, under conditions of anxiety, in which a subject manufactures a report or answer that seems appropriate.

Conflict A situation in which two or more incompatible motive conditions are operating at the same time.

Conformity Responding in accordance with a group's expectations or opinions.

Conjunctive concept A complex concept based upon the simultaneous presence of two or more stimulus properties.

Conscience In Freud's theory of personality, the part of the superego that reminds the person of what is unacceptable behavior.

Conscious An activity or condition is conscious if the individual is aware of it and can recognize or describe it.

Consciousness The internal mental experiences of which a person is aware.

Conservation According to Piaget, the principle that if nothing is added or taken away from an amount, it remains the same.

Consumer psychology A branch of psychology concerned with market research or consumers' buying habits.

Contact comfort The need of many young organisms to have something warm and soft to cling to; apparently a combination motive.

Contingency In operant conditioning, a situation in which reinforcement is not delivered unless certain responses are made; in statistics, the concept of causality or dependency that indicates there is a meaningful relationship between two variables.

Continuity Perceptual principle that indicates that if all elements in a set of stimuli go in the same direction, they are judged to be part of the same group.

Control group In a scientific experiment, those subjects whose responses are used as a basis for comparison; the experimenter compares the responses of the control group with the responses of experimental groups.

Convergent thinking Thinking aimed at finding a known solution to a problem.

Conversion disorder The transformation of psychological anxiety into a physical reaction.

Cooperation Working with or assisting someone else in an attempt to reach a mutually satisfying goal.

Corpus callosum The broad band of fibers that connect the cerebral hemispheres.

Correlation The tendency of two (or more) variables to vary together (concomitantly); also the numerical representation of the relationship between these two variables.

Cortex The most recently developed portion of the brain; involved with higher mental processes, such as thinking.

Cortical lobes The four somewhat arbitrarily designated divisions of the cortex.

Counseling psychology The branch of psychology that assists people in coping with normal personal problems.

Countermovement An attempt to resist social change.

Creativity Original, purposeful, worthwhile, and unique approaches to problem solving and other activities.

Cretinism A physiologically caused form of mental retardation resulting from a prenatal lack of iodine.

Criterion An absolute standard of performance used to evaluate a subject's performance on a test.

Critical period A state during which an organism is able to learn a new behavior; this state is limited in time: it has both a beginning and an end.

Cross-sectional study In developmental psychology, an investigation that makes use of subjects of different age groups to determine how age, the independent variable, affects behavior.

Crossing-over A process in which genes that were previously linked become unlinked or linked with a different set of genes.

Crowding Studied by psychologists, the deprivation of personal space in which to move; also the deprivation of privacy.

Crystallized intelligence Intelligence used in the application of already-learned materials; usually considered to be rigid or unchanging.

Cultural relativity The principle that proposes an individual's behavior must be judged according to the cultural setting in which it occurs.

Culture-fair tests Tests that try to use items that should be equally well known to all subjects taking the test, regardless of their cultural or subcultural background.

Culture-free tests Tests that attempt to eliminate entirely the introduction of any biases created by cultural or subcultural differences.

Cumulative record The tally or record of appropriate or satisfactory operant responses made in a given time period.

Curve of forgetting The plot of retention of a response over a period of time; usually greatest loss of retention occurs soon after acquisition is completed.

Cycle of motivation A proposal explaining many motive situations as a sequence of need, operant response, goal, and relief; the cycle often repeats itself.

Deductive reasoning The process of reasoning from the general principle to specific cases.

Deep structure The meaning transmitted by words used in a language.

Defense mechanisms See Ego defense mechanisms.

Delay of reinforcement A period of time between the response and reinforcement in a contingency situation.

Delayed conditioning In classical conditioning, a trial in which the onset of the CS precedes the UCS, with the CS staying on at least until the UCS has occurred.

Delusion A false belief.

Dendrite The branched fibers that serve as the signal receiving portion of a neuron.

Denial A defense mechanism; the person refuses to recognize stimuli that threaten the ego.

Deoxyribonucleic acid (DNA) A chemical that is the basic building block of life, and becomes organized into genes and chromosomes.

Dependent influence A change in a person's attitudes or behaviors that occurs because of the social characteristics of a model or group.

Dependent variable The measured response in an experiment.

Depolarization The process by which the electrical charge of a neuron reverses during the passage of an action potential.

Depression A mental state characterized by despondent, low-activity patterns of behavior.

Deprivation Doing without; in developmental psychology, a significant reduction of stimulation or opportunity; in motivation, often measured in terms of the time since the motive was last satisfied.

Descriptive statistics Measures or techniques that allow a summary portrayal of collected data.

Detachment The development of independent behavior by a child; often occurs when an adult of high attachment status is nearby.

Detection theory A theory stressing the effects of motivation, stimulus probability, and extraneous stimuli on the decision regarding the presence or absence of a given stimulus or a change in stimulus value.

Developmental psychology A branch of psychology that concentrates on changes of behavior through a time span, such as childhood or adolescence.

Developmental scale Reports of average or typical behavior based upon data collected from large groups of individuals.

Deviation IQ The value of intelligence established by using normal probability distributions of scores obtained for various age levels.

Difference threshold The minimum change in stimulus value that can be correctly identified as a change 50 percent of the time; also known as the just noticeable difference, or j.n.d.

Differentiation Responding to the original stimulus, but not to the other, similar stimuli, also called discrimination.

Directed thinking Thinking that occurs for a purpose, as in problem solving.

Directional hypothesis A prediction that a specific change in the conditions of an experiment will result in a particular change in the outcome of the experiment.

Discrimination See Differentiation.

Discriminative stimulus A cue stimulus that indicates when it is either appropriate or inappropriate to make an operant response.

Disinhibition In modeling, observing a response and learning that the response is appropriate to a given situation.

Disjunctive concept A complex concept based upon the simultaneous consideration of two or more stimulus properties, but in which the presence of any one stimulus property is adequate to qualify the stimulus as an instance of the concept.

Displacement Directing aggressive tendencies toward an innocent object rather than the one that produced the aggressive feeling.

Displacement activity An irrelevant response made in the presence of two simultaneous but incompatible releaser stimuli.

Dissociative disorder A disorder in which anxiety-producing thoughts or actions are banished completely, as in amnesia or fugue states.

Distribution of practice Interspersing periods of rest between periods of practicing new learning.

Divergent thinking Thinking devoted to finding a new or different (previously unknown) solution to a problem.

Dominant gene The gene in a pair of unlike genes that acts as the controller, directing development of a certain characteristic.

Double-blind control An experimental situation in which both the subjects and those who administer the experiment are unaware of how or when the variables are manipulated.

Dream analysis In psychoanalysis, the procedure of interpreting the meaning of dreams reported by the patient.

Drive The state resulting from physiological need; less specifically, the general wish to reach some goal.

Dyad A group of two people.

Early childhood The period of postnatal development from approximately age two to age six.

Ectomorphy The body type describing a thin, fragile person.

Educational psychology A branch of psychology that applies psychological principles in an attempt to improve the learning experience.

Effectance motives Motives that originate in the desire to increase one's ability to deal with the environment, such as the motive to explore unknown territory.

Ego In Freud's theory of personality, the problem solving part of personality, which operates according to the reality principle.

Ego defense mechanisms Actions or techniques that allow an individual to protect the self-image or cope with anxiety.

Egocentrism According to Piaget, the young child's belief that nothing exists outside himself and that the self is the cause of all actions.

Electrical stimulation of the brain (ESB) The process of implanting electrodes into brain tissue and delivering mild electric shocks.

Electrooculogram (EOG) A device that records the movement of the eyes when the eyelids are closed.

Electroconvulsive shock therapy (ECT) A medical therapy involving the passing of an electric current through the patient's brain; this produces unconsciousness, followed by a series of convulsions.

Electroencephalogram (EEG) A technique used to measure the electrical activity of the brain.

Embryo The developing organism during the early weeks of pregnancy (see also Embryonic stage).

Embryonic stage The second period in prenatal development, from approximately the third week after conception until the end of the sixth week.

Emotion A complex state of arousal, usually marked by a heightened state of internal feelings.

Empathy The quality of feeling as another feels, to experience another's reality from that other person's point of view.

Empirical Anything that is directly observable or measurable.

Encounter group A therapy in which normal people meet together to try to increase interpersonal skills and self-awareness.

Endocrine glands Glands that secrete hormones directly into the bloodstream.

Endomorphy The body type describing the soft, round person.

Engineering psychology A branch of psychology that concentrates on the relationships between people and machines.

Enrichment In developmental psychology, stimulation or opportunity considerably above normal levels.

Environment Any external factors or conditions that may influence an organism.

Environmental psychology The branch of psychology that studies public and personal space to better understand the context of an individual's behaviors and experiences.

Equity theory In social psychology, the idea that we measure the costs and benefits of our actions to establish a sense of fairness.

Escape response Any response made by an organism in order to get away from an already-present aversive stimulus.

Ethology The study of organisms in their natural habitats.

Eugenics The science of "improving" the human species through selective breeding.

Exhibitionism The practice of purposely exposing the genitals in a public or semipublic setting.

Existential model An explanation of abnormal personality patterns that stresses the influence of present events rather than past experiences.

Exocrine glands Glands that secrete fluids onto the body's surface or into its cavities.

Experimental group In a scientific experiment, those subjects who respond to an independent variable that is "specially" manipulated by the experimenter; the responses of the experimental group can then be compared with the responses of the control group.

Experimental method A technique involving the controlled comparison of conditions to determine if the variable investigated affects the results obtained.

Experimental neurosis Neurotic patterns exhibited by subjects forced to differentiate between two very similar stimuli; first pointed out by Pavlov.

Experimental psychology The branch of psychology that uses the scientific method to explore fundamental questions of human and animal behavior and mental processes.

Experimenter bias Any bias, intentional or unintentional, on the part of a researcher conducting an experiment.

Expressive language Words that convey a message.

Extinction In classical conditioning, both the procedure of presenting the CS alone repeatedly and the result of this procedure, which returns the CR to its original (preconditioning) level; more generally, the termination of reinforcement for a conditioned response.

Extraneous variable A condition that may affect the outcome of an experiment but that is irrelevant to the experiment.

Extrasensory perception (ESP) Manipulation or interpretation of the environment in the absence of regular sensory processes.

Extraversion According to Jung (his spelling), the personality trait of being concerned primarily with outside objects and people in the world.

Factor analysis A statistical technique involving the use of correlations to determine common factors or traits.

Family therapy A group therapy involving members of the same family.

Fear One of the basic emotions; a response in the general class of anxiety or dread.

Feature extraction Identification of the most important aspects of a total stimulus configuration.

Feedback An organism's knowledge of the results of its response.

Fetal stage The third period in prenatal development, from approximately the seventh week until delivery; in a full-term pregnancy (of 38 weeks), the last 32 weeks.

Fetus The label for the baby-to-be during the last 32 weeks of full-term pregnancy.

Figure-ground relationship The interconnection of the principal stimulus and the stimuli that surround it.

Fixation In Freud's theory of personality, the carryover of effect from one of the psychosexual stages to the adult personality, so that the adult's libidinal energy must in part be expended to satisfy motives appropriate to the earlier stage.

Fixed schedules Partial reinforcement schedules that remain unchanged.

Fixed-action pattern (FAP) Unvarying sequences of movement, keyed by a releaser, or sign, stimulus; FAPs are species-specific.

Flavor A combination of taste and smell; a term often used when discussing food.

Fluid intelligence Intelligence that can adjust to new situations; usually considered as flexible or adaptive thinking.

Forced compliance The theory that conflict between one's public and private beliefs creates dissonance and leads to attitude change.

Formal group A gathering of people in which formal titles, rules, and other designations are significant.

Formal operational stage According to Piaget, the fourth (and final) stage of cognitive development, from approximately age eleven to age thirteen (or cognitive adulthood).

Fovea The area in the center of the retina containing only cones; the point of maximum visual acuity.

Fraternal twins Two children conceived independently as two separate zygotes but born at approximately the same time.

Free association A psychoanalytic technique in which the client says whatever comes to mind, letting each thought lead to the next.

Free recall A process in which learned materials are later recalled in any order the subject chooses.

Frequency distribution Graphic or tabular representation of the number of cases found in each class interval of a distribution.

Frequency polygon A line graph representing a frequency distribution.

Freudian slips Mistakes of memory, expression, forgetting, etc. thought by Freud to represent unconscious conflict trying to express itself.

Frontal lobe The area of the cortex from the front of the central fissure to the front of the lateral fissure.

Fugue A form of amnesia involving both loss of memory and actual physical flight from home, often for an extended period of time.

Functional autonomy A situation in which a response that was made originally to satisfy some motive becomes motivating in and of itself.

Functional fixedness A type of set in which a subject is unable to use some object in a novel manner.

Functional psychoses Psychotic reactions provoked by psychological or experiential influences.

Functionalism A system of psychology that studied the purposes of behavior and the adaptation of an organism to the environment.

Galvanic skin response (GSR) A change in the electrical resistance of the skin as a result of the autonomic changes that produce sweating.

Gender role Those characteristics thought to be masculine or feminine, as determined by social standards.

General factor (G) According to Spearman, the general factor of intelligence which takes in many specific factors; also called the G factor.

Generalized anxiety disorder A condition in which an individual experiences a general anxiety and sense of worry.

Generative thinking The creation of new systems of thought.

Genes The basic "information-bearing" units of heredity; carried within chromosomes.

Genetic counseling Counseling in which potential parents are advised of the likelihood that their children will be normal; based on chromosomal studies of one or both parents.

Genetics The study of the transmission of hereditary characteristics through generations.

Genuineness The therapist's personality quality of giving of oneself, of being real in the therapeutic situation.

Germ cells In the female, the egg; in the male, the sperm.

Germinal stage The first period in prenatal development; from conception until approximately the end of the second week.

Gestalt psychology A system of psychology that adopts a holistic approach to the study of behavior.

Gestalt therapy A therapy technique that emphasizes the patient's responsibilities for behavior; based upon perception of the total personality.

Gifted subjects Those subjects whose scores are more than 2 standard deviations above the mean of an intelligence test.

Goal In motivation, the thing believed to satisfy a motive condition.

Goal specificity The desire to satisfy a motive condition with a particular reinforcement rather than with any reinforcement that would satisfy.

Gonads Endocrine glands that control sexual and reproductive behaviors.

Graded potential The sum of the excitation and inhibition at a given synapse.

Group dynamics The general term describing social interactions within groups.

Group test Psychological tests administered to more than one subject at the same time.

Group therapy Any therapy in which more than one patient is present in the therapy setting at the same time.

Groupthink An atmosphere found in the discussions of some groups; an air of invulnerability and unanimity of decision in group discussion.

Habit A long-term learned tendency to respond in a predictable way.

Habituation A change of behavioral pattern in which an organism ceases to respond with an FAP to an inappropriate stimulus.

Hallucination Perception of "stimuli" that do not exist.

Hallucinogenic drugs Those drugs that have as a major characteristic the production of hallucinations.

Halo effect The influence that the judged attractiveness of an individual has on people's expectations regarding that individual's behavior and on their perception of his or her additional positive qualities.

Hebephrenia Psychotic behavior showing wild or silly responses, often accompanied by hallucinations and delusions.

Heredity The genetic transmission of characteristics from parent to offspring.

Hierarchy of needs A proposal by the psychologist Abraham Maslow that arranges motives in an order of importance; those lower in the hierarchy must be satisfied before the higher ones can be satisfied.

Higher-order conditioning A conditioning procedure in which a new CS is paired with a well-established CS from a previous instance of classical conditioning; the new CS comes to elicit the same type of CR.

Histogram A bar graph representing a frequency distribution.

Homeostasis A state of physiological balance.

Hormones Distinctive chemicals, secreted by endocrine glands, that carry information ("instructions") to certain areas of the body.

Humanism An emphasis on positive, constructive human capacities; the basis for humanistic psychology.

Humanistic psychology Also called the "third force," the approach to psychology that emphasizes the study of the individual as a whole person, usually in the process of growth.

Hypnosis A technique (or group of techniques) for inducing an altered state of consciousness that is characterized by increased suggestibility, relaxation or alertness, and possible distortion of reality.

Hypochondriasis The neurotic belief that one has serious illness when one really does not.

Hypothalamus A small area of the brain that controls many of our basic drives, such as sex, hunger, thirst, and rage.

Hypothesis A tentative explanation of a relationship, or a proposition that a relationship exists; an experiment should be designed so that a hypothesis can be either confirmed or disconfirmed.

Id In Freud's theory of personality, the most primitive or instinctive part of personality, operating according to the pleasure principle.

Identical twins Twins who are the result of a single fertilization and therefore have identical genetic make-ups.

Identity crisis According to Erikson, the adolescent's attempt to find a unique identity within the social context.

Illusion Stimuli that exist in a configuration that creates an incorrect interpretation by the person perceiving it (misperception).

Imagery Internal representations of visual stimuli.

Implosion therapy A technique involving pairing of the worst possible anxiety-producing stimuli with a nonthreatening setting.

Imprinting Learning that occurs by instinct during a critical learning period.

Incest Having sexual relations with one's relative.

Independence When a person's responses are not influenced one way or another by social expectations or opinions.

Independent influence A change in a person's attitudes or behaviors that occurs because a perceived message itself (rather than the sender of the message) is persuasive.

Independent variable A condition manipulated by the experimenter; the experimenter manipulates the independent variable to determine the effect of such manipulations on the dependent variable.

Individual differences The term used to describe variations among people in traits and developmental stages common to the entire population.

Individual psychology The system developed by Alfred Adler that incorporates social striving with individual psychological growth.

Individual test Psychological tests given by the test administrator to only one subject at a time.

Inductive reasoning The process of arriving at general principles from specific cases or facts.

Industrial psychology A branch of psychology that applies psychological principles to the solution of work-related problems.

Infancy The first period of postnatal development, from birth to approximately two years of age.

Infantile autism Psychotic patterns of behavior shown by children under age ten; poor communication, no desire for personal contact, and a desire for status quo are characteristic symptoms.

Inferential statistics Measures or techniques that allow for the analysis or evaluation of relationships existing within a sample of data or between samples of data; can be used to make predictions.

Inferiority complex From Adler's theory of personality, the concept that a person may experience feelings of deficiency and be reinforced in such a belief by others in society.

Inferiority feelings According to Alfred Adler, the inborn sense of inadequacy common to all children, but which may become problematical later in life.

Informal group A casual gathering of people in which there are no formal rules or titles; however, unwritten guidelines may exist for the members of this group.

Information-processing approach A method of studying retention and memory by using computer simulations.

Inhibition In modeling, observing a response and learning that the response is inappropriate to a given situation.

Inner speech Internal representations of verbal stimuli.

Inoculation effect A set created by first exposure to mild arguments so that later, a person can resist stronger arguments.

Insight In problem solving, the phenomenon in which a subject knows the problem, has a period of no apparent progress, and then suddenly finds a solution.

Instinct An innate (inborn) condition that regularly provokes specific, complex responses from all members of a species when a distinctive stimulus pattern occurs.

Instrumental conditioning A learning process that involves changing the probability of a response by manipulating the consequences of that response; also called operant conditioning and Skinnerian conditioning.

Instrumental response A response leading toward a goal.

Intellectualization A defense mechanism; the person protects the ego by avoiding the reality of another person, seeing him or her as an object instead.

Intelligence Those enduring characteristics that allow an individual to solve problems.

Intelligence quotient (IQ) The ratio obtained by dividing mental age by chronological age and then multiplying by 100; more generally, the numerical value determined from a test of intelligence.

Intelligence tests Tests designed to measure intelligence; usually consist of a series of aptitude tests that predict academic ability.

Interrole conflict The situation where an individual is confronted with expectations based upon two (or more) different roles that cannot be fulfilled simultaneously.

Interposition A monocular depth cue in which one object appears closer to the viewer because it partly blocks the view of another object.

Interstimulus interval (ISI) In classical conditioning, the time between the onset of the CS and the onset of the UCS.

Interval schedules Partial reinforcement schedules in which reinforcement is delivered after a response that has been made at the end of a given time period.

Intrarole conflict The situation where an individual is confronted with two or more expectations that arise from only one role but that cannot be fulfilled simultaneously.

Introspection A method of psychological investigation in which subjects report on their own responses to stimuli.

Introversion According to Jung, the personality trait of being primarily concerned with one's inner world.

Introversion-extraversion Proposed by Jung, the continuum representing how responsive an individual is to stimuli within or outside of the self.

Intuitive judgment Decision based upon statistical data and other information, and the feelings of the psychologist giving a test.

James-Lange theory of emotion A theory proposing that emotion-producing stimuli generate physical reactions, which in sum are perceived as felt emotions.

Justification reaction A rationalization that allows a person to justify his or her lack of helping behavior.

Kinesthesis The sensations concerned with body position and body movement.

Knowledge of results (KR) Any information about the effect of a response; also called feedback.

Latency stage In Freud's theory of personality, the period extending from the end of the phallic stage to the onset of puberty; during this period, libidinal energies are quiet.

Latent dream content The meaning of a dream, contrasted with the manifest dream content reported by the dreamer.

Later childhood The period of postnatal development from approximately age six until age twelve (the onset of puberty).

Lateral fissure A deep convolution running from the lower front of the brain toward the center side.

Law of effect Thorndike's proposal that a response followed by the presence of a satisfying stimulus or the termination of an annoying stimulus will become conditioned.

Learned helplessness The principle that as animals or people learn that they cannot control the events that affect them, they ultimately lose hope and experience a sense of depression.

Learned motives Conditions that result from experience and initiate, guide, and maintain behaviors; often called social motives.

Learning A relatively permanent change in behavior as a result of experience.

Learning curve A graphic representation of the change in acquisition of a response as a function of time or number of trials.

Learning to learn A general form of transfer of training; learning the general principles of how to go about performing a task.

Level of significance In statistics, the criterion chosen to determine if the experimental results are due to chance.

Libido In Freud's theory of personality, the fundamental drive that provides psychic energy; libido has a basically sexual nature.

Lie detector A device that measures physiological reactions such as heart rate or GSR; these reactions supposedly reveal when the responder has lied.

Life-style According to Alfred Adler, an individual's organized patterns, themes, behaviors, and orientations that are expressed through his or her life activities.

Limbic system Circuits which extend from the cortex to the lower brain centers.

Linear program Any programmed learning situation that progresses in the same way for each subject.

Lithium carbonate A drug used in the treatment of bipolar affective disorder (manic-depression).

Live modeling One organism copying a behavior of another organism that is physically present and observed.

Long-term storage In memory, when material is retained for over 30 seconds (and sometimes for as long as one lives).

Longitudinal study An investigation conducted over a fairly long period of time, using the same subjects throughout; the study may be used to determine how age, the independent variable, affects behavior.

Major tranquilizers Also known as antipsychotic drugs, these medications lessen psychotic symptoms and generally allow more normal levels of functioning.

Mania Elated, hyperactive patterns of behavior.

Manifest dream content The material reported by the dreamer, contrasted with the latent dream content; the events but not the underlying meaning of the dream.

Masochism Deriving sexual gratification through experiencing pain or psychological humiliation.

Matched sampling A technique for selecting subjects by which an experimenter makes sure that each group in the experiment contains the same number of subjects who possess a certain characteristic that might influence the outcome.

Maternal behavior A combination motive, the behavior a mother shows to her newborn offspring.

Maturation In development psychology, the physical development of the body.

Mean The average score in a distribution of scores; calculated by summing all the scores and dividing that sum by the number of scores.

Meaningfulness In verbal learning, the number of associations evoked by material that is being learned.

Median The middle score in a distribution of scores; the number of scores above and below it are equal, and the score is at the fiftieth percentile.

Medical therapies Therapies that involve the use of physical procedures to try to treat abnormal personality problems.

Meditation Techniques used to focus or concentrate conscious processes.

Medulla The brain stem, responsible for many of our involuntary responses, such as breathing and digestion.

Memory The storage and later measured retention of a response that was previously acquired.

Menarche A girl's first menstruation.

Mental age A measurement of a person's performance on an intelligence test; the basis for measurement is the chronological age at which people typically can pass a specific test.

Mental retardation A designation for exceptional subjects whose IQ scores are more than -2 standard deviations below the mean of a normal probability distribution of intelligence test scores.

Meprobamate A class of drugs used to treat anxiety.

Mesomorphy The body type describing the muscular, rugged person.

Milieu therapy A type of therapy that tries to incorporate the social standards of a culture or community into the hospital or treatment setting.

Minor tranquilizers Also known as antianxiety drugs, used to lessen a patient's level of anxiety; especially useful in conjunction with psychotherapy.

Mitosis The process of cell division involving differentiation and the halving of chromosomes.

Mode The score that occurs most frequently in a distribution; there may be more than one mode in a distribution.

Model status The standing or position accorded the model by the observer.

Modeling The observation and subsequent incorporation and display of a response or response sequence; other names for modeling are observational learning, learning by imitation, and identification learning.

Mongolism A chromosomally caused form of mental retardation in which the child is conceived with 47 chromosomes rather than with the normal 46; also called Down syndrome.

Monoamine oxidase inhibitors A group of antidepressant drugs, used to treat the symptoms of long-term depression.

Monocular depth cues Cues to depth perception that are dependent upon only one eye; perspective and interposition are examples.

Mood disorders Conditions typified by mood swings; great elation or deep depression, often occurring in cycles.

Morphemes The smallest meaningful units of a language.

Motivation Conditions that initiate, guide, or maintain behaviors, usually until some goal is reached or the response has been blocked.

Multiple approach-avoidance conflict A situation in which a subject must choose between two (or more) stimulus situations, each of which has both positive and negative values.

Multiple personality A dissociative disorder in which the individual has more than one distinct personality; usually each personality knows little or nothing about the others.

Multiple schedules Partial reinforcement schedules that require the subject to satisfy two or more independent schedules that are presented successively, each cued.

Mutation A spontaneous, sudden change in heredity pattern.

Myelin (myelinization) A fatty substance that covers many axons, usually surrounding the axon in a beadlike arrangement. Myelinization is the process of development of this substance.

nAch The need for achievement; a motivation.

Narcissistic personality disorder A disorder characterized by a preoccupation with success, extreme feelings of self-importance, and a lack of interpersonal empathy.

Narcotic drugs Those drugs that can be used as painkillers, such as heroin or morphine.

Natural selection The evolutionary process by which traits that aid the organism recur in future generations, while those that are unsuitable do not; often summarized by the phrase "survival of the fittest."

Naturalistic observation The careful observation of events not manipulated by the observer.

Nature-nurture controversy The dispute over the relative importance of heredity and environment in determining human traits.

Need A physiological deficit; less specifically, some condition for which satisfaction is desired.

Negative reinforcement A type of event in which the removal or absence of a stimulus condition strengthens or maintains a response.

Negative skew A distribution in which most of the scores are found at the upper (higher) end of the measurement scale.

Nerve A collection of neuron fibers (axons and dendrites).

Neuron The basic structural unit of the nervous system, composed of a cell body, an axon, and one or more dendrites.

Neurotic disorders A category of abnormal personality patterns characterized by a high level of anxiety in one particular area but the ability to continue functioning in daily activities.

Noise In detection theory, the term used to describe any extraneous stimuli.

Nonconformity Response in a manner opposite to a group's opinions or expectations.

Noncontingent reinforcement Reinforcement that follows a response but is not dependent upon that response.

Nonsense syllable A consonant-vowel-consonant sequence that does not make a word.

Normal behavior Used interchangeably to mean behavior that is typical or behavior that is considered healthy and adaptive.

Normal curve The graphic representation of the normal probability distribution.

Normal probability distribution An idealized distribution based upon data collected from large samples; most scores are at or near the mean, with a few scores at the extremes; often used for making statistical inferences.

Norms The scores, obtained by a representative group taking a particular test, that serve as the standard against which an individual's score can be compared.

Null hypothesis A prediction that a specific change in the conditions of an experiment will not result in a change in the outcome.

Obedience to authority The tendency of an individual to accept the commands of an authority figure, even when they contradict common sense or ethics.

Object permanence The recognition a child develops that things continue to exist even when they are not readily apparent.

Objective Free from bias or prejudice.

Objectivity The quality or state in which judgments made are free from bias or the influence of personal feeling.

Obsession An unwanted but not preventable thought pattern that recurs often.

Occipital lobe The lower back portion of the cortex.

Oedipus complex In Freud's theory of personality, the child's sexual desire for the opposite-sex parent and rivalry with the same-sex parent; successful resolution occurs when the child identifies with the same-sex parent.

Opening-up meditation An attempt to produce continuous attention to all aspects of the stimulus environment.

Operant conditioning In general, acquisition of voluntary responses made to achieve a reinforcement.

Operant-conditioning chamber An apparatus used for experimental testing of operant conditioning; several varieties exist.

Oral stage In Freud's theory of personality, the period from birth to the second year of life, when all libidinal energy is expended primarily to satisfy mouth-oriented activity.

Ordinal position The position of one's birth order in the family (first born, middle born, last born).

Ordinate The y-axis, or vertical axis, of a graph.

Organic psychosis Psychotic reactions provoked by physical disorders.

Orienting response (OR) In classical conditioning, any of a number of adjustment responses made when the CS first occurs.

Overlearning The amount of practice occurring after a performance criterion has been reached.

Paired-associate learning A learning technique in which particular stimuli are linked with specific responses.

Paper-and-pencil tests Psychological tests that use written or check-type answers only.

Paradoxical sleep The period of sleep, also called REM sleep, during which a sleeper dreams.

Parallel sensory processing Sensory processing when several stimuli are attended to simultaneously.

Paranoia An abnormal personality pattern characterized by feelings of persecution and grandeur.

Paraprofessional The designation of a person with relatively little training who works (often as a volunteer) to help individuals confront personal problems.

Parasympathetic system That part of the autonomic nervous system primarily involved with the recuperative functions of the body.

Parietal lobe The area of the cortex from the rear of the central fissure to the central back of the brain.

Parsimony Economy of explanation; a parsimonious explanation is preferred to a more complex one if both explain a situation equally well.

Partial reinforcement In classical conditioning, when the CS is presented on every trial, but the UCS occurs on only some of the trials; more generally, reinforcement for some, but not all responses that are judged "correct."

Partial reinforcement effect (PRE) The finding that responses conditioned under partial reinforcement are more resistant to extinction than are those conditioned under continuous reinforcement.

Pedophilia Sexual relations with children.

Peer-group influence The attachment to and the effects of age mates; increasingly important as a child grows older.

Percentile The point below which falls a given percentage of the total number of scores in a distribution.

Perception Basically, the interpretation or understanding of sensory receptions.

Perceptual constancies Understanding the stability of an object's size, shape, color, brightness, etc., despite changing stimulus conditions.

Performance The responses that an organism actually shows; may or may not reveal what the organism has learned.

Peripheral nervous system (PNS) Those nerves outside the central nervous system; it has two subdivisions, the somatic and autonomic systems.

Persona The role a person plays in society, or the "face" presented to the external world; also, for Carl Jung, an archetype.

Personal space The physical distance surrounding a person; often considered by the person as his or her "own."

Personal unconscious In Jung's theory of personality, the part of personality that holds memories and repressed desires.

Personality Those enduring characteristics that are representative of a person's behavior; they may be developed from unique or common experiences and the effects of environmental and hereditary influences.

Personality disorders A classification of abnormal personality patterns characterized by the person's inability to act in accordance with societal standards. Contrasted with neurotic disorders by their integration with the person's total outlook on life or character.

Personality tests Tests designed to determine the attributes that are unique, enduring, and typical of a particular individual.

Perspective A monocular depth cue in which perception of distance is based upon previous knowledge of size-distance and shape-slant relationships.

Persuasion The process of trying to change attitudes.

Phallic stage In Freud's theory of personality, the period when libidinal energy centers on the genitalia; the period of the Oedipus complex.

Pharmacological therapy Also called chemotherapy, the use of drugs to change brain chemistry or behavior and feelings.

Phenothiazines A family of drugs, sometimes called "major tranquilizers," used to treat psychotic symptoms.

Phobia An intense, compelling fear of some situation or object; the fear is more intense than the circumstance appears to warrant.

Phonemes The basic sound or inflection components of a spoken language.

Phrenology The discipline that "maps" the human skull in an attempt to label brain functions and their consequent effects on human behaviors.

Physiognomy The study of the shape of the face and head as indicators of personality traits.

Physiological motives Inborn, unlearned motives that arise from basic biological needs.

Physiological psychology A branch of psychology that studies the physiological, or bodily, foundations of behavior.

Pituitary gland Often called the "master gland," a pea-sized area of the brain responsible for controlling many of our important hormonal and behavioral functions.

Placebo A chemically inert material that has the same appearance as an active drug; allows psychologists to test the effects of the expectations of subjects who believe they are actually taking a drug; by analogy, the "placebo effect" is any situation in which subjects believe they are experiencing a manipulation by the experimenter when in fact they are not.

Plateau In a learning curve, a period of little or no change in performance preceded and followed by periods of performance improvement.

Play therapy A therapy technique used mostly with children; personality patterns are expressed by the children in unrestricted play situations.

Pleasure One of the basic emotions; a response ranging from mild delight to ecstasy.

Pleasure principle In Freud's theory of personality, seeking pleasure and avoiding pain regardless of social dictates; a property of the id.

Population The entire group from which samples may be chosen; all of a group.

Positive regard In Carl Rogers' theory of personality, the concept of acceptance by others; may be unconditional (unrestricted) or conditional (restricted).

Positive reinforcement A type of event in which the presence of a stimulus condition strengthens or maintains a response.

Positive skew A distribution in which most of the scores are found at the lower end of the measurement scale used.

Postnatal After birth; the period of time from delivery until death.

Power In modeling, potential influence.

Power tests Psychological tests in which the time limit for completion is not considered an important variable.

Preoperational stage According to Piaget, the second stage of cognitive development, from approximately age two to age seven, in which a child learns to represent things by language, drawing, and other symbolic activities.

Precipitating factors Stimuli that actually initiate behavioral patterns.

Precognition The correct prediction of events that have not yet occurred.

Preconscious According to Freud, memories that are readily accessible to consciousness.

Predispositions The background characteristics of a person that serve to influence personality patterns; also called predisposing factors.

Prejudice An overgeneralized and inappropriate learned reaction to a social stimulus.

Prenatal Before birth; the period of time from conception to delivery.

Preparedness An evolutionary concept regarding the organism's readiness to learn; used to try to explain why some learning occurs easily while other learning may be quite difficult.

Primacy effect In learning, the finding that materials presented first will be acquired and remembered well.

Primary motives Unlearned motives, drives that satisfy basic physiological needs (e.g., hunger, thirst, sleep, etc.).

Primary stimulus generalization Stimulus generalization based upon the physical properties of the stimulus.

Principle of least interest In a dyadic relationship, an attempt to account for situations where the person with the least involvement establishes the conditions, and the other accepts these in order to maintain the relationship.

Privacy The need for aloneness and personal space; opposite of crowding.

Private logic According to Alfred Adler, a person's unique (and not always correct) logical assumptions and personal processes of logical reasoning.

Proactive inhibition (PI) The interfering effect that one learning task has on the retention of a later-learned task.

Problem-solving The recognition and establishment of some goal, followed by attempts to reach that goal.

Programmatic reasoning Reasoning using already-existing systems of thought.

Programmed learning A special learning technique that usually involves small steps, immediate feedback, and a high level of reinforcement for performance.

Progressive-part method In learning, the practice of mastering one part, then a second, and so on, in a building- block manner.

Projection Attributing one's own unacceptable motives to others; seeing in others the motives that dominate the self.

Projective tests Personality tests in which ambiguous stimuli are presented to a subject who is asked to describe each or tell a story about each; supposedly, the reactions will reveal personality characteristics the individual has projected onto each stimulus.

Pronounceability In verbal learning, the characteristics of a word that make it either difficult or easy to pronounce.

Prosocial behavior Helping behavior.

Proximity The real or perceived distance between one person and another; more generally, the perceived "nearness" of two or more stimuli.

Proximo-distal trend The tendency for the central portions of the body to develop before and more quickly than the peripheral portions.

Psychiatrist A medical doctor with advanced training in the use of psychotropic medications, medical therapies, and psychotherapies.

Psychiatry A medical specialty dealing with the diagnosis and treatment of behavioral and mental disorders.

Psychoactive drugs Any of a number of drugs that can cause subjective or psychological effects for a person.

Psychoanalysis A form of psychotherapy originated by Sigmund Freud; stresses the importance of early-childhood experiences and unconscious motives in the development of personality.

Psychoanalyst A psychiatrist trained at a special institute in the techniques developed by Freud.

Psychodynamic model As proposed by Freud, an explanation of abnormal personality patterns based upon the concept of unconscious conflicts.

Psychokinesis The capacity to make objects move by using only thought processes.

Psycholinguistics The study of the relationship between organisms and their language; concerned with the acquisition, structure, and usage of language.

Psychological testing The use of some measurement technique to try to assess a behavioral characteristic.

Psychology The scientific study of all behavior.

Psychometric psychology The branch of psychology that specializes in testing and measuring human abilities and traits.

Psychopath A self-centered person without care and concern for others, and lacking a sense of guilt.

Psychopathology of everyday life The slips of the tongue, forgetting, or other common daily mistakes that, to psychoanalysts, reveal aspects of the patient's unconscious conflicts.

Psychopharmacology The study of the psychological effects of drugs.

Psychosexual disorder Sexual behavior viewed by clinicians as detrimental to the person and/or others; socially disapproved sexual activities.

Psychosexual stages In Freud's theory of personality, a series of phases in the development of personality.

Psychotic disorders An abnormal personality pattern characterized by loss of contact with reality.

Psychosomatic disorder A physical illness brought about by a psychological cause.

Psychosurgery A medical therapy involving the surgical destruction of brain tissue.

Psychotherapy Use of psychological methods to try to treat abnormal personality patterns.

Psychotropic drugs A general term for drugs used to change mood, behavior, or symptoms of an abnormal psychological condition.

Puberty The physiological changes associated with adolescence; marked by the development of the capacity to reproduce and by the appearance of secondary sex characteristics.

Public opinion poll A questioning of a sample from a population regarding attitudes toward a particular topic.

Punishment A type of event in which delivery of an aversive stimulus is contingent upon a certain response.

Qualitative measurement As a measure of retention, using a subjective judgment to assess such skills as musical, literary, and creative, abilities.

Quota sampling A statistical method in which different attributes of the population are represented in the sample in proportion to their numbers in the population at large; also called stratified sampling.

Random sample In statistics, the use of subjects or a group selected from the population by drawing numbers "out of a hat" or using a table of random numbers; all members of the population have an equal chance of being chosen.

Range A measure of variability calculated by determining the difference between the highest and lowest scores in a distribution.

Rapid-eye-movement sleep (REM) The period during sleep when there is rapid movement of the eyes; often the period in which dreaming occurs.

Rational-emotive therapy (RET) Developed by Albert Ellis, a therapy technique that examines illogical thinking and the "propaganda" from one's past.

Rationalization Acting because of one unacceptable motive while crediting that action to some more acceptable motive.

Reaction formation A defense mechanism; the person acts in a way that totally contradicts unconcious feelings.

Readiness The state in which an organism is ready and able to learn a new behavior; once readiness is reached, the organism will always have the ability to learn the new behavior.

Reality principle In Freud's theory of personality, seeking pleasure and avoiding pain in socially acceptable manners; a property of the ego.

Reasoning Attempts to solve a problem by combining two or more aspects from past experience or successful past reasoning.

Recall As a measure of retention, the ability to arrive at the correct response with a minimum cue statement.

Recency effect In studies of memory, the principle that the most recently presented information is remembered best or is considered most significant. In learning theory, the finding that materials presented last will be acquired and remembered best.

Receptive language What is understood from words that are used.

Receptor A specialized nerve ending that is sensitive to a particular type of stimulus.

Recessive gene The gene in a pair of unlike genes that does not usually affect the process of development.

Recognition As a measure of retention, the ability to recognize one correct answer out of a choice of many.

Redirection An organism's inappropriate responding in the presence of a single releaser stimulus.

Refractory phase The recovery period of time required by a neuron before another signal may be conducted.

Regression In statistics, use of the knowledge of a previously obtained correlation and the value of one variable to predict the value of some other variable. In Freud's theory, acting in a manner appropriate to someone of a younger age.

Relational concept A complex concept based upon the relation between two features of a stimulus situation.

Relative refractory period The time during a neuron's refractory recovery phase when it can be activated once again, but only if the excitation is stronger than normal.

Reliability The consistency of results when a psychological test or other measuring technique is used more than once.

Reminiscence An improvement in performance following practice and a period of rest.

Repression The use of psychic energy to keep anxiety-producing memories from conscious recognition; motivated forgetting.

Resistance In psychoanalysis, the phenomenon in which the patient does not wish to discuss a particular topic.

Response generalization Responding to the original stimulus not only with the original response, but with other, similar responses.

Resting potential The nonactivated state of a neuron, in which the inside of the cell is slightly negative in potential when compared to the outside.

Retention The storage of learning over some period of time.

Retention interval The period of time during which new learning is stored.

Reticular activating system (RAS) A system of interconnected neurons in the lower center of the brain believed to be partly responsible for emotional arousal and other basic behaviors.

Retina That part of the eye containing the receptors for vision; located at the back of the eyeball.

Retinal disparity The difference between the visual images striking the retinas of the two eyes.

Retroactive inhibition (RI) The interference effect that a later learning task has on the retention of a previously learned task.

Retrospective study An investigation involving recollected data reported by people who were significant in a person's life.

Risky shift A group decision that is more venturesome than what could have been predicted from the responses of any one individual in the group.

Rods The visual receptors that function primarily in dim or dark conditions; they are located toward the periphery of the eye and operate only in a black-and-white dimension.

Role The expected range of responding that accompanies a particular status.

Role of arguments The effect of discussion upon a group decision; generally the decision follows the strongest arguments.

Romeo and Juliet effect The principle that parental opposition increases the attractiveness of romantic partners to each other.

Rorschach inkblot test A projective test using ten inkblots as stimuli.

Sadism Achieving sexual gratification by inflicting pain on one's partner.

Sample A group selected from a population; the attempt should be made to make the sample as representative as possible of the population.

Sampling Selection of subjects from a population; in general, the experimenter attempts to make the sample as representative of the total population as possible.

Savings score As a measure of retention, a ratio between the number of trials required for relearning and the number required for the original learning.

Scapegoating Displacement of aggression from the precipitating cause to some available person or minority group.

Scattergram The pictorial representation of a correlation.

Schedules of reinforcement Ways of arranging partial reinforcement in operant conditioning situations.

Schizoid personality A disorder marked by the inability to hold warm or caring feelings for others.

Schizophrenia The most common of psychotic reactions, often characterized by pronounced loss of contact with reality, delusions, and hallucinations.

Scholastic tests Aptitude tests used to predict future performance in academic pursuits.

School psychology A branch of psychology that specializes in testing, counseling, and guiding students.

Scoring profile The presentation of a summary of the results collected from administration of a test battery.

Secondary appraisal An interpretation of the causes of an emotion; may change the explanation from the one that was first proposed.

Secondary motives Learned drives that vary from one person to another as a result of social needs and learning.

Secondary reinforcer A previously neutral stimulus that, once paired with a reinforcer, comes to take on reinforcing properties.

Secondary sex characteristics Physiological characteristics that arise during puberty, distinguishing children from adults.

Secondary stimulus generalization Stimulus generalization based upon the subject's knowledge of language or some other type of symbol.

Selection In genetics, the principle that survival-oriented traits tend to predominate over time.

Selective attention A sensory state in which an organism attends to certain aspects of the environment while ignoring others.

Selective breeding The process of mating in genetic combinations that are likely to produce favorable offspring.

Selective exposure A person's ability to select from the stimuli available what he or she will perceive and process.

Self theory A theory of personality based upon the human's desire to achieve complete realization of potentials.

Self-actualization The realization of one's full potential, according to humanistic theory.

Self-arousal In modeling, a motive condition that arises out of the observation and retention of the behaviors of others.

Self-fulfilling prophecy A theory proposing that a person will act in accordance with expectations that have been expressed about anticipated behaviors.

Semicircular canals Three tubes located in the inner ear; they are filled with fluid and are sensitive to changes in body and head orientation.

Sensations The processes that detect, judge, and identify stimuli.

Sensorimotor stage According to Piaget, the first stage of cognitive development; from birth to about age two.

Sensory adaptation The process of adjustment to unusual, usually persistent levels of stimulation.

Sensory deprivation Doing without stimulation; extreme restriction of the sensory environment.

Sensory gating A brain process that reduces the input into certain sensory systems while allowing other systems to remain fully functioning.

Sensory overload Excessive stimulation; extremely high levels of a stimulus.

Sensory storage The notion that learned or perceived items are held in an unprocessed sensory form before being categorized or interpreted by the mind.

Sequential attention Sensory processing in which single units of information are treated in succession.

Serial learning Learning in which materials are presented in a particular order or sequence that must be followed.

Seriation According to Piaget, the ability to arrange elements in order of increasing or decreasing size.

Set The temporary tendency to respond in a certain manner.

Sexual deviation Any sexual behavior judged as deviant according to a particular society's standards.

Shadow According to Jung, the archetype that represents the animal instincts in human beings.

Shaping Reinforcing closer and closer approximations of a desired behavior.

Short-term storage In memory, the retention that extends from 1 to 30 seconds after exposure to a stimulus item.

Sign A signal that has inherent meaning because its characteristics are related to naturally occurring events.

Signal A stimulus that can be used for communication.

Similarity In learning, the principle that some materials are more easily learned because they are much like previously learned materials.

Simple attitude A set opinion such as "good/bad" or "yes/no."

Simple concept A concept concerned with a single property only.

Simulation Attempts to use a computer program to duplicate the processing (thinking) stage in problem solving; more generally, attempts to use mechanical means to imitate or represent human behaviors or situations.

Simultaneous conditioning A classical-conditioning procedure when the ISI equals zero; that is, the CS and UCS occur at the same time.

Single-blind control An experimental situation in which the subjects are unaware of how or when the variables are manipulated by the experimenter.

Situational tests Personality tests in which the subject is placed in a prepared circumstance and is asked to react; the subject's responses are assessed for various personality characteristics.

Skew A distribution in which the scores occur with greater frequency at one end of the distribution.

Social change A significant alteration of social structure.

Social comparison In situations of uncertainty, seeking out others to determine the similarity or difference of reactions.

Social exchange The interaction of two people, usually involving some feelings of superiority and inferiority on the part of each.

Social facilitation Instances where the presence of others appears to help performance of a particular response.

Social interest According to Alfred Adler, a mix of inborn and acquired motivations to contribute to the social good and to succeed in the world with others.

Social interference Instances where the presence of others appears to hinder performance of a particular response.

Social-learning model An explanation of abnormal personality patterns based primarily upon learning principles.

Social-learning theories A group of theories joined together by the belief that much of our motivation and behavior is the result of what we learn by our experiences; contrasted with psychoanalytic theory or humanistic theory.

Social motives Motives that are learned as a consequence of interacting with others.

Social movement An attempt to cause social change.

Social psychology A branch of psychology that studies the effects of group membership on an individual's behavior.

Socialization The general process of learning and establishing values and norms within a culture.

Somatic system That part of the peripheral nervous system concerned with sensory and motor functions.

Somatic therapies See Medical therapies.

Somatoform disorders Disorders that manifest a physical symptom without an organic cause.

Somatotonia The personality accompanying mesomorphy; an aggressive, direct person.

Specific factors According to Spearman, the specific factors of intelligence—also called the S factors—which are all included under the general factor (G).

Speed tests Psychological tests in which the time limit for completion is considered an important variable.

Split-brain experiments Research conducted when the corpus callosum has been severed, creating two entirely separate hemispheres which function independently.

Spontaneous recovery A phenomenon in which, after a period of rest following extinction, the CR reappears when the CS is presented alone.

Spontaneous remission Recovery from abnormal personality patterns without any therapy.

Standard deviation A measure of variability based upon the differences of each score from the mean.

Standardization The process of testing with a consistent pattern, and the establishment of norms.

State-dependent learning The association of learned materials with the environment in which they were learned.

Statistical judgment Decisions based solely on statistical (or numerical or data-based) information.

Statistics The discipline that deals with the collection, analysis, interpretation, and presentation of numerical data.

Status A person's position or function.

Stereotype A relatively rigid, overgeneralized interpretation of some aspect of reality, especially persons or groups.

Stimulation needs A class of motives in which a person seems to require certain levels of sensory stimulation.

Stimulus generalization Responding not only to the original stimulus, but to other, similar stimuli.

Stratified sampling A technique for selecting subjects in such a way that significant subgroups within the population are accurately reflected in the composition of each group in the experiment; also called quota sampling.

Stress inoculation A process in cognitive therapy in which a person conditions himself or herself not to react physiologically or psychologically to stressful stimuli.

Structuralism A system of psychology that studied the adult, normal, human mind by using the method of introspection.

Subjective Influenced by some bias or prejudice.

Subjectivity The quality or state in which judgments made are affected by bias, prejudice, or personal feeling.

Subliminal perception The supposed understanding or interpretation of stimuli that occur at a level slightly below the threshold value.

Substance use disorders With regard to drugs, behaviors involving abuse or pathological use of the drug and/or dependency on it.

Superego In Freud's theory of personality, the part of the personality concerned with ideal behavior and what is not acceptable behavior (ego ideal and conscience).

Superstitious behavior Behavior in which an organism performs as if a particular response causes reinforcement, but in fact there is no contingency.

Surface structure The arrangement of words in a language.

Syllables The smallest speech units to which the receiver usually attends.

Symbol Any specified stimulus that has become a commonly accepted representation for some object, event, action, or idea.

Symbolic learning In modeling, learning a behavior without actually observing it; verbal descriptions are used to establish the modeled response.

Symmetrical distribution In statistics, a frequency distribution arranged in a similar pattern on either side of the middle of the distribution.

Sympathetic system That part of the autonomic nervous system that acts primarily when the person is aroused.

Synapse The gap between the axon of one cell and a dendrite of the next.

Synaptic vesicles Openings at the end of an axon from which transmitter substances are discharged.

System of psychology Any particular body of theories of psychology used in the organization or interpretation of all of behavior.

Systematic desensitization Step-by-step classical conditioning in which a series of anxiety-producing stimuli (CS) are paired with relaxation (UCS).

Taste buds Receptors for taste; located in the pits of the tongue.

Telepathy The transfer of thought from one person to another without the use of regular sensory channels.

Temporal conditioning A classical-conditioning procedure in which the UCS occurs at regular intervals; these regular intervals are treated as the CS.

Temporal lobe The area of the cortex from in front of the occipital lobe to the rear of the lateral fissure.

Territoriality The tendency of a person, animal, or group to consider a region its own, to fight to preserve it, and to close it to nonmembers.

Test battery The combination of several different psychological tests into a series presented to a subject.

Texture gradient The change in the appearance of texture based upon distance from the viewer; a monocular depth cue.

Thalamus The part of the brain that regulates sleep and wakefulness (with the limbic system) and relays sensory information to the cortex.

Thematic Apperception Test (TAT) A projective test using twenty monochromatic, ambiguous pictures as stimuli.

Theory A general principle, based upon evidence or observation, suggested as an explanation for phenomena.

Thinking A personal process of symbolic mediation, often attributed to the mind.

Threshold The level of stimulation necessary for reception to occur.

Thyroid gland   An endocrine gland responsible for controlling the body's rate of metabolism.

Tip-of-the-tongue phenomenon   The inability to remember completely something that is close to conscious recall.

Token economy   A behavior modification technique in which secondary reinforcers (tokens) can later be traded in for rewards.

Trace conditioning   A classical-conditioning procedure in which the onset and cessation of the CS occur before the UCS is presented.

Traditional therapy group   A psychotherapy group in which many of the methods of traditional psychotherapy are applied in a group context.

Trait theory   An attempt to categorize personality using the presence or absence of several characteristics.

Transduction   The change of stimulus energy into an action potential.

Transfer of training   The effect of learning one task upon the learning of another task.

Transference   In psychoanalysis, the phenomenon in which the patient develops a strong emotional attachment (reminiscent of an earlier emotional attachment) to the therapist.

Transmitter substance   A chemical discharged from an axon's synaptic vesicles; may be either excitatory or inhibitory.

Transpersonal unconscious   According to Jung, the inborn categories handed down from generation to generation as expressions of the human race; same as collective unconscious.

Transsexualism   Feeling trapped in the body of the wrong sex.

Transvestism   Wearing the clothes of the opposite sex.

Triad   A group of three people.

Trichromatic theory   The most popular explanation of color vision, based upon the idea that there are three types of cones that are sensitive respectively to red, green, and blue.

Tricyclics   A group of antidepressant drugs, used to treat long-range symptoms of depression.

Type theory   An attempt to categorize personality by the presence or absence of one characteristic.

Typology   The discipline that correlates body type with personality and social characteristics.

Unconditional positive regard   See Positive regard.

Unconditioned response (UCR)   In classical conditioning, the response elicited by the UCS.

Unconditioned stimulus (UCS)   In classical conditioning, the stimulus that is response-producing on the first and every other trial.

Unconscious Conditions of which the individual is unaware or barely aware, yet which seem to influence behavior.

Unconscious motives According to Freud, motives of which we are unaware because they are emanating from the unconscious mind.

Unlearned motives Conditions that are inborn or innate and that initiate, guide, and maintain behaviors.

Vacuum activity The appearance of an FAP when no releaser stimulus has occurred.

Validity The capacity of a test to measure what it claims to measure (or predict what it claims to predict).

Variability In statistics, the extent to which scores are dispersed in a distribution. In biology, the changes made in the genetic make-up over several generations.

Variable schedules Partial reinforcement schedules that can change, usually around some average value.

Vestibular sense Balance; the function of the three semicircular canals and the vestibular sacs.

Vicarious learning The experience of observing and understanding another's response and the consequences of that response.

Viscerotonia The personality accompanying endomorphy; a cheerful person seeking a passive, accepting environment.

Vocational tests Aptitude tests used to predict future performance in a job or career.

Von Restorff effect Exceptional retention of an especially distinctive stimulus found in a serial list; also called the isolation effect.

Warm-up Any of a number of experiences that serve to prepare an organism for performance of a response.

Wish fulfillment In psychoanalysis, the principle that through our dreams we attempt to fulfill our unconscious wishes.

Yerkes-Dodson Law In the psychology of emotion, the principle that optimal performance is obtained for relatively simple tasks when arousal level is high and for complex tasks when the arousal level is low.

Zygote The single cell formed by the uniting of a sperm cell and an egg cell at the moment of conception.

Index